Windows® 95

CHEAT SHEET

by Joe Kraynak

que®

A Division of Macmillan Computer Publishing
201 W. 103rd Street, Indianapolis, Indiana 46290 USA

International Standard Book Number: 0-7897-0371-8

Library of Congress Catalog Card Number: 94-73799

99 98 97   10 9 8 7 6 5

Interpretation of the printing code: the rightmost number of the first series of numbers is the year of the book's printing; the rightmost number of the second series of numbers is the number of the book's printing. For example, a printing code of 95-1 shows that the first printing of the book occurred in 1995.

Printed in the United States of America.

Publisher   *Roland Elgey*

Vice-President and Publisher   *Marie Butler-Knight*

Editorial Services Director   *Elizabeth Keaffaber*

Publishing Manager   *Barry Pruett*

Managing Editor   *Michael Cunningham*

Development Editor   *Faithe Wempen*

Technical Editor   *C. Herbert Feltner*

Production Editor   *Phil Kitchel*

Copy Editor   *Barry Childs-Helton*

Cover Designer   *Scott Cook*

Book Designer   *Barbara Kordesh*

Indexers   *Virginia Bess, Mary Jane Frisby, Kathy Venable*

Production Team   *Angela D. Bannan, Amy Cornwell, Maxine Dillingham, Darren Jackson, Bob LaRoche, Bobbi Satterfield, Michael Thomas, Karen York*

Contents

Part 3   Using the Windows 95 Accessories

Part 5   Using the Windows Control Panel

Part 7 Telecomputing with Windows 95

Part 8 Tricks and Traps

Introduction

Windows 95 is billed as *the* graphical, user-friendly interface of the 90s. It has a desktop on which you can spread all your work and flip from one project to the next by poking around with your mouse. When you start using Windows, however, things may not seem all that easy. Where do you poke with the mouse? How do you poke? Where did the document you were just working on disappear to, and how can you get it back?

As you grip your mouse tighter and tighter, the last thing you need is a book that's packed with fluff. You need a book that cuts through the drivel, presents the information you need, and lets you skip the details. You need the *Windows 95 Cheat Sheet*.

This Book Is Different

Most computer books on the market are designed to make you work. Interesting or significant details are buried under mounds of text that you must dig through to unearth what you need. The *Cheat Sheet* is different:

- **Headings** appear in the left-hand margin of each page, labeling each section. This makes it easy to find (and skip) information.

- **Step-by-step instructions** lead you through each task. You don't have to wade through paragraphs to figure out what to do next.

- **Lots of pictures** help you see what's going on as you perform a task, and act as checkpoints so you can make sure you've done things right.

- **Paragraphs** are used sparingly and are kept brief, so you don't have to dig through text to find the important points.

- **Highlighting** is used to call your attention to important information.

- A **Cheat Sheet** at the beginning of each chapter gives a quick rundown of the steps you need to perform for the essential tasks in the chapter.

- **Basic Survival** tasks are covered first in each chapter. That way, you can easily avoid the more advanced material.

- **Beyond Survival** at the end of each chapter covers advanced features that tell you how to use a feature more efficiently, or customize it for a specific use.

- **Hand-written tips** in the left-hand column provide quick ways of performing a task or call your attention to important text.

- **Tear-out Cheat Sheet** at the back of this book contains the most important concepts, tips, and step-by-step instructions for working in Windows.

Something for Everyone

Just because this book is easy to use, don't think of it as just another beginner's Windows book. Every chapter of the Windows 95 Cheat Sheet contains advanced tips that give you more control and a deeper understanding of Windows. You'll learn how to save loads of time with your right mouse button, how to share information between two programs simply by dragging it across the screen, how to choose a wallpaper design for Windows, how to optimize your computer's memory, and much more.

In addition, this book contains a six-chapter section at the end that's devoted exclusively to advanced features, tricks, and troubleshooting in Windows 95.

How to Use This Book

This book is designed for users who like to skip around, and who need to find information in a hurry. However, it also has an overall structure that allows you to concentrate on certain aspects of Windows:

- **To install Windows**, see the appendix at the back of the book. Because so many computers come with Windows pre-installed, we chose to move the installation to the back to keep it out of the way.

- **To master Windows basics**, such as how to start Windows, select commands from menus, get help, and run applications, see "Part 1: Windows 95 Basics."

- **To install and set up programs to run in Windows**, skip to "Part 2: Working with Programs." In this part, you learn how to install Windows programs, set up DOS programs to run under Windows, and go to the DOS prompt.

- **To use the programs that come with Windows**, look to "Part 3: Using the Windows 95 Accessories." You'll learn how to use WordPad (the word processor), Paint (the graphics program), Cardfile (the address book), and much more. You'll even learn how to use the programs together.

- **To manage your disks, folders, and files**, skip to Part 4 to learn how to use the Windows Explorer and My Computer, Windows 95's new disk and file management tool. You'll learn how to format floppy disks, create folders on a disk, and copy files by dragging them with the mouse pointer from one disk or folder to another.

- **To control the look and behavior of Windows**, see "Part 5: Using the Windows Control Panel." You'll learn how to change your screen colors, add fancy wallpaper backgrounds, and have Windows use your hard disk as memory. You'll even learn how to turn on Windows screen savers, and use a password to prevent unauthorized use of your computer.

- **For advanced tips on protecting your files and speeding up your computer,** check out "Part 6: Maintaining Your Computer." In this part, you learn how to back up and restore files using Microsoft Backup, fix disk problems with ScanDisk, improve your hard disk speed with Defragmenter, and increase your hard disk space with DriveSpace.

- **To set up and use your modem,** see "Part 7: Telecomputing with Windows 95." Here, you'll learn how to make Windows 95 detect your modem, and set it up to dial phone and fax numbers. You'll connect to Microsoft's new online service, called The Microsoft Network, and you'll learn how to use Windows 95's built-in fax program to send and receive faxes. You'll also learn how to use your modem and Windows as a programmable phone.

- **To optimize your system, troubleshoot problems, or have fun,** turn to "Part 8: Tricks and Traps." You'll learn how to get stubborn DOS applications up and running, speed up Windows, solve printer problems, and even view a brief Windows animation sequence.

No matter which section you turn to, you'll find the information you need in the easily accessible Cheat Sheet format.

Acknowledgments

Many individuals contributed their knowledge and expertise to this book. Special thanks goes to the development editors: Seta Frantz who set me on the right direction with this book and Faithe Wempen for her valuable ideas, insights, and in-depth knowledge of Windows 95. Thanks to Barry Childs-Helton (copy editor) for his language expertise and timely reality checks, and to Phil Kitchel (production editor) for carefully managing this production, and for having the best music in the hall. Oh yeah, and thanks to my boss, Barry Pruett (publishing manager) for not being bossy.

PART 1

Windows 95 Basics

From its inception and through its recent metamorphosis, Windows has been billed as the friendly interface of the '90s—the Mac of the PC world. That's partially true; Windows is friendly to anyone who has used it for awhile. But I've seen beginning users fumble around as much in Windows as they do in DOS. And if you're making the transition from Windows 3.1 (or 3.11) to Windows 95, you might flounder even more in the initial stages. To help you get started, this part helps you master the basics:

1. Starting and Restarting Windows 95

2. Using the Start Button and Taskbar

3. Running and Switching Between Programs

4. Entering Commands in Windows 95

5. Arranging Windows

6. Working with Icons

7. Dumping Objects in the Recycle Bin

8. Getting Help

Cheat Sheet

Starting Windows 95

1. Press the power button or flip the switch on your monitor.
2. Press the power button or flip the switch on your system unit.
3. Wait for the Welcome to Windows 95 dialog box to appear (unless you have disabled it).
4. Click on the Close button.

Using a Mouse

- **Point**   To roll the mouse on your desk until the tip of the mouse pointer touches the desired object.
- **Click**   To press and release the left mouse button once without moving the mouse.
- **Right-click**   To press and release the right mouse button once without moving the mouse.
- **Double-click**   To press and release the left mouse button twice quickly without moving the mouse.
- **Drag**   To hold down the left mouse button and move the mouse.

Shutting Down Windows 95

1. Click on the Start button at the bottom of the screen.
2. Click on Shut Down.
3. Click on the Yes button.
4. Turn off the system unit and the monitor.

Restarting Windows 95

1. Click on the Start button at the bottom of the screen.
2. Click on Shut Down.
3. Click on Restart the computer?.
4. Click on the Yes button.

Starting and Restarting Windows 95

Before you can do anything in Windows, you have to start it. In this chapter, you'll learn the basic Windows startup procedure. You'll also learn how to restart Windows when you run into trouble, how to start in DOS mode, and how to step through the startup commands.

Basic Survival

Starting Windows 95

Windows 95 pretty much "takes control of your television set." When you turn on your computer, Windows 95 starts automatically, presenting you with its new, improved interface. Although the operation is fairly simple, let's walk through it just to see what happens.

1. Flip the power switch on your monitor or press the power button to turn it on. (By turning the monitor on first, you prevent any electrical surges from the monitor startup from shooting through your system unit.)

2. Flip the power switch or press the power button on your system unit to turn it on. Your monitor displays some startup commands, and then the Welcome to Windows 95 dialog box appears, displaying the Tip of the Day.

    (If you set up Windows 95 to ask for a password on startup, you'll have to enter your name and password, and click on OK to start. Another way: you can usually start simply by clicking on the OK button.)

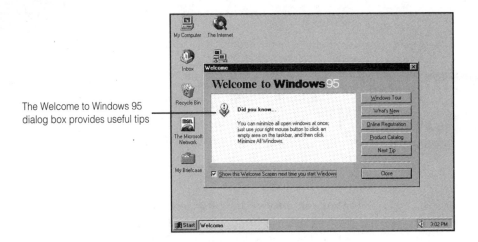

The Welcome to Windows 95 dialog box provides useful tips

3. Read the tip, and then click on one or more of the following options/ buttons:

> **Show this Welcome Screen next time you start Windows**   Click on this option (remove the check mark from the box) to prevent the Welcome screen from appearing on startup.
>
> **Windows Tour**   If you're new to Windows 95, click here for a tutorial.
>
> **What's New**   If you're making the transition from Windows 3.1 to Windows 95, this option provides a quick overview of what has changed.
>
> **Online Registration**   If you have a modem, you can click here to register your copy of Windows 95 over the phone, instead of by mail.
>
> **Product Catalog**   Click here for more information about Microsoft products (CD-ROM version only).
>
> **Next Tip**   Click here to view the next tip of the day. These tips provide useful timesaving suggestions for using Windows 95.
>
> **Close**   Closes this Welcome dialog box so you can get at the Windows 95 screen.

At "Starting Windows 95 message," press F8   You can have your computer run the startup commands one by one, asking you to confirm each command; just press the F8 key when you see the **Starting Windows 95** message.

If you have trouble starting Windows 95, skip ahead to the section "Dealing with Startup Problems."

Using Your Mouse

To do anything in Windows, you need to learn how to use your mouse. Here's a quick list of the basic mouse moves:

- **Point**   To place the tip of the mouse pointer over the desired object or command.

- **Click**   To press and release the mouse button (usually the left button) without moving the mouse. You usually click to highlight something.

- **Right-click**   To click the right mouse button. When you right-click on an area of the screen or on an object, Windows 95 displays a *shortcut menu*, which provides a list of commands you can enter to affect that object.

- **Double-click**   To press and release the mouse button twice quickly without moving the mouse. Because double-clicking is such a hassle, Windows 95 is designed to reduce the need for double-clicking.

- **Drag**   To hold down the left mouse button and move the mouse. You usually drag to move an object or draw a line or shape.

Shutting Down Windows 95

I know, you just started Windows, so why would you decide to shut it down so fast? You don't have to shut down Windows right now, but you should know how. Here's what you do:

1. If you were working in any programs, click on File near the top of the program's window, and then click on Save to save your work. For more details about opening menus and selecting commands, see Chapter 4, "Entering Commands in Windows 95."

2. Exit any DOS applications you may have run from Windows. (Refer to the DOS application's manual to learn how to do this.)

3. Click on Windows' Start button, and then click on Shut Down. The Shut Down Windows dialog box appears, asking you to confirm.

Windows lets you shut
down or restart

4. Click on the Yes button to confirm. Windows closes and displays a message saying that it's okay to turn off your computer.

5. Turn off the system unit, and then turn off your monitor and printer.

Beyond Survival

Starting Another Program When You Start Windows

You can start Windows and another program at the same time by telling Windows which command to enter at startup. For example, to start Windows and start WordPad (the word processing application that comes with Windows), do the following:

1. Click on the Start button (in the lower left corner of the screen), and then point to Settings.

2. Click on Taskbar. The Taskbar Properties dialog box appears.

3. Click on the Start Menu Programs tab. The dialog box options change, enabling you to add a program to the Start menu.

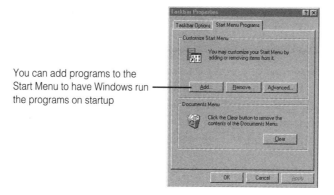

You can add programs to the Start Menu to have Windows run the programs on startup

4. Click on the Add button, and Windows asks you to specify the path to the file that starts the program.

5. Click on the Browse button to pick the program file from a list. (The file that runs WordPad is named Write, and it is in the folder named Windows.)

6. Click on the arrow to the right of the scroll bar to bring the Windows folder into view.

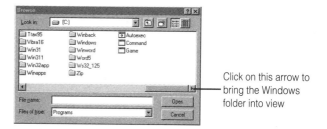

Click on this arrow to bring the Windows folder into view

7. Double-click on the Windows folder.

8. Use the scroll bar to bring the Write icon into view, and double-click on it.

9. Click on the Next button, and then double-click the Startup folder.

10. Type the name of the program as you want it to appear on the Startup menu, and then click on Finish.

11. When you're finished, click on the OK button.

The next time you turn on your computer or restart Windows, the specified program will run automatically.

Dealing with Startup Problems

If Windows just won't start and you end up with a blank screen or an error message, you have to figure out some way to coax Windows into starting. First, try starting Windows in *safe mode*. When Windows starts in safe mode, it runs with some basic settings, using a standard VGA monitor and the Microsoft mouse driver. Here's what you do to restart in safe mode:

1. Press the Reset button on your computer (or turn the system unit's power off, wait 30 seconds, and turn it back on).

2. Wait till you see the **Starting Windows 95** message, and then press and release the F8 key.

3. Press 3 to select safe mode, and then press Enter. Windows starts in safe mode, and a dialog box appears telling you so. At each corner of the Windows desktop, **Safe Mode** is displayed.

4. Click on the OK button to close the dialog box.

In safe mode, you won't be able to use CD-ROM drives, printers, sound cards, or other such devices.

After you restart Windows, you have to track down and correct the problem that was preventing Windows from starting in the first place. Usually you can have Windows solve the problem itself: just shut down Windows (again) and restart it. If that doesn't work, see Chapter 61, "Troubleshooting Common Windows Problems."

Making a Floppy Startup Disk

If you installed Windows 95 yourself, you probably remember the installation program asking if you wanted to create a *startup disk* (a disk you can use to start Windows in the event you can't start from your hard drive). If you chose not to or if Windows 95 came installed on your system, you should make a floppy startup disk in case anything happens to the startup files on your hard disk. To make a startup disk, follow these steps:

1. Click on the Start button and select Settings.

2. Click on Control Panel. The Control Panel window appears.

3. Double-click on the Add/Remove Programs icon, and the Add/Remove Programs Properties dialog box appears.

4. Click on the Startup Disk tab, and then click on Create Disk. A dialog box appears, prompting you to insert Windows Disk 1 in one of the drives.

5. Follow the on-screen instructions to complete the operation.

6. Remove the new startup disk from your floppy disk drive, and label it. Store the disk in a clean, dry place away from any magnets.

Starting in DOS Mode

You bought Windows 95 so you could run cutting-edge Windows programs, right? So why would you want to run in DOS mode? If you can't get an older DOS program or game to run under Windows 95, you might have to start your computer in DOS mode and run the application the old-fashioned way: from the DOS prompt. To start in DOS mode, follow these steps:

1. Turn on your monitor and system unit, and then wait till you see the **Starting Windows 95** message.

2. Press the F8 key, and a message appears, asking how you want to start.

3. Press one of the following keys to continue:

> Select Step-by-Step Confirmation and hit Enter to proceed step-by-step through the startup commands.

> Select Command Prompt Only and hit Enter to skip the startup commands (in CONFIG.SYS and AUTOEXEC.BAT) and go directly to the DOS prompt.

> Select Safe Mode Command Prompt Only and hit Enter to start in safe mode and display the command prompt.

> If you installed Windows 95 in a separate directory (instead of installing it over your previous Windows version) and you want to run your old version of DOS, select Previous Version of MS-DOS and press Enter.

Cheat Sheet

What's on the Windows Desktop?

Use My Computer to see the files and programs that are on your disks.

Drag files, folders, or other objects to the Recycle Bin to delete them.

If your computer is networked, you'll see this icon.

If you installed Windows on a laptop computer, use My Briefcase to transfer files to a desktop computer.

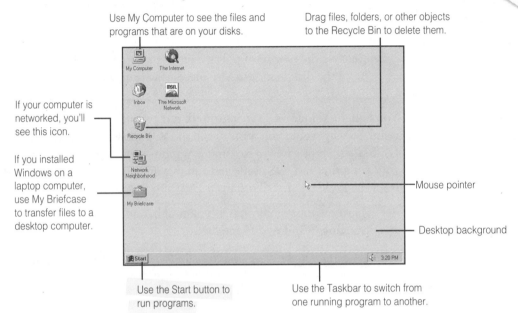

Mouse pointer

Desktop background

Use the Start button to run programs.

Use the Taskbar to switch from one running program to another.

Using the Start Button

When you move the mouse pointer over a menu item that has a submenu, the submenu automatically opens.

Click on the Start button to open this menu.

Click on a program's name to run it

Using the Taskbar

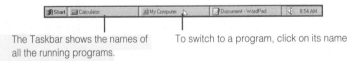

The Taskbar shows the names of all the running programs.

To switch to a program, click on its name

Using the Start Button and Taskbar

2

If you've ever seen the old Windows 3.1 desktop, you probably noticed that Windows 95 has a cleaner look. Gone are the program group windows and icons that cluttered the screen and buried the windows you were trying to get at. In some ways, this new look is very appealing.

However, if you're an experienced Windows 3.1 user, you're probably somewhat miffed by this new, "improved" look. Where are the familiar program groups? How are you supposed to run your applications (now called "programs")?!

Whether you're new to Windows or an experienced Windows user, this chapter will help you make a smooth transition to the new Windows desktop. Maybe it will even convince you that the new desktop really is better than the old one.

Basic Survival

Surveying the Desktop

Before you panic, sit back and take a look at the Windows 95 desktop. Notice that most of the desktop is empty. You'll learn how to clutter it yourself in Chapter 14. For now, just appreciate the open expanse. As you scan the screen, take note of the following three objects:

- **My Computer** is an icon that gives you access to your disk drives. In Chapter 28, you'll learn how to use this icon to organize your files and find programs.

- The **Recycle Bin** is an on-screen trash can. To delete a file, icon, or other object, move the mouse pointer over the object, hold down the left mouse button, and drag the object over the Recycle Bin icon. When you release the mouse button, the object is placed in the Recycle Bin. You can rummage through the bin to recover items, or empty the bin when you're sure you no longer need the discarded items. Check out Chapter 7 for details.

- **Start** button is an on-screen button that you can click on to view a list of all the programs installed in Windows 95. Simply click on a program to run it.

You may have additional icons, such as Network Neighborhood, the Microsoft Network, Inbox, the Internet, and My Briefcase, on your desktop (see the following figure). Network Neighborhood appears only if you chose to install a Windows 95 network component when you installed Windows. My Briefcase enables you to quickly transfer files between a laptop and desktop computer. The others are communications options. If these items are not installed and you want to install them (or if they are installed and you want to remove them), refer to the Installation appendix at the back of this book, and to Chapter 63, "Uncluttering Your Disk."

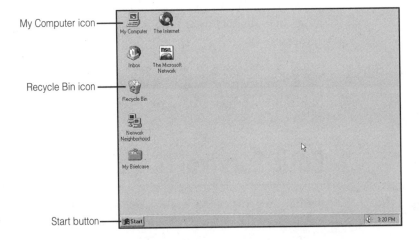

Using the Start
Button

The Start button is the core of the Windows 95 interface. You use this button to install and run your programs, customize windows, arrange files, install new hardware, and perform all other Windows tasks. Think of this as the Windows kiosk, a one-stop control center for your computer. To use the Start button, follow these steps:

1. Click on the Start button. The Start menu opens and remains open until you click on another item on the menu or click outside the menu.

2. Move the mouse pointer over the desired item. If you move the mouse pointer over a submenu item (an item followed by a right-pointing arrow), a submenu automatically opens.

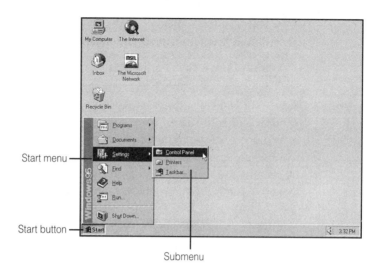

Start menu —

Start button —

Submenu

3. Keep moving the mouse pointer until it is over the desired item, and then click the left mouse button.

Notice that the Start menu contains several items. The following list describes each item and its function:

- **Programs** is a menu that contains a list of programs installed in Windows 95. To run a program, click on its name. Windows runs each program in its own window and displays the names of all open windows on the Taskbar.

- **Documents** contains a list of recently opened *documents* (files you create and edit). To open a document, select it from the Documents submenu. (Not all programs can add documents to this submenu.)

- **Settings** gives you access to the tools you need to control your printer, mouse, and display; to install programs; to install new hardware; and to perform any other system configurations. Part 5, "Using the Windows Control Panel," discusses system settings in detail.

- **Find** does just what it says it does: it helps you find misplaced files and programs.

- **Help** displays a Help window, which provides complete online documentation that you can search for specific information. Chapter 8 explains in detail how to get help in Windows 95.

- **Run** displays a dialog box that you can use to run programs not listed on the Programs menu. See Chapter 3 for details.

- **Shut Down** closes or restarts Windows 95 (as you learned in Chapter 1).

Using the Taskbar

Whenever you run a program, Windows displays the program in its own window and adds the program's name to the Taskbar. If you've ever worked in Windows 3.1, you know how easy it used to be to bury a running program window under a stack of windows. The Taskbar prevents this from happening by keeping the names of all running programs available at the bottom of the screen. To switch to a program, simply click on its name in the Taskbar.

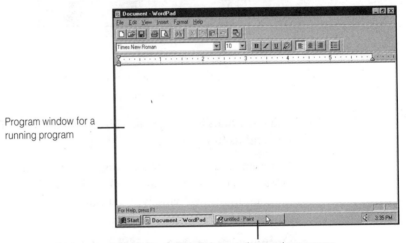

Program window for a
running program

To switch to another running program,
click on its name in the Taskbar.

Beyond Survival

Customizing the Taskbar

Although the Taskbar is a useful tool, you may want to change its position on the screen or make it take up less room. To take control of the Taskbar, follow these steps:

1. To move the Taskbar, move the mouse pointer over any blank area of the Taskbar (the area just to the left of the clock works well, or grab the clock itself).

2. Press and hold the left mouse button, and drag the Taskbar to the left, right, or top of the screen until the outline is in the desired position.

3. Release the mouse button, and Windows moves the Taskbar to its new location.

Right-click in blank area of taskbar and select Properties

4. To further customize the Taskbar, click on the Start button, move the mouse pointer over Settings, and click on Taskbar. The Taskbar Properties dialog box appears, as shown in the following figure.

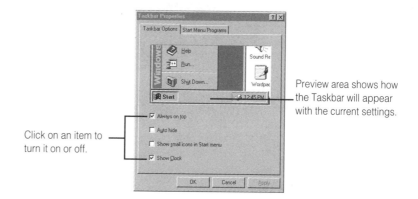

Click on an item to turn it on or off.

Preview area shows how the Taskbar will appear with the current settings.

5. Click on any of the following options to turn them on or off (a check mark in the check box indicates that the item is on):

Always on Top keeps the Taskbar on top of the desktop, so you can always see it. (Keep this option on.)

Auto Hide reduces the height of the Taskbar when you're working in your programs so it takes up less screen space. To redisplay the Taskbar (full height), point at the area where the Taskbar should be.

Show Small Icons on Start Menu reduces the size of the icons (little pictures) on the Start menu.

Show Clock displays the current time on the right side of the Taskbar.

6. Click on the OK button to save your changes.

Cheat Sheet

Running a Program from the Start Menu

2. Move the mouse pointer over Programs.

4. Click on the program's name.

1. Click on the Start button.

3. Move the mouse pointer over a submenu name.

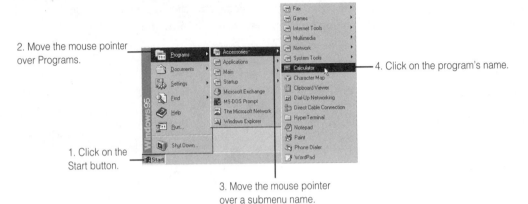

Running a Program That's Not on the Start Menu

1. Click on the Start button.

2. Click on Run.

3. Type the program's drive letter followed by a colon.

4. Click on the Browse button.

5. Double-click on the folder that contains the program's files to open it.

6. Double-click on the program's icon.

7. Click on the OK button.

Switching to a Running Program

- Click on the program's name in the Taskbar.
- Click anywhere inside the program's window.
- Hold down the Alt key and press Tab repeatedly until the desired program is selected.

Exiting a Windows Program

- Click on File in the menu bar, and then click on Exit.
- Click on the Close button (the button with the **X** on it, in the upper-right corner of the window).

3

Running and Switching Between Programs

Face it: you didn't buy Windows to play around with little pictures. You bought Windows so you could run *Windows programs*—programs that let you do something practical with your computer, like type a letter or balance your budget. In this chapter, you'll learn the basics of running a program and switching from one running program to another.

Basic Survival

Starting a Program from the Start Menu

The Start menu contains icons for all the programs installed in Windows 95. To run a program:

1. Click on the Start button.

2. Move the mouse pointer over Programs. The Programs menu opens, displaying additional submenu and program names.

3. If the program is on a submenu (the name has an arrow to the right of it), move the mouse pointer over the submenu's name. The submenu opens.

The Start menu ———

The Programs submenu

4. Click on the name of the program you want to run. Windows runs the program and displays it in its own program window.

Press first letter of name to select program

On the Programs submenu, the programs are arranged alphabetically by name (submenu names appear first; individual program names follow). You can quickly highlight a folder or program name by pressing the key that corresponds to the first letter of its name. If two or more items start with the same letter, keep pressing the letters of the program's name until the desired item is highlighted. Then press Enter to open the submenu or run the program.

Running a Program That's Not on the Start Menu

During the Windows installation, Windows tried to create entries on the Start menu for most of your programs. If the program you want to run is on the Start menu (or one of its submenus), you can run it by performing the steps in the previous section. If the program you want to run is not on the menu, skip ahead to the section called "Finding a Program That's Not on the Menu" later in this chapter, or turn to Chapter 9 to learn how to add the program to the Programs menu. If you're in a hurry, follow these steps to run the program right now:

1. Click on the Start button and click on Run. The Run dialog box appears.

2. Type the letter of the drive where the program's files are stored, followed by a colon. For example, type **c:**.

3. Click on the Browse button. The Browse dialog box appears, showing all the folders (a.k.a. *directories*) on the specified drive.

4. Double-click on the folder that contains the program's files.

Alt + Spacebar to run DOS program in a window (not full-screen)

5. Click on the name of the file that runs the program, and then click on Open. The Browse dialog box closes, and the file's name is added to the Run dialog box.

6. Click on the OK button, and Windows runs the program.

Type the drive letter here,
then click Browse.

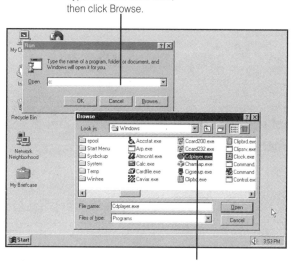

Double-click on the file that
runs the program, or click on
it and then click Open.

Exiting a Windows Program

When you finish working in a program, you should exit it properly to avoid losing any work. Most programs have safeguards that warn you if you're about to exit without saving your file. However, if you exit improperly (by turning off your computer, for instance), you bypass these safeguards. To exit a program, take one of the following steps:

- Click on File in the program's menu bar, and then click on Exit.

- Click on the Close button in the upper-right corner of the window (it's the button with the **X** on it).

- To exit from a DOS program, use the program's Exit or Quit command (usually on the File menu). Using the Close button can cause you to lose data.

- If you happen to end up at the DOS prompt (something like **C:\>**), type **exit**, and then press Enter.

Alt + F4
same as file, Exit

19

You can also exit a program quickly by double-clicking on the window's Control-menu box (the icon in the upper-left corner of the window).

Beyond Survival

Finding a Program That's Not on the Menu

In Chapter 9, "Installing and Setting Up Programs," you'll learn how to add installed programs to the Programs menu. For now, if you can't find a program you want to run, use the Find command on the Start menu to search for it. These steps tell you how.

1. Click on the Start button.

2. Move the mouse pointer over Find, and then click on Files or Folders. The Find dialog box appears.

3. Type the name or partial name of the program file that runs the program. For example, to find your fax program, you might type **fax**.

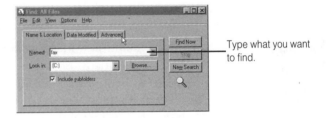

Type what you want to find.

4. Click on the Advanced tab.

5. Click on the arrow to the right of Of type, and click on Application.

6. Click on the Find Now button. Windows searches your disk for program files that match your instructions and displays a list of the files it finds.

7. Double-click on the file that runs the desired program. Windows runs the program.

Switching Between Programs

One of the things users like best about Windows is that it lets you run two or more programs at the same time. When you run multiple programs, however, you can easily get lost in a stack of windows. To switch to a specific program, do one of the following:

- Click anywhere inside the program's window (if you can see it).

- Click on the program's name inside the Taskbar.

- Right-click on a blank area of the Taskbar (not on a button or the clock) and choose one of the top three options (Cascade, Tile Horizontally, or Tile Vertically) to view all the windows. Then click inside the desired window.

- Hold down the Alt key and press the Tab key one or more times until the title of the desired program appears. Then release the Alt key.

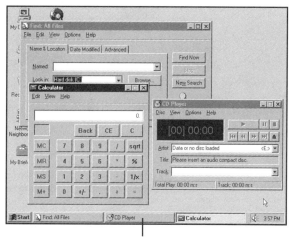

Click on the program's
name in the Taskbar

If you have trouble quitting a program, try changing to the program and pressing Ctrl+Alt+Del. This action displays the Close Program dialog box, which lists the names of all running programs. Click on the name of the program that's giving you trouble, and then click on the End Task button. This usually shuts down only the problem program, leaving Windows and your other programs unscathed.

Cheat Sheet

Selecting Menu Commands

1. Click on the name of the menu you want to open.

2. Click on the desired command.

3. If a submenu opens, click on the desired submenu option.

Backing Out of a Menu

- Click anywhere outside the menu.
- Press Esc once or twice.

Using Shortcut Menus

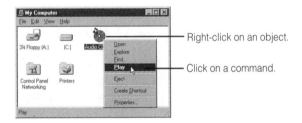

Right-click on an object.

Click on a command.

Responding to Dialog Boxes

Click on a tab to see a group of related options.

Type a setting or name in a text box.

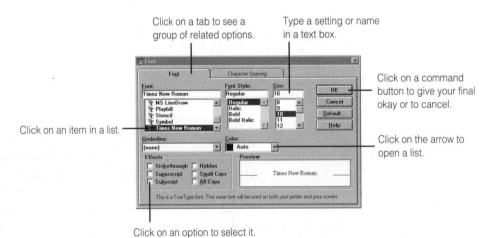

Click on a command button to give your final okay or to cancel.

Click on an item in a list.

Click on the arrow to open a list.

Click on an option to select it.

Entering Commands in Windows 95

4

In Windows, you enter commands not by typing them but by selecting them from *pull-down menus* or new *shortcut menus*. In this chapter, you'll learn how to select commands and how to respond to dialog boxes—boxes that request additional information.

Basic Survival

Selecting Commands from Pull-Down Menus

Just below the title bar of most windows is a *menu bar* that contains the names of several pull-down menus. Most menu bars include the following menus: File, Edit, Format, Window, and Help. Each menu contains several related commands. To enter a command, you can perform any one of the following steps:

- Click on the menu name, and then click on the desired command.

- Move the mouse pointer over the menu name, press and hold the mouse button, drag over the desired command, and release the mouse button.

- Hold down the Alt key and press the underlined letter in the menu's name, release the Alt key, and press the underlined letter in the name of the command or option you want to select.

Many menu options have corresponding *shortcut keys* that you can use to bypass the menu system. These shortcut key combinations are listed on the menus, so you can wean yourself from the menus.

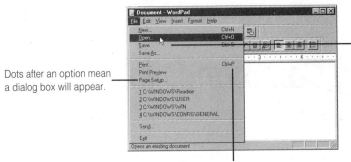

Dots after an option mean a dialog box will appear.

You can drag over an option's name and release the mouse button.

Use these shortcut key combinations to bypass the menu altogether.

You may notice that not all the options on the menu appear the same. Some options are followed by an arrow or an ellipsis (...). Other options appear light gray instead of black. Here is a rundown of some of the variations you may encounter:

Light gray options are unavailable for what you are currently doing. For example, if you want to copy a chunk of text but have not yet selected the text, the Copy command is not available.

Options with an arrow open a *submenu* that requires you to select another option.

Options with a check mark are currently active (turned on). To turn the option off, select it. This removes the check mark and closes the menu.

Options followed by an ellipsis (...) open a *dialog box* that requests additional information.

Cancelling Menus

If you open a menu and then decide that you do not want to select an option, you have several choices:

- Click on the menu name (or anywhere outside the menu) to close it.

- Press the Alt key or F10.

Press Esc to cancel menu

- Press Esc to back out of the menu. You may have to press it two or more times to deactivate the menu bar.

- Once a menu is open, you can open a different menu instead by moving the mouse pointer over its name. Or use the left arrow key to open the menu to the left, or the right arrow key to open the menu to the right.

Responding to Dialog Boxes

If you choose a command that is followed by an ellipsis (...), the program displays a *dialog box* that requests additional information.

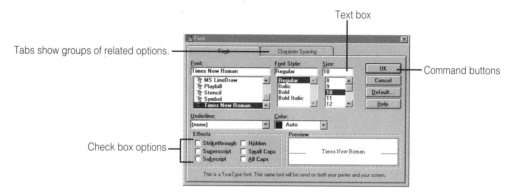

Text box

Tabs show groups of related options.

Command buttons

Check box options

Dialog boxes are chock-full of all sorts of interesting objects. Here's a list of all the items you might encounter, though you'll see only two or three items in any given dialog box:

Tabs: Each tab contains a group of related options. To switch to a set of options, click on its tab.

Text boxes: A text box is sort of a "fill in the blank": it is where you type text, such as the name of a file. To replace an entry in a text box, double-click inside it and then type your entry. To edit an entry, click inside the text box, use the arrow keys to move the insertion point, and type your correction.

Option buttons: Option buttons look like Cheerios. You click on a button to turn it on. You can turn on only one option in a group.

Check boxes: Check boxes enable you to turn an option on or off. Click inside a check box to turn it on if it's off, or off if it's on. You can select more than one check box in a group.

List box: A list box presents two or more options. Click on the option you want. If the list is long, you'll see a *scroll bar*. Click on the scroll bar arrows to move up or down in the list.

Drop-down list box: This list box displays only one item and hides the rest of the items. Click on the arrow to the right of the box to display the rest of the list, and then click on the item you want.

Spin box: A spin box is a text box with controls. You can usually type a setting in the text box or use the up or down arrow key to change the setting.

Command buttons: Most dialog boxes have at least three buttons: OK to confirm your selections, Cancel to quit, and Help to get help.

To get around in a dialog box, you can click on items with the mouse, use the Tab key to move from item to item (Shift+Tab to move back), or hold down the Alt key and press the underlined letter in the option's name.

Right-Clicking for Shortcut Menus

For some time now, Windows programs have been making use of the right mouse button to display *shortcut menus*. These menus contain commands that specifically relate to the selected object, so you don't have to search through the menu bar to find available commands. Now, Windows 95 itself is also using right-click shortcut menus. To use a shortcut menu, follow these steps:

1. Move the mouse pointer over the object you want to control.

2. Click the right mouse button, and a shortcut menu pops up. The options on the menu vary depending on the object you clicked on. For example, if you click on the clock in the Taskbar (all the way on the right), you see the menu in the following figure.

This shortcut menu displays your options when you right-click on the clock.

3. Click (right or left mouse button) on the desired option. What happens next depends on the option you select. Windows may carry out the command, or display a dialog box asking for more information.

4. To close a shortcut menu without entering a command, press the Esc key or left-click outside the menu.

I'll use these shortcut menus extensively throughout this book to show quick ways to perform tasks. For now, just keep in mind that options are usually just a right-click away.

Beyond Survival

Finding a File in a Dialog Box

One of the most common (and confusing) dialog boxes you will encounter is the one you get when you try to select a file.

Click on this button to move up the folder tree.

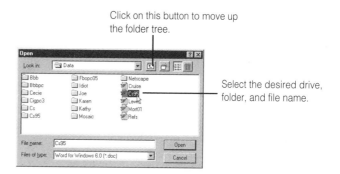

Select the desired drive, folder, and file name.

To respond to such a dialog box, follow these steps:

1. Click on the arrow to the right of the Drives or Look in list, and then click on the letter of the desired drive.

2. In the Folders list, double-click on the desired folder. (To move up the directory tree, double-click on the drive letter or folder at the top of the list, or press the Backspace key.)

3. To view the names of only those files that end with a specific extension, click on the arrow to the right of the Files of type list, and click on the desired file type.

4. Perform one of the following steps:

    • If you are saving a file, click inside the File Name text box, and type the name you want to use for the file.

    • If you are selecting an existing file, click on the desired file in the File Name list, or type its name in the text box.

5. Click on the OK button.

Moving a Dialog Box

Sometimes a dialog box blocks your view, preventing you from seeing an important message or an object that's behind it. In such cases, you can move the dialog box by *dragging* its title bar. Simply move the mouse pointer inside the dialog box title bar, hold down the mouse button, and move the mouse.

Selecting Multiple Items in a List

Some dialog box lists allow you to select more than one item at a time. To select two or more items, do one of the following:

- To select neighboring items in the list, click on the first item you want to select, press and hold the Shift key, and click on the last item.

- To select non-neighboring items, hold down the Ctrl key while clicking on each desired item.

Using Toolbars (in Some Programs)

Many programs include *toolbars* that are usually just below the menu bar or on the left or right side of the program's window. These toolbars provide a quick way to enter commonly used commands. For example, instead of opening the File menu and selecting Print, you can simply click on a toolbar button.

In most programs, if you rest the mouse pointer on a button, a description of the button appears in the lower left corner of the window or right next to the button.

Click on a tool to bypass the menu system

Rest the mouse pointer on a button to see its name

Toolbars offer quick access to commands

Cheat Sheet

Arranging Windows

1. Open all the Windows you want to arrange.
2. Right-click on a blank area of the Taskbar.
3. Click on one of the following window arrangements:

   Cascade (to view overlapping windows)

   Tile Horizontally (to view windows one above the other)

   Tile Vertically (to view windows side by side)

Sizing a Window

1. Position the mouse pointer over a window border so the pointer turns into a double-headed arrow.
2. Hold down the left mouse button.
3. Move the mouse until the window is the desired size.
4. Release the mouse button.

Quick Sizing Options

Click on the Maximize button to make the window full-screen size.

Click on the Minimize button to make the window into an icon.

Click on the Restore button to return a maximized window to its previous size.

Click on the Close button to close the window and exit the program.

Moving a Window

1. Place the mouse pointer inside the window's title bar.
2. Hold down the left mouse button.
3. Move the mouse until the window is in the desired position.
4. Release the mouse button.

5

Arranging Windows

Working with Windows is like working with a deck of cards. Whenever you run an application, open a group window, or create a file, you open another window that may hide an existing window. In order to manage all these windows, you need to know how to "fan the deck." In this chapter, you'll learn how to take control of your windows by moving, sizing, and rearranging them to your liking.

Basic Survival

Types of Windows

Windows uses two types of windows: *program windows* and *document windows*. A program window contains a running program. For example, when you run Word for Windows, a program window opens. A document window contains a file you open or create in the program. For example, you type text in Word for Windows in a document window; most Windows applications let you work on two or more documents in separate windows.

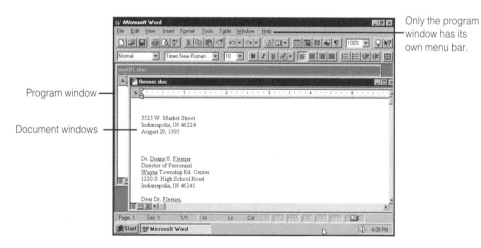

Only the program window has its own menu bar.

Program window

Document windows

Opening and Closing Windows

When Windows runs a program, it opens the program in its own *program window*. Usually the program window contains a *document window* you can use to start your work. Also, whenever you open a file you've created, the program displays it in its own document window (inside the program window). Program and document windows behave a little differently. When you close a program window, for example, you exit the program; when you close a document window, you simply close the file (the program remains running).

To close a program window (quit the program), perform one of the following steps:

- Open the File menu and select Exit.

- Press Alt+F4.

- Click on the Close button in the upper-right corner of the window.

- Click on the Control-menu icon in the upper-left corner of the window, and click on Close.

- Double-click on the Control-menu icon.

Alt + F4 = Exit

Right-click inside title bar to open Control menu

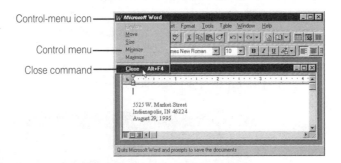

Control-menu icon

Control menu

Close command

To close a document window, click on its Close button. Most programs also have a Close option on the File menu that closes the current document window. Switch to the window you want to close; then open the File menu and select Close.

If you close a window that contains a file you were working on—but did not save—a warning message appears, giving you a chance to save the file. Click on the Yes button, enter the selection to name the file, and then type a name and location for the file (refer to Lesson 10 for details).

If you exit without saving,
you are warned.

Cascading or Tiling Windows

Windows knows how easy it is to lose a window in a stack, so it gives you three possible window arrangements: cascading, tiled horizontally, or tiled vertically. "Tiled" places the windows side by side, whereas "cascading" overlaps the windows, showing only a portion of each window. To choose an arrangement for your windows, here's what you do:

1. Open all the Windows you want to arrange. (Windows that are closed or minimized will not be arranged.)

2. Right-click on a blank area in the Taskbar. The Taskbar's pop-up menu appears.

3. Click on Cascade, Tile Horizontally, or Tile Vertically. Windows rearranges all open program windows as specified.

To return to the previous window arrangement, right-click on a blank area of the Taskbar and click on the Undo option.

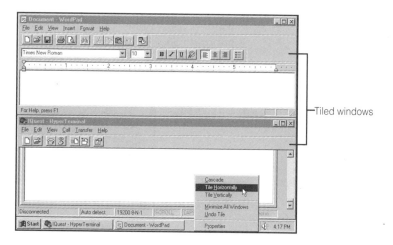

Tiled windows

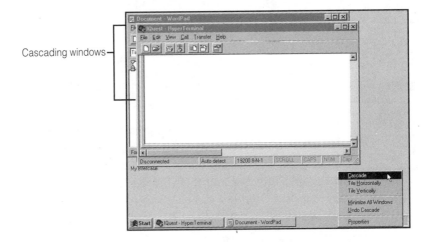

Cascading windows

The tiled and cascading arrangements make it easy to change from one window to another. You simply click on the desired window, and it jumps to the front of the stack. If you cannot see a portion of a window, you can change to it simply by clicking on the program name in the Taskbar.

Moving Windows

Although the Tile and Cascade commands enable you to arrange windows quickly, they give you little control over the actual position of the windows. You can move a window more precisely by dragging the window's title bar. Simply place the tip of the mouse pointer anywhere inside the title bar, press and hold the left mouse button, and move the mouse. An outline of the window appears, indicating the window's new position. When you reach the position you want the window in, release the mouse button, and the window is relocated.

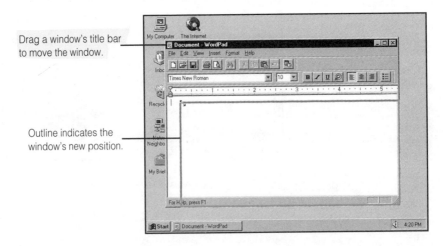

Drag a window's title bar to move the window.

Outline indicates the window's new position.

Sizing Windows

While you're rearranging your windows, you may want to resize them. The easiest way to resize a window is to place the mouse pointer over one of the window's borders, press and hold the mouse button, and drag the border. (Note that if the window is maximized, you can't resize it; click on the window's Restore button, and then drag its border.)

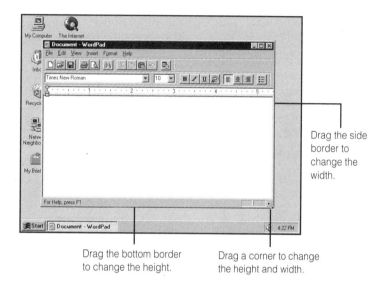

Drag the side border to change the width.

Drag the bottom border to change the height.

Drag a corner to change the height and width.

For a fast-and-loose resizing job, use the following buttons, located in the upper right corner of the window:

Maximize button makes the window full-screen size. The Maximize button is then replaced by the Restore button.

Minimize button reduces the window to icon size. You can restore the window by double-clicking on the icon, or by clicking on it and select-ing Restore.

Restore button returns a maximized window to the size it was before you clicked on the Maximize button.

Close button closes the window and exits the program. The program's name is removed from the Taskbar.

Right-click on blank Taskbar and select Minimize All Windows

If you want to minimize all of your open windows, right-click on a blank area of the Taskbar and click on Minimize All Windows.

Beyond Survival

Controlling Windows with the Keyboard

If you don't like to take your fingers off the keyboard, you can use keystrokes to move and resize windows:

1. Press Alt+Spacebar to open the current window's Control menu.

2. Press the underlined letter in the desired option name: Restore, Move, Size, Minimize, or Maximize.

3. If you choose Move or Size, use the arrow keys to move or resize the window, and then press Enter.

Window Panes (in Some Programs)

Some programs, including the new Windows Explorer, use window *panes* to separate a window into two or more sections. You can drag the pane border to change the relative size of the sections, just as you drag window borders.

Panes

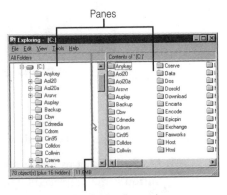

Drag the dividing line to change
the relative size of the sections.

Changing the Border Width

If your window borders are too narrow or too thick for your liking, you can change the border thickness. (A thicker border often makes it easier to position the mouse pointer correctly for resizing windows.) Here's what you do:

1. Click on the Start button.

2. Move the mouse pointer over Settings, and then click on Control Panel. The Windows Control Panel appears.

3. Double-click on the Display icon. The Display Properties dialog box appears.

4. Click on the Appearance tab.

5. Click on the arrow to the right of the Item list, and click on Active Window Border.

6. Click on the up arrow to the right of the Size spin box to increase the size of the border. (The preview area shows the border's new size.)

7. Click on the OK button to save your settings.

For more information about how you can change the look of your Windows 95 desktop and your individual windows, see Chapter 39, "Changing the Display Settings."

The Appearance tab

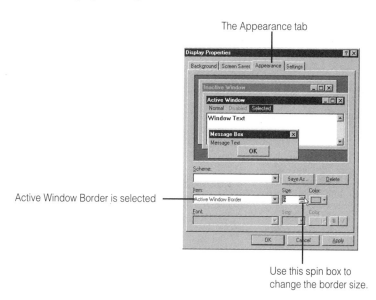

Active Window Border is selected

Use this spin box to change the border size.

Cheat Sheet

Understanding Icon Types

- **Shortcut icons** are clones of original icons; you place them on the Windows desktop, on the Programs menu, or in another folder or window. They provide quick access to your programs, documents, printers, and other resources.

- **Disk icons** open a window that shows you the names of the files and folders (directories) on the selected disk.

- **Folder icons** represent directories that contain groups of related files.

- **Program icons** represent programs you can run. Double-click on a program icon to run the program.

- **Document icons** are for the files you create. Double-clicking on a document icon runs the program in which the document was created and opens the document in that program.

Displaying Icons in My Computer

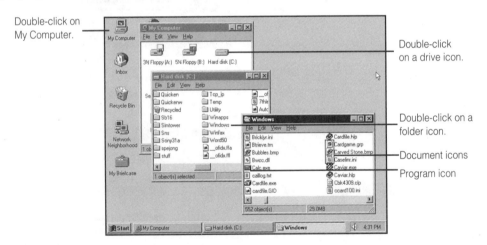

Double-click on My Computer.

Double-click on a drive icon.

Double-click on a folder icon.

Document icons

Program icon

Arranging Icons

1. Right-click inside the window that contains the icons you want to rearrange.

2. To sort the icons (for example, by size or name), point to Arrange Icons and click on the desired sort order.

3. To arrange the icons in a grid, right-click inside the window and click on Line Up Icons.

6

Working with Icons

As you work with Windows 95, you'll notice all sorts of tiny pictures, called *icons*, that pepper the screen. In this chapter, you'll learn how to control the size, position, and appearance of these icons.

Basic Survival

Types of Icons

Windows comes with five basic types of icons: shortcut icons, disk icons, folder icons, program icons, and document icons. These icons are graphic representations of files and programs. To run a program or open a document (file), you simply double-click on its icon. Here's a rundown of the various types of icons you'll encounter:

- **Shortcut icons** are copies of original icons; you place them on the Windows desktop, on the Programs menu, or in another folder or window. They provide quick access to your programs, documents, printers, and other resources. In Chapter 12, you'll learn how to drag icons to the desktop to create your own shortcut icons.

- **Disk icons** open a window that shows you the names of the files and folders (directories) on the selected disk. Before you click on a disk icon, make sure there's a disk in the drive; if there isn't, you'll receive an error message.

- **Folder icons** represent *folders* (directories) that contain groups of related files and other folders. To view the contents of a folder, double-click on it.

- **Program icons** represent programs you can run. You typically bump into program items on the Programs menu and in program folders. To run the program, double-click on its icon.

- **Document icons** are for the files you create. Usually, a particular document type is *associated* with a specific program. If you double-click on a document file, Windows runs the associated program and opens

Double-click on an icon to "run" it

the document. In Chapter 37, "Running Programs from Windows Explorer," you'll learn how to associate documents to programs.

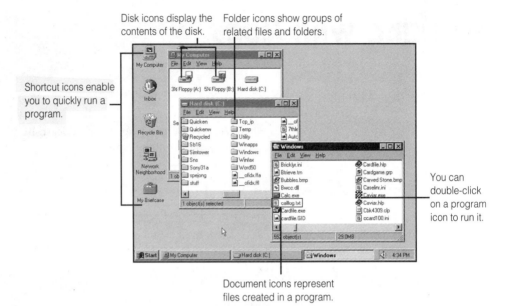

Disk icons display the contents of the disk.

Folder icons show groups of related files and folders.

Shortcut icons enable you to quickly run a program.

You can double-click on a program icon to run it.

Document icons represent files created in a program.

Displaying Icons in My Computer

In case you haven't noticed, there's an icon in the upper-left corner of the Windows desktop that's labeled My Computer. If this icon is buried under a stack of windows, simply right-click on a blank area in the Taskbar and click on Minimize All Windows. Windows 95 minimizes all the windows and you can see the My Computer icon again.

The My Computer icon gives you access to all the folders (directories), files, and programs on your computer. All you have to do is sift through the icons. To access a program or file, here's what you do:

1. Double-click on My Computer. The My Computer window appears, displaying icons for all the drives on your computer plus a folder for installed printers and for the Control Panel.

2. To view the contents of a floppy drive or CD-ROM drive, make sure there's a disk in the drive.

3. Double-click on the icon for the drive. Another window opens on top of the first, displaying the files and folders on the selected drive.

4. To view the contents of a folder, double-click on its icon.

5. To run a program or open a document, double-click on its icon.

You'll learn more about using My Computer to manage your disks, folders, and files in Part 4 of this book. For now, you'll use My Computer to learn the basics of dealing with Windows icons.

Arranging Icons

Like windows themselves, icons can overlap, which may result in some icons getting lost in the stack. If this happens, you can take the following steps to sort the icons and arrange them in a grid on-screen:

1. Right-click anywhere inside the window that contains the icons.

2. To arrange the icons by name, size, or some other feature, place the mouse pointer over Arrange Icons, and then click on the desired sorting configuration.

3. To arrange the icons in an on-screen (invisible) grid so they won't overlap, right-click inside the window and click on Line up Icons.

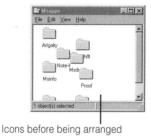
Icons before being arranged

Icons after being arranged

Moving and Copying Icons

Up to this point, icons have played a very static role, pretty much holding their position. However, on the Windows 95 desktop, icons are actually dynamic; you can move them from one window to another, between disks, and even to the desktop simply by dragging them. To copy or move an icon, here's what you do:

1. Open the window that contains the icon you want to move and make sure the destination window or icon is visible.

2. Move the mouse pointer over the icon you want to copy or move.

Press Ctrl to copy an icon

3. To copy the icon, hold down the Ctrl key while performing the next step.

41

4. Press and hold the left mouse button, and drag the icon where you want it.

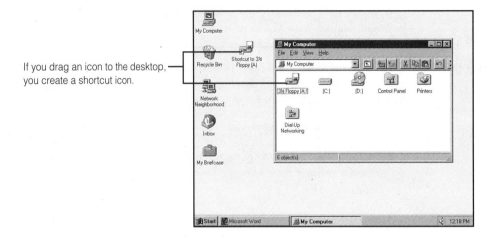

If you drag an icon to the desktop, you create a shortcut icon.

5. Release the mouse button. If you dragged the icon to the Windows desktop, you'll see the following message, showing that you are about to create a *shortcut*. A shortcut is a clone icon that you can use to quickly select an item from the desktop without opening multiple windows. Click on the Yes button.

As you copy or move icons, one icon might cover another. You can drag the top icon off the other icon, or you can have Windows rearrange the icons as explained in the previous section.

Beyond Survival

Changing the Spacing Between Icons

When Windows arranges icons, it spaces them on an invisible grid 43 pixels apart, so they don't overlap. To increase or decrease the spacing between icons, follow these steps:

1. Right-click anywhere on the desktop. The Desktop shortcut menu pops up.

2. Click on Properties and then click on the Appearance tab.

3. Open the Item drop-down list and click on Icon Spacing (Horizontal) or Icon Spacing (Vertical).

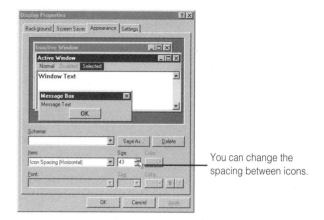

You can change the
spacing between icons.

4. Click on the up or down arrow to the right of the Size spin box to increase or decrease the spacing between icons.

5. Click on the OK button when you're done.

Changing the Way Icons Are Displayed

Windows typically uses small icons for windows that contain lots of icons, and large icons for windows that contain few icons. Also, Windows typically arranges icons alphabetically by name (placing folder icons first, followed by file icons). You can control the size and arrangement of icons in a specific window by performing the following steps:

1. Click on View in the menu bar.

Right-click inside window and point to View

2. Click on the desired icon display: Large Icons, Small Icons, List, or Details. List is similar to Small Icons; Small Icons arranges items horizontally in rows, whereas List arranges them vertically in columns. Details provides additional information about files and folders, including the date the file or folder was last modified.

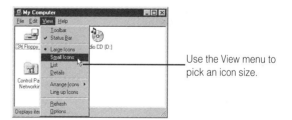

Use the View menu to
pick an icon size.

Cheat Sheet

Understanding the Recycle Bin

- The Recycle Bin is disk storage that acts as a buffer area for deleted files.
- Drag icons to the Recycle Bin icon to delete them and any files they point to.
- If you accidentally delete a file by dragging it to the Recycle Bin, you can retrieve the file by opening the Bin and dragging the icon out.
- Because the Recycle Bin uses disk space, you should empty the Bin regularly.
- You can customize the Recycle Bin so it uses more or less disk space.

Selecting Icons to Drag to the Recycle Bin

- Click on an icon to select it.
- Hold down the Ctrl key and click on additional icons to select them.
- Drag a selection box around several icons to select a group.
- To select neighboring icons, click on the first icon, press and hold the Shift key, and click on the last one in the group.

Dragging Icons to the Recycle Bin

1. Place the mouse pointer over one of the selected icons.
2. Press and hold the left mouse button and drag the icons over the Recycle Bin icon.
3. Release the mouse button.

Restoring Items from the Recycle Bin

1. Double-click on the Recycle Bin icon.
2. Select the items you want to restore.
3. Open the File menu and click on Restore.

Emptying the Recycle Bin

1. Double-click on the Recycle Bin icon.
2. Click on File in the menu bar.
3. Click on Empty Recycle Bin.

7

Dumping Objects in the Recycle Bin

In addition to the My Computer icon, the Windows desktop contains an icon labeled Recycle Bin. This nifty little device enables you to quickly delete items on the desktop or in Windows and just as quickly restore them (if you deleted an object by mistake). In this chapter, you'll learn how to use the Recycle Bin to delete and retrieve files and other objects, empty the Recycle Bin, and even customize the Bin to behave as you wish.

Basic Survival

Selecting Objects to Delete

To dump a single item into the Recycle Bin, you can simply drag it over the Recycle Bin icon and release the mouse button. However, if you want to delete several items at once, you must first select them. You can use any of several techniques to select multiple objects:

- Click on the first item you want to select, press and hold the Ctrl key, and click on any additional items. You can select files, folders, disks, and shortcuts (icons that appear on the desktop).

- To select neighboring items in a list, click on the first item, press and hold the Shift key, and click on the last item in the group. Windows highlights the first and last items and all items in between.

  Note: In List view, Shift+click selects columns of neighboring items. In Small Icon view, Shift+click selects rows of neighboring items.

- Position the mouse pointer at the upper-left side of the first item you want to select, press and hold the mouse button, and drag over the other items. A box appears as you drag. When all the items are surrounded by the box, release the mouse button. (This method of selecting a group of neighboring objects is new in Windows 95.)

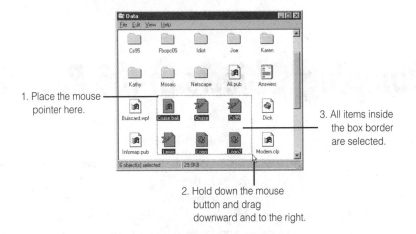

1. Place the mouse pointer here.

3. All items inside the box border are selected.

2. Hold down the mouse button and drag downward and to the right.

Pitching Objects into the Recycle Bin

After you select the object or objects you want to delete, you can dump them into the Recycle Bin. In most cases, dragging icons to the Recycle Bin deletes the icon and any file it points to; if you delete a shortcut icon, however, only the icon is removed (the files remain intact). To delete selected objects, here's what you do:

1. Place the mouse pointer over any one of the selected objects.

2. Press and hold the left mouse button and drag the items over the Recycle Bin icon. The Recycle Bin icon appears highlighted to show that the mouse is positioned properly.

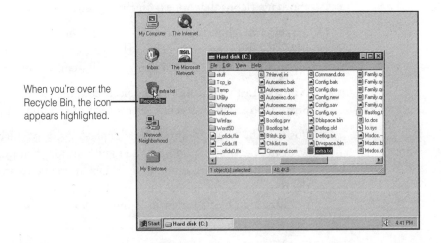

When you're over the Recycle Bin, the icon appears highlighted.

Right-click on selected object and select Delete

3. Release the mouse button and the items are moved to the Recycle Bin.

The items you place in the Recycle Bin remain there (even after you turn off your computer) until you dump the Recycle Bin. If you need to, you can retrieve the objects as explained in the next section.

Recycling Deleted Objects

The Recycle Bin is like the bin where you store recyclable aluminum cans until you take them to the recycling center. Just as you have the option of getting rid of the materials in that bin or pulling them out to reuse them, you have the option of dumping (recycling) or saving (undeleting) objects you put in the Recycle Bin. So if you accidentally place something in the Recycle Bin, you can follow these steps to restore the deleted item to its original location:

1. Double-click on the Recycle Bin icon. The Recycle Bin window appears, displaying the Recycle Bin's contents.

2. Select the items you want to undelete, as explained earlier in this lesson.

You can select items to restore
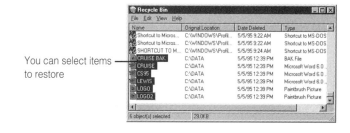

Right-click on selected object and select Restore

3. Open the File menu and click on Restore. The selected items are undeleted and placed in their original locations.

You don't have to restore deleted items to their original disks or folders. To restore to a different location, simply select the items you want to restore and drag them to the disk or folder icon where you want them placed.

Dumping the Recycle Bin

Keep in mind that the Recycle Bin is actually a storage area on your disk drive. As such, it can become cluttered with files and other objects that consume precious disk space. On a regular basis, you should review the contents of the Recycle Bin and dump any items you're sure you don't need. When you're sure you don't need anything in the Bin, follow these steps to dump the contents:

1. Double-click on the Recycle Bin icon.

To empty Recycle
Bin quickly,
right-click on
Recycle Bin icon;
click on Empty
Recycle Bin

2. Open the File menu and click on Empty Recycle Bin. A dialog box appears, asking for your confirmation.

3. Click on the Yes button. Windows removes the icons from your disk.

If you want to delete some (not all) objects from the Recycle Bin, first select the items you want to delete, as explained earlier in this lesson. Then open the File menu and select Delete. When the confirmation dialog box appears, click on the Yes button.

Beyond Survival

Changing the Recycle Bin's Properties

Empty Recycle Bin
regularly to prevent
disk clutter

The Recycle Bin is initially set up to use 10 percent of each of your hard drive's space for deleted files. It's also set up to display a confirmation dialog box whenever you dump files into it. To change either of these settings, perform the following steps:

1. Right-click on the Recycle Bin icon or on a blank area inside the Recycle Bin window.

2. Click on Properties. The Recycle Bin Properties dialog box appears. If you have more than one hard drive, you'll have a tab for each drive.

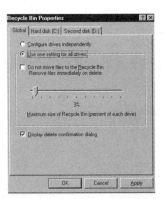

3. To enter the same settings for all the hard drives on your system, click on Use one setting for all drives. To use different settings for each drive, click on Configure drives independently, and then click on the tab for the drive whose settings you want to change.

4. The Do not move files to the Recycle Bin option can be dangerous. It tells Windows to automatically delete files you drag to the Recycle Bin (which means you can't restore them). Choose this option only if you're really tight on disk space and you never accidentally delete files.

5. To change the percentage of the drive used by the Recycle Bin, drag the pointer along the Maximum size of Recycle Bin scale until it displays the desired percentage. For example, 10 percent of a 500MB disk drive is 50 megabytes. When the Recycle Bin contents exceed this amount, the Recycle Bin automatically deletes the oldest deleted files.

6. To prevent the confirmation dialog box from appearing when you dump items into the Recycle Bin, click on Display delete confirmation dialog box to remove the check mark.

7. Click on the OK button to save your changes and close the dialog box, or click on Apply to save your changes and leave the dialog box open.

Cheat Sheet

Getting Help

1. Click on the Start button.
2. Click on Help.
3. Click on the Contents tab.
4. Double-click on the desired help type: Introducing Windows, How To, Tips and Tricks, or Troubleshooting.
5. Keep double-clicking on items until you view the Help screen you need.

Skipping Around in the Help System

- Click on a topic with a button next to it to display information about the topic.
- To go back to the previous Help screen, click on the Back button.
- To go back to the first Help screen, click on the Help Topics button.
- Click on a dotted-underlined term to display a pop-up box with a definition.

Getting Context-Sensitive Help

- Display the dialog box for which you want help, and then press the F1 key.
- If the window or dialog box has a question mark button in its title bar, click on the button, and then click on the item for which you want help.

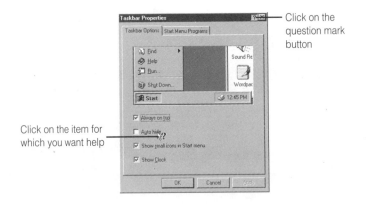

Click on the question mark button

Click on the item for which you want help

8

Getting Help

Windows contains an online Help system that can answer most of your questions. It offers a table of contents, index, and even a Find feature that can help you search for specific information. In this chapter, you'll get a crash course on using the Help system.

Basic Survival

Using the Help Table of Contents

The easiest way to get general help for using Windows 95 is to use the Help Table of Contents. Here's what you do:

1. Click on the Start button, and then click on Help. The Help Topics window appears.

2. Click on the Contents tab, and Windows displays a list of topics for which you can get help.

3. Double-click on the type of help you want: Introducing Windows, How To, Tips and Tricks, or Troubleshooting. The item expands to show a list of Help topics.

4. Keep double-clicking on items until the desired Help window appears.

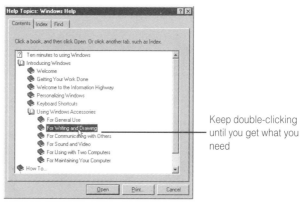

Keep double-clicking until you get what you need

*Fl for Help Contents;
Fl again for help
using Help*

5. To go back to the Help Topics window, click on the Help Topics button. Then you can select a different topic by double-clicking on it.

6. To exit Help, click on the Close button in the upper-right corner of the Help window.

Jumping Around in the Help System

Many Help windows contain links, called *jumps*, that display related information. Some links have a button next to them. If you click on the button, Windows opens a Help screen with detailed information about that item. Other links appear as green underlined terms. If you click on one of these links, a small window appears, displaying additional information or instructions.

If you see a button that has an arrow on it, you can click on the button to run a Windows program (or Windows setup utility) directly from the Help system. The Help window stays open, providing additional information on how to use the program or utility to perform a specific task.

Click on this button to run a
Windows program or setup utility

Click on this link for
a new Help window

Click on this link
for additional
information

In addition to using jumps to skip around in the Help system, you can use the Back button to view previous Help windows. Simply click on the button to go back one screen. To go back to the first Help window, click on the Help Topics button.

Click on the Back button to
view the previous Help screen

Click on Help Topics to go
back to the first Help screen

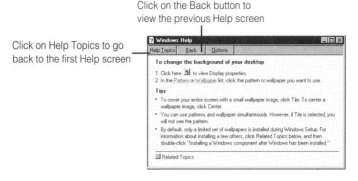

Getting Context-Sensitive Help

If you want specific help in a window or dialog box, Windows can provide *context-sensitive* help. When you request context-sensitive help, Windows "senses" the task you're currently trying to perform and offers specific instructions for that task. To obtain context-sensitive help, follow these steps:

1. Display the dialog box you want help with, and click on the specific option for which you want help.

2. Press the F1 key. Windows displays a Help window that contains information pertaining to that menu option or dialog box.

To print a Help topic, select Options, Print Topic

Here's another way to get context-sensitive help: in the upper-right corner of many dialog boxes and windows is a button that has a question mark on it. You can also use this button to get context-sensitive help. Simply click on the button, and then click on the item for which you want help. A pop-up window appears on top of the dialog box, explaining the selected option.

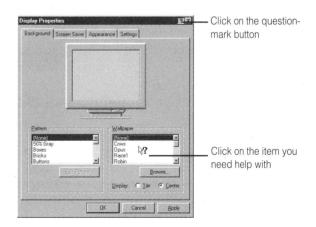

Click on the question-mark button

Click on the item you need help with

Beyond Survival

**Searching for
Specific
Information**

If you know the name of the topic for which you want help, you can search specifically for that topic. Here's what you do:

1. Click on the Start button and then click on Help. The Help Topics dialog box appears.

2. Click on the Find tab. A list of options appears, in which you search for information.

   (The first time you click on the Find tab, the Find Setup Wizard dialog box appears, asking you to specify how detailed you want the Find feature to be. Follow the on-screen instructions to proceed.)

3. In the Type the word(s) you want to find text box, start typing the topic's name. As you type, the lists at the bottom of the dialog box change to show the topics that match your entry.

4. In the first list (Select some matching words to narrow your search) click on a word or phrase, or Ctrl+click on each word or phrase you want to search for.

5. In the Click a topic list, click on the help topic you want to display.

6. Click on the Display button. Windows displays help for the selected topic.

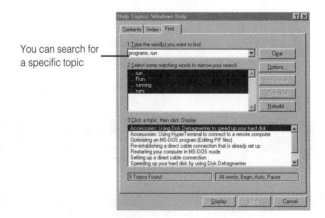

You can search for
a specific topic

In addition to using the Find tab to search for information, you can use the Index tab. This tab provides an extensive list of Help topics arranged in alphabetical order. In the Type the first few letters of the word you're looking for text box, type a few letters. As you type, Windows highlights the first item in the list that contains your text. When the desired Help topic scrolls into view, stop typing, and then double-click on the topic.

Keeping the Help Window on Top

As you're performing a task, it's often helpful to keep the Help window on top of other windows and dialog boxes so you can refer to the instructions as you perform the task. To keep the Help window on top, click on the Options button, move the mouse pointer over Keep Help on Top, and click on On Top.

Using Bookmarks and History Lists (Sometimes)

Some programs come with more advanced Help systems that enable you to use *bookmarks* and a *history list* to go back to Help topics you've previously read. A bookmark provides a way of marking a page so you can go back to that page by simply selecting your bookmark from a list. A history list is a log of all the Help topics you've viewed; you select a topic from the list to return to it.

No bookmarks or history list? Use the Back button.

If you're using a program that offers bookmarks and history lists, follow these steps to add a bookmark to a topic:

1. Display the Help topic you want to flag.

2. Open the Bookmark menu and select Define. A dialog box appears, asking you for a name.

3. Type a descriptive name for the bookmark and press Enter.

4. To return to the topic, display any Help window, open the Bookmark menu, and select your bookmark.

History lists are a little easier to deal with than bookmarks are, because you don't have to create them; the program creates the list for you. To go back to an item in the history list, perform the following steps:

1. Click on the History button.

2. Click on the topic you want to revisit.

PART 2

Working with Programs

In the previous part, you learned how easy it is to run programs in Windows. You simply open the Start menu, point to Programs, and click on the program you want to run. There's more to running programs, however, than just clicking on them. You need to know how to install and set up new programs; save, open, and print documents; add programs to the menu; work with DOS programs; and add shortcuts to the desktop so you can quickly run the programs you use most often. In this part, you'll get some hands-on experience with the following tasks:

Cheat Sheet

Installing a Program

1. Exit all other programs.
2. Write-protect your program disks.
3. Insert your program disk 1 into drive A or B, or into the CD-ROM drive.
4. Click on the Start button.
5. Move the mouse pointer over Settings, and then click on Control Panel.
6. Double-click on the Add/Remove Programs icon.
7. Click on the Install/Uninstall tab if it is not already selected.
8. Click on the Install button, and then click on Next.
9. Click on the Finish button.
10. Follow the installation instructions that appear on-screen.

Adding a Program to the Programs Menu

1. If the program is not installed, install it, as explained in the previous steps. This adds it to the Programs menu.
2. Click on the Start button.
3. Move the mouse pointer over Settings, and then click on Taskbar.
4. Click on the Start Menu Programs tab.
5. Click on the Add button.
6. Click on the Browse button.
7. Use the window that appears to change to the drive and folder that contains the program files.
8. Double-click on the file that runs the program.
9. Click on the Next button.
10. Click on the menu or submenu on which you want the item to appear, and click on the Next button.
11. Type the program name as you want it to appear on the menu, and click on the Finish button.
12. Click on the OK button to save your change.

Installing and Setting Up Programs

Before you can use any program, you have to install it. The installation process consists of copying the program files from floppy disks to your hard disk, and (usually) decompressing the files to make them usable. Most programs come with an Install or Setup utility that does everything for you. In this chapter, you will learn how to run the Install or Setup program in Windows, and how to add program names to the Start menu (so you can run them by selecting them with a click of your mouse).

For information on how to install or uninstall programs that are a part of Windows 95 (such as WordPad, Paint, and games), see Chapter 63, "Uncluttering Your Disk," and the installation appendix at the back of this book.

Basic Survival

Installing a Windows or DOS Program

Whenever you get a new program, you must install it before you can use it. Most programs come with a setup or install program that copies the program files to a directory on your hard disk, prepares the files for use, and adds the icons required to run the program to the Programs menu. Take the following steps to start the installation program for your new (or old) program:

1. Exit all other Windows programs. (Windows saves disk space by allowing programs to share some files. If these files are being used, and Windows needs to change them during the installation, you'll run into problems.)

2. Insert your program disk 1 into drive A or B, or insert your CD into the CD-ROM drive. If your drive has a door or caddy, close it.

3. Click on the Start button. This opens the Start menu.

4. Move the mouse pointer over Settings, and then click on Control Panel. The Control Panel window appears.

5. Double-click on the Add/Remove Programs icon. The Add/Remove Programs Properties dialog box appears. (This dialog box will lead you through the installation.)

6. Click on the Install/Uninstall tab if it is not already selected.

7. Click on the Install button, and then click on Next. Windows checks your floppy drive and CD-ROM drive (if you have one) for an IN-STALL or SETUP file, and inserts its name in the Command line for installation program text box.

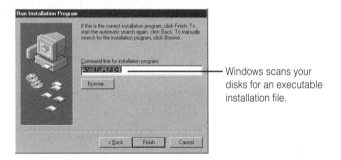

Windows scans your disks for an executable installation file.

Click on Browse
to look for files

8. If you don't see INSTALL.EXE, SETUP.EXE, or a similar name in the Command Line text box, click on the Browse button, and use the dialog box that appears to select the correct installation file. Then click on the OK button.

9. Click on the Finish button.

10. Follow the installation instructions that appear on-screen.

If you have trouble running a DOS program after installing it, refer to Chapter 62, "Running Stubborn DOS Games and Programs," to learn how to enter settings that affect the way Windows runs the program.

Adding a Program to the Programs Menu

If, for some odd reason, one of your installed programs doesn't show up on the Programs menu (sometimes, DOS programs seem to be left out), you can add it to the menu. The following steps show how:

1. Click on the Start button.

2. Move the mouse pointer over Settings, and then click on Taskbar. The Taskbar Properties dialog box appears.

3. Click on the Start Menu Programs tab. The Start Menu Programs options appear.

4. Click on the Add button. The Create Shortcut dialog box appears, prompting you to specify the location and name of the file that runs the program.

5. Click on the Browse button. The Browse dialog box appears, showing a list of files and folders on the current drive.

6. If the file is on a different drive, open the Look In drop-down list, and click on the letter of the drive. Windows updates the list of files and folders for the selected drive.

Select the folder and file name of the program you want to run.

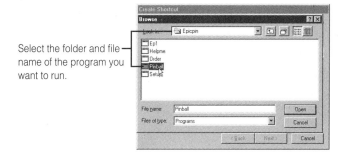

7. From the list, double-click on the folder where the program files are stored.

8. Click on the name of the file that runs the program, and then click on the Open button. You return to the Create Shortcut dialog box.

9. Click on the Next button. The Select Program Folder dialog box appears, prompting you to select the menu or submenu in which you want to place the program. (You can place the program directly on the Programs menu or on one of its submenus.)

10. Click on Programs to place the program directly on the Programs menu, or click on the submenu (folder) on which you want the program to appear. (To create a new submenu, click on the New Folder button, and type a name for the submenu.)

11. Click on the Next button. The Select a Title for the Program dialog box appears, prompting you to type a name for the program.

12. Type the program name as you want it to appear on the menu, and click on the Finish button.

13. Click on the OK button to save your change. The item is now on the Programs menu or the selected submenu on the Programs menu.

Removing a Program from the Programs Menu

If your Programs menu is getting cluttered with programs you never use, you can remove programs and submenus from the menu. Fortunately, it's a lot easier to remove a program from the Program's menu than it is to add one. Here's what you do:

1. Click on the Start button.

2. Move the mouse pointer over Settings, and then click on Taskbar. The Taskbar Properties dialog box appears.

3. Click on the Start Menu Programs tab. The Start Menu Programs options appear.

4. Click on the Remove button. The Remove Shortcuts/Folders dialog box appears, prompting you to select the item you want to remove.

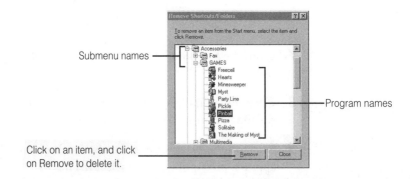

Submenu names

Program names

Click on an item, and click on Remove to delete it.

5. If the item is on a submenu, click on the plus sign to the left of the submenu's name. This opens the submenu folder, displaying its contents.

6. Click on the program or submenu (folder) you want to remove.

7. Click on the Remove button. A dialog box might appear (if you chose to delete a submenu that contains programs or additional submenus), asking you to confirm the deletion.

8. If you see the confirmation dialog box, click on the Yes button. Windows removes the item and places it in the Recycle Bin.

9. Repeat steps 5 to 8 to remove additional items, and then click on the Close button. You return to the Taskbar Properties dialog box.

10. Click on the OK button.

Beyond Survival

Regrouping Items on the Programs Menu

With its many submenus, the Programs menu can get a little difficult to navigate. Sometimes, you don't want to have to go through a series of submenus to run your favorite programs. To remedy the situation, you can regroup items on the Programs menu. For example, you can move an item from the System Tools submenu to the Programs menu, so you don't have to open the Accessories and System Tools submenus. To regroup items, take the following steps:

1. Click on the Start button.

2. Move the mouse pointer over Settings, and then click on Taskbar. The Taskbar Properties dialog box appears.

3. Click on the Start Menu Programs tab. The Start Menu Programs options appear.

4. Click on the Advanced button. Windows runs Explorer, its file management utility, which you'll learn more about in Part 4.

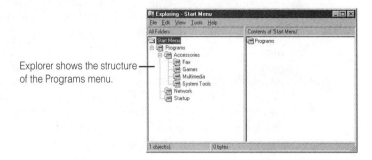

Explorer shows the structure of the Programs menu.

5. If the item you want to move is on a submenu, click on the plus sign to the left of the submenu's name. This opens the submenu folder, displaying its contents.

To move a submenu to top of Programs menu: drag submenus folder over Programs folder

6. Move the mouse pointer over the item you want to move, hold down the left mouse button, and drag the item over the Programs folder or over the submenu folder in which you want the item placed.

7. Release the mouse button. The item is placed inside the selected folder.

Uninstalling Windows Applications

To uninstall a program in Windows 95, take the following steps:

1. Click on the Start button.

2. Move the mouse pointer over Settings, and then click on Control Panel. The Control Panel window appears.

3. Double-click on the Add/Remove Programs icon. The Add/Remove Programs Properties dialog box appears.

4. Click on the Install/Uninstall tab, if it is not already selected. At the bottom of the screen is a list of programs you can have Windows uninstall.

5. Click on the program you want to remove. (Ctrl+click on any additional programs you want to uninstall.)

6. Click on the Remove button.

7. Follow the on-screen instructions to complete the process.

Cheat Sheet

Saving a File

1. Click on File in the program's menu bar.
2. Click on Save.
3. Type a name for the file.
4. Click on the OK button.

Opening a Saved File

1. Click on File in the program's menu bar.
2. Click on Open.
3. Click on the arrow to the right of the Look In option, and click on the letter of the drive that contains the file.
4. Double-click on the folder that contains the file.
5. Click on the name of the file you want to open.
6. Click on the Open button.

Printing a File

1. Create or open the file you want to print.
2. Click on File in the menu bar.
3. Click on Print.
4. Click on the OK button.

10

Saving, Opening, and Printing Documents

In Chapter 3, you learned how to run programs and switch between them. In this chapter, you'll learn how to perform basic tasks in most applications; these include saving, opening, and printing files. In addition, you'll learn about Windows 95's new document handling feature.

Basic Survival

Saving a Document File

In most programs, you create something, such as a picture or a business letter. You should save your work to disk early and often (at least every 10 minutes) to prevent it from getting obliterated when you quit the program, exit Windows, or lose power. The procedure for saving a file is the same in most Windows programs:

1. Click on File in the program's menu bar.

2. Click on Save.

3. Type a name for the file in the File Name text box. (Windows 95 allows for long file names, complete with spaces; you're no longer limited to the old eight-character file names.)

4. (Optional) To specify where you want the file saved, select a drive from the Save In drop-down list, and double-click on the folder in which you want the file saved.

5. Click on the OK button.

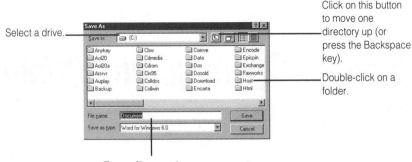

Select a drive.

Click on this button
to move one
directory up (or
press the Backspace
key).

Double-click on a
folder.

Type a file name here.

*In most
programs,
press
Ctrl+S to
save file*

Once you've named a file, you don't have to name it again or tell your
program where to store it. When you open the File menu and select Save, the
program saves the file to its original location, and uses its original name.

Opening a Saved Document

If you saved and closed a file, and later decide you want to work with it, you
have to run the program you used to create the file; then you can open it.
Once the program is running, perform the following steps to open the file:

1. Click on File in the program's menu bar.

2. Click on Open. The Open File dialog box appears.

3. Click on the arrow to the right of the Look in list, and then click on the
drive where the file is stored.

4. Double-click on the folder that contains the document file.

5. Click on the name of the document file you want to open.

*In most
programs,
press
Ctrl+O to
open file*

6. Click on the Open button. The program opens the file and displays it
on-screen.

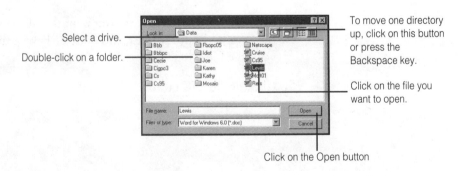

Select a drive.

Double-click on a folder.

To move one directory
up, click on this button
or press the
Backspace key.

Click on the file you
want to open.

Click on the Open button

Printing a Document

Once you have opened a file and displayed it on-screen, you can print it. To print in most programs, do the following:

1. Make sure your printer is turned on and has paper. If your printer has an On Line light, make sure it is lit (not blinking).

2. Click on File in the program's menu bar.

3. Click on Print. In most programs, a Print dialog box will appear. If you print from a basic text editing program (such as Notepad), printing starts immediately.

Select which pages you want to print.

You can select a different printer.

Type the number of copies.

4. Select your printing preferences.

5. Click on the OK button.

Press Ctrl+P to print file

When you installed Windows, it asked you to pick a printer. If you changed printers—or Windows fails to print your document—you may need to select a different printer. Refer to Chapter 46, "Setting Up and Selecting a Printer," for details.

Beyond Survival

Opening Documents from the Documents Menu

If you've worked with Windows programs before, you probably know that most programs keep a list of most-recently-opened documents at the bottom of the File menu. Now, Windows 95 offers a similar feature that allows you to open recent documents quickly; you don't even have to run a program to open the document. Here's what you do:

1. Click on the Start button.

2. Move the mouse pointer over Documents. The Documents menu opens, showing a list of the fifteen documents you most recently worked on. (*Documents* are any data files, including individual spreadsheets, letters, and graphics.)

3. Click on the document you want to open. Windows runs the program used to create the document, and then opens the document in that program.

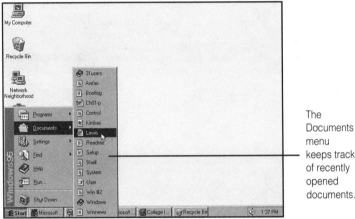

The Documents menu keeps track of recently opened documents.

If document not listed, open Start menu; click on Find.

In Chapter 12, you'll learn how to make shortcut icons for your documents and place them permanently on the Windows desktop. Then you can open a document simply by double-clicking on its icon.

Removing Documents from the Documents Menu

You can clear the documents from the Documents menu at any time, and start over. Clearing these documents does not delete them; it only removes their names from the menu. To clear the menu, take the following steps:

1. Click on the Start button.

2. Move the mouse pointer over Settings, and then click on Taskbar. The Taskbar Properties dialog box appears.

3. Click on the Start Menu Programs tab.

4. Click on the Clear button. Windows removes the document names from the menu.

5. Click on the OK button to close the Taskbar Properties dialog box.

Cheat Sheet

Going to the DOS Prompt

1. Click on the Start button.
2. Move the mouse pointer over Programs.
3. Click on MS-DOS Prompt.

Running Programs at the DOS Prompt

1. Change to the drive containing the program's files: type the drive letter and a colon; then press Enter.
2. Change to the directory (folder) containing the files: type **cd** and the name of the directory, and then press Enter.
3. Type the required command and press Enter.
4. (Optional) To run the DOS session in a window, press Alt+Enter.
5. (Optional) To switch to another program or return to Windows, press Ctrl+Esc.

Exiting the DOS Prompt

1. Quit any DOS programs you ran from the prompt.
2. Type **exit**.
3. Press Enter.

11

Going to the DOS Prompt

If you are having trouble totally abandoning DOS, Windows provides a way of stepping out to a DOS prompt. That way, you can run programs and perform other tasks at the DOS prompt, the same (almost) as you could before you ran Windows. In this chapter, you'll learn how to display the DOS prompt, run programs, and return to Windows.

Basic Survival

Displaying the DOS Prompt

To go to the DOS prompt, here's what you do:

1. Click on the Start button (in the Taskbar).

2. Move the mouse pointer over Programs. The Programs submenu opens.

3. Click on MS-DOS Prompt.

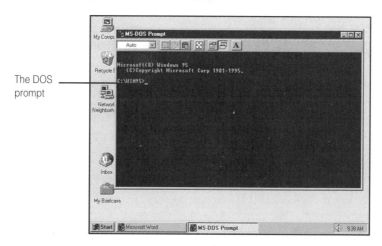

The DOS prompt

Some Restrictions May Apply...

Before you jump out to the DOS prompt and try to live the rest of your computing life from it, you should know a few facts and warnings.

First, there are two ways to run a DOS program: by clicking on an icon for it from within Windows, and by going to the DOS prompt and running it there. There's a lot to be said for the former method. When you run a DOS program from Windows by clicking on its icon, Windows runs the program with settings that make it run efficiently. (You can change these settings, as explained in Chapter 13, "Changing an Object's Properties," and in Chapter 62, "Running Stubborn DOS Games and Programs.") If you run the program from the DOS prompt (instead of by using its icon), Windows uses the generic settings used for opening the DOS prompt window, and you may encounter problems with your DOS program.

It's better to run programs from Windows

Second, some programs and utilities are not designed to run under Windows. Examples include defragmentation programs, disk-optimization utilities, DOS-file undelete programs, and most programs that will change your system settings. In most cases, you should avoid using utility programs that are designed to run from DOS. Use the Windows 95 utility programs instead, or use utilities designed specifically for Windows 95. Instead of using the DOS Defrag program, for example, use the Windows Defragmenter, as explained in Chapter 53.

Running a DOS Program from the DOS Prompt

Once you've decided to run a program at the DOS prompt, perform the following steps:

1. Change to the drive that contains the program's files. To change to drive C, for example, type **c:** and press Enter.

2. Change to the directory that contains the program's files. To change to the \WORD directory, for example, type **cd\word** and press Enter.

3. Type the command required to run the program, and then press Enter. This starts the program.

Getting Back to Windows 95

Switch apps:
Hold down
Alt, press
Tab till
desired app
name appears

You can go back to the Windows, or switch from your DOS program to a running Windows program, just as you can with any other program. If the DOS window is full-screen (you can't see the Taskbar), press Ctrl+Esc, and then click on the desired program in the Taskbar. If you want to quit the DOS prompt entirely, here's what you do:

1. Quit any DOS programs you ran from the prompt.

2. Type **exit**.

3. Press Enter.

Beyond Survival

Running a DOS Program in a Window

Alt+Enter =
DOS in a
window

When you run a DOS program from the DOS prompt, sometimes it starts in full-screen mode, not in a window. You can run the program in a window, however, by pressing Alt+Enter. This approach not only makes it easier to work with other Windows programs, it gives you a Control-menu box you can click on for access to Windows commands. To return the window to full-screen view, press Alt+Enter again.

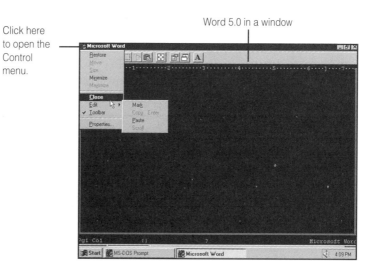

Click here to open the Control menu.

Word 5.0 in a window

Copying and Pasting Data from DOS Programs

If you choose to run a DOS program in a window, you can use the Windows Clipboard to copy data from the documents you've opened in the DOS program to other documents (including those created using Windows programs). Here's what you do:

1. In the DOS program, open the document that contains the data you want to copy.

2. Click on the Control-menu box, move the mouse pointer over Edit, and then click on Mark.

3. Drag the mouse pointer over the data you want to copy.

4. Click on the Control-menu box, move the mouse pointer over Edit, and then click on Copy.

5. Open the document into which you want to paste the copied data. (If you created the document in another program, you may have to run that program and open the document.)

6. Move the insertion point to where you want the data pasted.

7. Enter the program's Paste command (usually on the Edit menu in Windows programs). If you are pasting the data in a DOS program, click on the Control-menu box, move the mouse pointer over Edit, and then click on Paste.

For more information about how to cut, copy, and paste data, see Chapter 17, "Moving, Copying, and Sharing Information."

Getting Help for DOS Commands

If there's a DOS command you need help with, you can view Help at the DOS prompt. Simply type one of the following command lines:

- Type the name of the DOS command, followed by /?. Then press Enter. For example, type **dir /?** and press Enter.

- If the information scrolls by too fast to read, type **|more** after the question mark. For example, type **dir /? |more** and press Enter.

DOS provides help for its many commands.

- If you're not sure which command you need help with, type **help** and press Enter to view an index of commands. Press the PgDn key to view more commands. Press the Tab key to move the cursor to the desired command, and then press Enter. Press the F1 key to view instructions on how to use the DOS Help system.

If you're interested in running DOS so that it uses less memory or runs with specific settings in place, refer to Chapter 62, "Running Stubborn DOS Games and Programs." You can right-click inside the MS-DOS Prompt title bar, and select Properties to display a dialog box that lets you control the way DOS behaves. Chapter 62 explains the procedure in greater detail.

Cheat Sheet

Shortcut Facts

- Shortcuts are icons that point to a program or document.
- You can place shortcuts on the Windows desktop (or on a menu) to make programs and documents easily accessible.
- Deleting a shortcut does not delete the program or document.

Adding a Shortcut to the Desktop

1. Double-click on the My Computer icon.
2. Double-click on the icon for the drive where the program or document is stored.
3. Open the folder that contains the document icon (or the icon for the file that runs the program).
4. Right-click on the icon; then click on Create Shortcut. A shortcut icon appears.
5. Drag the shortcut icon to a blank area on the Windows desktop.

Deleting a Shortcut

1. Drag the shortcut icon over the Recycle Bin icon.
2. Release the mouse button.
3. If asked, click on the Yes button to confirm.

Changing a Shortcut's Properties

1. Right-click on the shortcut icon.
2. Click on Properties.
3. Use the dialog box that appears to enter the desired shortcut settings.
4. Click on the OK button.

Saving Time with Shortcuts

12

Admittedly, the Start menu is a time-consuming way to run your programs. You have to move through at least two submenus to find the icon that runs your program. To save time, you should consider placing icons for the programs you use most on the Windows desktop. These icons, called *shortcuts*, allow you to run programs and open documents quickly, without using the Start menu. You simply double-click on the icon on the Windows desktop. In this chapter, you'll learn how to create and work with shortcuts.

Basic Survival

Creating a Shortcut

You can place shortcuts on the Windows desktop, in a folder, or even on a menu. You can create shortcuts for just about anything on your computer: a document file, a program, a folder, or even a disk. For example, you can create an icon for drive C, to provide easy access to your files. Or, you can create a shortcut for a folder that contains icons for the programs and document files you use most often.

The following steps explain how to create a shortcut and place it on the desktop to provide easy access to programs and documents:

1. Double-click on the My Computer icon. (You can also use the Windows Explorer, as explained in Part 4.)

2. Double-click on the icon for the drive where the program or document is stored.

3. Double-click on the folder that contains the document icon (or the icon for the file that runs the program). Keep double-clicking on folder icons until you see the file you want.

4. Right-click on the icon; then click on Create Shortcut. Windows creates the shortcut icon and places it in the window. (Windows cannot create shortcuts in some windows. In such cases, Windows displays a dialog

79

box asking if you want the shortcut placed on the desktop instead; click on Yes.)

5. Move the mouse pointer over the shortcut icon, hold down the left mouse button, and drag the icon to a blank area on the Windows desktop.

6. Release the mouse button. The shortcut icon is moved to the Windows desktop. You can now drag the icon anywhere on the desktop to reposition it.

A quicker way to create shortcuts is simply to right-drag the icon to where you want the shortcut placed. When you release the right mouse button, a shortcut menu appears; click on Create Shortcut(s) Here to create the new shortcut.

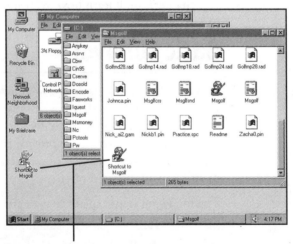

Drag the shortcut icon to a blank area on the desktop.

After creating a shortcut, you don't have to leave it on the desktop. You can drag the shortcut to another window to move it to a different folder if you prefer.

If you create a shortcut for a document, the document must be *associated* with a program in order to automatically open the document. Windows associates some types of files with specific programs. For example, Windows opens any files that end in .PCX in Windows Paint; any documents that end in .DOC, Windows opens in WordPad (unless they have been linked to other programs such as Word for Windows). If you have document files that you want to open in a specific program, refer to Chapter 37, "Running Programs from Windows Explorer" to learn how to create file associations.

Creating a Shortcut in a Folder

Sometimes you may want to place a shortcut inside another folder, to make a document or program easily accessible from that folder. For example, say you keep all your spreadsheet files in one folder, and you have another folder for household records. You can create a shortcut in your household records folder that points to the budget spreadsheet in your spreadsheets folder.

You can create a shortcut inside a folder by using the steps just shown, or by using the Shortcut Wizard, as explained in the following steps. (A *Wizard* is a Windows helper that leads you through a task step-by-step.)

1. Double-click on My Computer.

2. Double-click on the icon for the drive that contains the folder into which you want the shortcut inserted.

3. Double-click on the icon for the folder in which you want the new shortcut placed.

4. Click on File in the menu bar.

5. Move the mouse pointer over New, and then click on Shortcut. The Create Shortcut dialog box appears, prompting you to select the name and location of the file you want to open or run.

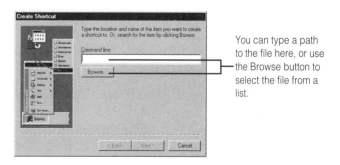

You can type a path to the file here, or use the Browse button to select the file from a list.

6. Click on the Browse button. The Browse dialog box appears, prompting you to select the drive, folder, and name of the file.

7. In the Look In drop-down list, select the letter of the drive where the file is stored.

8. From the folders list, double-click on folder icons until you've opened the folder that contains the file.

9. To display all files (rather than only program files), open the Files of type drop-down list, and click on All Files.

10. Click on the name of the file for which you want to create a shortcut, and then click on the Open button. You return to the Create Shortcut dialog box.

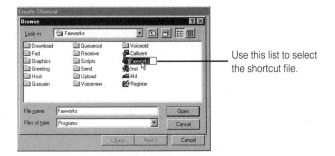

Use this list to select the shortcut file.

11. Click on the Next button. A dialog box appears, prompting you to type a name for the shortcut.

12. Type a name for the shortcut in the Select a Name for the Shortcut text box.

13. Click on the Finish button. Windows creates a shortcut for the selected file, and inserts it into the current window.

Deleting (and Restoring) Shortcuts

Unlike most Windows icons, shortcuts do not represent actual files; shortcuts merely point to those files. Therefore you can safely delete icons without deleting the files they point to. To delete a shortcut icon:

• Drag the shortcut icon over the Recycle Bin icon, and release the mouse button, or

• Right-click on the Shortcut icon, click on Delete, and click on the Yes button to confirm.

When you delete a shortcut icon, Windows places it in the Recycle Bin. As long as you don't empty the Recycle Bin, you can get your shortcut icon back. To learn how to restore items placed in the Recycle Bin, see Chapter 7, "Dumping Objects in the Recycle Bin."

Beyond Survival

Adding a Shortcut to the Programs Menu

You learned how to add program names to the Programs menu in Chapter 9. Maybe you didn't realize that you were actually adding shortcuts to the menu. Here's another way to add shortcuts to the Programs menu:

1. Right-click on the Start button, and then click on Open. The Start Menu window opens.

2. Double-click on the Programs folder; its contents appear.

3. Open the File menu and move the mouse pointer over New.

4. Click on Folder, type the name you want to use for the submenu, and press Enter. Windows creates a new folder inside the Programs folder; this folder will appear as a submenu.

5. Double-click the folder you just created. A blank window opens, showing the contents of the folder (presently nothing).

6. Open the File menu, move the mouse pointer over New, and then click on Shortcut. This starts the Shortcut Wizard (explained in "Creating a Shortcut in a Folder," earlier in this chapter).

7. Use the Shortcut Wizard to pick the file to use for the shortcut. ("Creating a Shortcut in a Folder" gives details.)

Once you've created your shortcut, Windows places it on the Programs menu in the submenu (folder) you created. You can run the program or open the document simply by opening the submenu and clicking on the shortcut.

Add program to top of Start menu: drag-and-drop its shortcut icon over Start button

If you want to place a shortcut at the top of the Start menu, simply drag the program's icon from a My Computer or Windows Explorer window, and put it over the Start button. When you release the mouse button, the shortcut appears at the top of the Start menu; you don't have to open the Programs menu to get at it.

Changing a Shortcut's Properties

Each shortcut has properties that tell Windows how to treat the associated file or run the program. You'll learn more about the properties of various objects in the next chapter, "Changing an Object's Properties." For now, just keep in mind that to change the properties of a shortcut, you can right-click on the shortcut and then click on Properties. When you do so, a dialog box appears and displays the shortcut's current properties (which you can change).

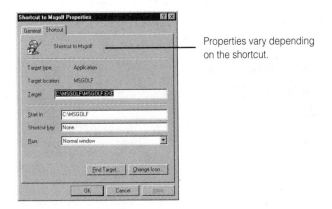

Properties vary depending
on the shortcut.

A shortcut's properties vary depending on the type of file the shortcut points
to. If the shortcut represents a Windows program, you'll usually get two
tabs—the first tab shows the properties of the file itself. The second (Shortcut) tab lets you change the way Windows runs the program; for example, you
can have Windows start the program in a maximized or minimized window.
For DOS programs, the Properties dialog box may have several tabs, telling
Windows which font to use, how much memory to give the program, and
additional parameters that control the program's operations. You'll learn more
about these properties in the next chapter.

Adding Folders to the Desktop

As you add shortcuts to the desktop, your desktop can become cluttered. Of
course, you can right-click on the desktop and select Arrange Icons to place
the icons in some sort of order. Another way to clear some of the items from
the desktop is to create a separate folder for your shortcuts. Here's what you
do:

1. Right-click on a blank area on the desktop. The desktop shortcut menu
appears.

2. Move the mouse pointer over New, and then click on Folder. Windows
places a new folder on the desktop, highlighting its name so you can
type a new name.

3. Type a name for the folder and then press Enter.

4. Select all the shortcut icons on the desktop that you want to move to the
new folder. (You can select multiple icons by Ctrl+clicking on them.)

5. Drag one of the selected shortcut icons from the desktop over the new folder icon. When you release the mouse button, Windows moves the shortcut icons to the new folder icon.

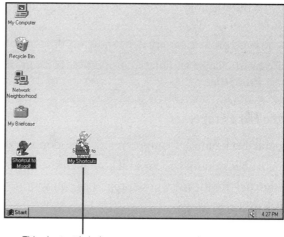

This shortcut is being
dragged onto a folder icon.

You can move or copy document icons, shortcut icons, and any other objects to your new folder simply by dragging them over the folder icon. To view the contents of the folder, double-click on its icon.

Cheat Sheet

Understanding Properties

- Each Windows object (icons, Taskbar, background, window, etc.) has properties that control the object.
- An object's properties vary depending on the type of object.
- To view or change an object's properties, you can right-click on the object and select Properties.

Checking a File's Properties

1. Double-click on My Computer, and then double-click on the desired drive's icon.
2. Double-click on folder icons till you open the folder that contains the file.
3. Right-click on the file whose properties you want to check.
4. Click on Properties.
5. Click on the Cancel button when you're done.

Changing the Properties of a DOS Program

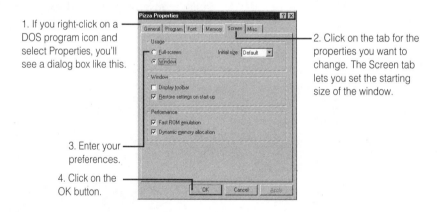

1. If you right-click on a DOS program icon and select Properties, you'll see a dialog box like this.

2. Click on the tab for the properties you want to change. The Screen tab lets you set the starting size of the window.

3. Enter your preferences.

4. Click on the OK button.

Checking the Display Properties

1. To change the display properties, right-click on a blank area of the desktop.
2. Click on Properties.
3. When a dialog box appears, use it to select your Windows display preferences.
4. Click on the OK button.

13

Changing an Object's Properties

As far as Windows is concerned, your desktop consists of a collection of *objects*, each of which you can control by its own settings. The Taskbar is one object; each icon and window is an object; Windows even treats the desktop itself as an object. You can control any of these objects by changing its *properties*. In this chapter, you'll learn how to change the properties of any Windows object. You'll also learn how to change the properties of a DOS program to make it run more efficiently.

Basic Survival

Right-Clicking for Properties

The procedure for changing an object's properties is fairly simple. You right-click on the object to view its shortcut menu, and then you click on Properties. This brings up a dialog box that allows you to change the object's properties. This dialog box varies according to the object you selected. As the figure below shows, you can right-click on any of several objects to change its properties.

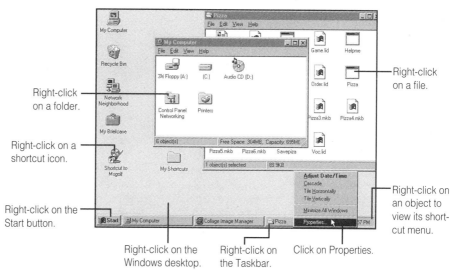

Right-click on a folder.

Right-click on a shortcut icon.

Right-click on the Start button.

Right-click on the Windows desktop.

Right-click on the Taskbar.

Right-click on a file.

Right-click on an object to view its shortcut menu.

Click on Properties.

Press Alt+Enter to view object's properties

The only trick here is that you have to be careful to right-click on the correct object. If you're trying to click on an icon and you click on the surrounding space (instead of the icon), the shortcut menu displays the Properties dialog box *for that window or for the desktop*, not for the icon. If you get the wrong menu, simply right-click again on the desired object.

Checking Out a File's Properties

If you need to know the size of a file or the date and time it was last edited, you can check its properties. Most document files and Windows program files don't allow you to change many file properties, but you can view the properties if you need information about the file. To view a file's properties, here's what you do:

1. Double-click on My Computer, and then double-click on the desired drive's icon.

2. Double-click on folder icons until you've opened the folder where the file is stored.

3. Right-click on the file whose properties you want to view, and click on Properties. The Properties dialog box appears, as shown here.

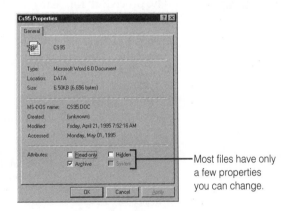

Most files have only a few properties you can change.

4. You can change any of the following file properties (attributes):

Read-only: To prevent anyone from changing the file, turn on this attribute. Windows will allow you to open and view the file, but not change it.

Hidden: Prevents the file's name from appearing in most lists. (The file's name will appear in Windows Explorer.)

System: Prevents the file from being changed or moved. System files are essential for the operation of your computer; leave this attribute on for any files already marked as system files.

Archive: Indicates whether a file has been backed up since it was last changed. The archive attribute—turned off when a file is backed up—turns on automatically when you edit the file. This tells the backup program that the file needs to be backed up.

5. Click on the OK or Cancel button.

Changing the Display Properties

In Chapter 39, "Changing the Display Settings," you'll learn how to change the Windows background, turn on a Windows screen saver, and change other display options. For a quick preview of the chapter, take the following steps:

1. Find a blank area of the Windows desktop, and right-click inside it. A shortcut menu appears.

2. Click on Properties. The Display Properties dialog box appears, as shown here. (Again, you'll learn more about display options in Chapter 39.)

3. Click on the OK button when you're done.

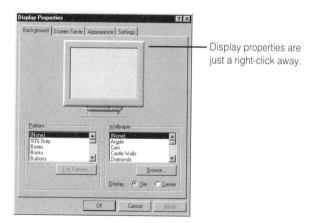

Display properties are just a right-click away.

Changing the Taskbar Properties

In Chapter 2, you learned how to change the Taskbar properties to control its behavior. In Chapter 9, you learned how to add programs to the Start menu. In both cases, you used the Start button to begin; you clicked on Start, pointed to Settings, and clicked on Taskbar. You could have saved yourself several steps by using the Taskbar's shortcut menu. Here's what you do:

1. Right-click on a blank area inside the Taskbar (a space between buttons).

2. Click on Properties. The Taskbar Properties dialog box appears, as you saw in Chapters 2 and 9.

3. Enter any changes you want to make, and then click on the OK button.

Beyond Survival

Changing the Properties of a DOS Program

If you ran DOS programs in Windows 3.1, you might be familiar with PIFs (short for *program information files*). Windows 3.1 used these files to control how DOS programs would run under Windows. Well, Windows 95 has largely done away with PIFs; instead, it assigns settings to each DOS program. You change these settings by changing the program file's properties.

If you have a DOS program that's giving you problems, consider changing its properties by taking the following steps:

1. Right-click on the icon you use to run the program. (This icon can be in a My Computer window, or it can be a shortcut icon on your desktop or in a folder.)

2. Click on Properties. The Properties dialog box for the DOS program file appears. As you can see, it has several tabs for various settings.

3. Click on the Program tab and enter any of the following settings:

   Cmd Line: This is the path to the drive, directory and name of the file that runs the program (you won't have to change this).

   Working: Enter the letter of the drive and the name of the folder that the program will save files to, or open files from.

   Batch File: If you want your program to run a macro or batch file when you start it, type the macro or file name here.

Shortcut Key: To assign a shortcut key to the program, click inside this text box, and press the shortcut key combination you want to use. You can use Ctrl+*key*, Ctrl+Shift+*key*, or Ctrl+Alt+*key*, where *key* stands for another key (such as A, B, C, 9, etc.).

Run: Pick the window size that you want the program to start with: Maximized, Minimized, or Normal.

Close on Exit: When this is on, Windows closes the program's window when you exit the program. Sometimes, you'll want the window left open so you can see what the program displayed just after you exited it.

Advanced: Use the advanced option only if you're having problems with the DOS program. (See Chapter 62, "Running Stubborn DOS Games and Programs," for details.)

Change Icon: If you don't like the look of the icon used for the program, click on this button to change it.

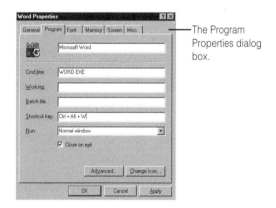

The Program Properties dialog box.

4. To control the look of the window (and the typeface used in the program window), click on the Font tab and select the following options:

Available Types: You can use standard (bitmapped fonts) for the on-screen text or Windows (TrueType) fonts. TrueType fonts look the same on-screen and in print. Click on Both Font Types to give yourself a wider selection.

Font Size: From the list, select the type size you want to use for the display. Keep an eye on the Window Preview area to see how the selected size affects the window. Look to the Font Preview area to see how the type will appear on-screen.

5. If you click on the Memory tab, you can control the amount of memory assigned to this program. It's best to leave these settings at Auto unless you're having trouble with the program. (See Chapter 62, "Running Stubborn DOS Games and Programs.")

6. Click on the Screen tab; enter any of these display settings:

Usage: Click on Full Screen if you want the program to take up the entire screen (as it does in DOS), or click on Window to display the program in a window (so you can switch easily to other programs and share data). The Initial Size drop-down list lets you set the *screen depth* (measured by text lines).

Window: Turn on Display Toolbar to have a toolbar appear at the top of the DOS window. This toolbar contains buttons for marking, copying, and pasting text, maximizing the window, and changing the screen fonts. Select Restore Settings on Startup if you want the window to reappear with the same settings when you restart it next time.

Performance: Turn on Fast ROM Emulation to have the display driver try to update the screen more quickly. If the program has trouble displaying text on the screen, turn this option off. Dynamic Memory Allocation helps manage memory when you switch to a different program. With Dynamic Memory Allocation turned on, Windows makes more memory available to other programs when this program is running in the background.

7. Click on the Misc tab and enter any changes to the following:

Foreground: If you want the screen saver to kick in when this program is active, turn on Allow Screen Saver. For more information about the Windows screen saver, see Chapter 39, "Changing the Display Settings."

Background: If you want this program to stop using system resources when it is not active, turn on Always Suspend.

Idle Sensitivity: This slide bar tells Windows how long to let this program remain idle before reassigning its resources to other (active) programs. Drag toward Low to make Windows wait longer: drag toward High to reassign resources sooner.

Windows Shortcut Keys: If the shortcut keys you use in this program conflict with Windows shortcut keys, you can turn off the Windows shortcut keys so that yours will be available.

Mouse: Turn on QuickEdit if you want to be able to select text with the mouse (without having to click on the Mark button in the toolbar). Turn on Exclusive Mode to make the mouse work only in this program (not in Windows); do this only if the mouse isn't working in the program.

Termination: Warn if Still Active tells Windows to display a warning message if you are about to quit the program with a Windows command (such as Close) rather than with the program's Exit command. Quitting from within the program is safer, because programs typically warn you if you are about to quit without saving your work. Keep this option on.

Other: Turn on Fast Pasting if you want Windows to paste copied or cut data faster into this program. If you're having trouble with the Paste command, turn this option off.

8. To save your settings, click on the **OK** button.

PART 3

Using the Windows 95 Accessories

When you purchase Windows 95, you not only get the most popular operating system on the market, you also get a collection of programs you can use to type documents, draw pictures, keep an address book, record sounds, and perform basic calculations. You even get a couple of very addictive games you can play while on break. In this part, you'll learn how to use these programs and perform the following tasks:

14. Typing and Printing with WordPad

15. Editing and Formatting Your WordPad Document

16. Making Pictures with Paint

17. Moving, Copying, and Sharing Information

18. Inserting Characters and Symbols with the Character Map

19. Go Figure with the Calculator

20. Tracking Time with the Clock

21. Editing Text with Notepad

22. Playing Audio CDs

23. Recording Sounds with the Sound Recorder

24. Going Multimedia with Media Player

Cheat Sheet

Starting WordPad

1. Click on the Start button.
2. Move the mouse pointer over Programs, and then move the pointer over Accessories.
3. Click on WordPad.

Typing Your Document

- Start typing.
- Press Enter only to end a paragraph. Do not press Enter at the end of each line.
- To move the insertion point, click where you want it or use the arrow keys.
- Use the Page Up or Page Down keys (or the scroll bar) to move up or down a page in the document.

Printing Your Document

1. Open the File menu and select Print.
2. Click on the OK button.

Saving Your Work

1. Open the File menu and select Save.
2. Type a name for the file.
3. Click on the Save button.

Opening a Saved File

1. Open the File menu and select Open.
2. Select the drive and folder that contain the file.
3. Click on the name of the file you want to open.
4. Click on the Open button.

14

Typing and Printing with WordPad

WordPad is a basic *word processing* program that allows you to type and print letters, articles, stories, and any other simple documents you want to create. WordPad provides *editing* tools that allow you to cut and paste text, *formatting* tools for styling your text and paragraphs, and *page layout* tools for setting margins. In this chapter, you will learn how to type, save, open, and print a document. In Chapter 15, you will learn how to change the look and layout of a document.

Basic Survival

Starting WordPad: What You'll See

To start WordPad, perform the following steps:

1. Click on the Start button. The Start menu opens.

2. Move the mouse pointer over Programs, and then move it over Accessories. The Accessories submenu appears.

3. Click on WordPad. The WordPad program window appears.

Click on Maximize button  for full-screen window

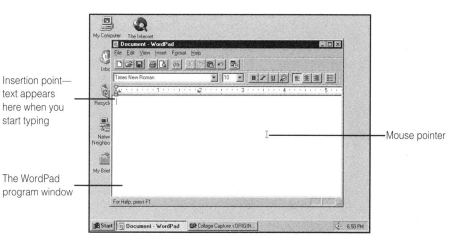

Insertion point— text appears here when you start typing

Mouse pointer

The WordPad program window

Typing Your Document

If you have already done some typing in a word processing program, you know what to do: start typing. If you have no experience with word processors, here are a few tips:

- Press Enter only to end a paragraph. The program automatically *wraps* text from one line to the next as you type.

- You can't move down if there is no text to move down to. Pressing the Enter key will move the insertion point down by creating new paragraphs.

- Text that floats off the top of the screen is NOT gone. Use the Page Up key or the scroll bar to view the text.

- To delete text, drag the mouse pointer over the text you want to delete, and then press the Del key. If you don't select text, press Del to delete one character to the right, or use Backspace to delete characters to the left.

- To move the insertion point, click where you want it, or use the up, down, left, or right arrow keys to move.

Press Enter to end a paragraph or insert a blank line.

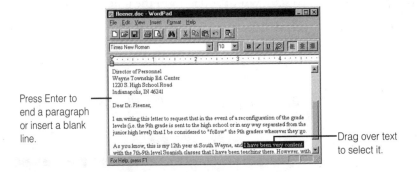

Drag over text to select it.

To exit WordPad, open the File menu and select Exit (or double-click on the Control-menu box).

Printing Your Document

You can print your document at any stage in the process of creating a document. Here's how you do it:

1. Make sure the document you want to print is displayed.

2. Open the File menu and select Print. The Print dialog box appears.

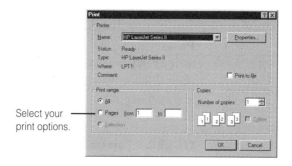

Select your print options.

3. In the Print Range section, select one of the following options:

All prints the entire document.

Selection prints only the selected portion of the document, assuming you dragged over some text before selecting the Print command.

Pages prints only the specified pages. If you select this option, type entries in the From and To boxes to specify which pages you want to print.

4. To print more than one copy of the document, type the desired number of copies in the Copies text box. On some printers, you can have the Printer collate the copies for you by clicking on the Collate option.

5. Next to the name of the selected printer is a button labeled Properties. To change the printer settings, click on this button to display a dialog box like the one shown here.

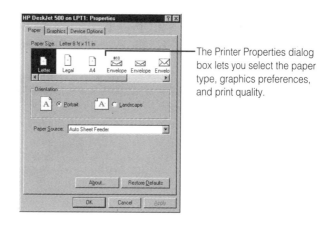

The Printer Properties dialog box lets you select the paper type, graphics preferences, and print quality.

6. Use the following tabs (yours may differ) to set your printer options:

Paper: Choose the paper size and type (for example, 8.5-by-11-inch or envelope). Choose the orientation: Portrait prints as a normal letter; Landscape prints sideways on a page. If you have two or more paper feed trays on your printer, select the correct tray.

Graphics: This tab lets you control the darkness of pictures on a page and how the colors in the picture are presented.

Device Options: This tab lets you control the print quality. You can usually choose a slow, high-quality output or a fast, low-quality output. Low-quality printouts are also less expensive because they use less ink. (For some printers, you may not be able to adjust the print quality for your text.)

Bypass Print dialog box: click on Print button

7. Click on the OK button. WordPad starts to print your document.

If you have trouble printing, refer to Chapters 46, 47, and 65, which explain (respectively) how to set up a printer, use the Windows Print Manager, and solve common printing problems.

Saving Your Work

As you type, what you type exists only in your computer's electronic memory (RAM). If the power goes off (even for an instant), you will lose your work. To avoid losing work, save it early and often. Here's what you do the first time you save the file:

1. Open the File menu and select Save. The Save As dialog box appears, prompting you to name the file.

Save files every 10 minutes

2. Type a name for the file in the File Name text box. (WordPad will add the extension .DOC to the end of the file name, automatically.)

Type a file name here.

3. (Optional) To specify where you want the file saved, select a drive from the Save In drop-down list and double-click on the folder you want to use in the window. (If you do not select a drive and folder, Windows uses the current drive and folder, usually C:\WINDOWS.)

4. Click on the Save button.

File/Save As makes copy of file

The next time you save your file, all you have to do is open the File menu and select Save (or press Ctrl+S). WordPad "remembers" the name and location of the file, so you don't have to retype it.

You can also use the File/Save As command to save a file. This allows you to save the file under another name, or to a different drive and folder. You can then edit the new file you created without changing the original.

Opening a Saved Document

Whenever you start WordPad, it displays a blank window in which you can start typing. To work on a file you already created and saved, you must open it. Here's how you open a file:

1. Open the File menu and select Open. The Open dialog box appears.

2. Click on the arrow to the right of the Look In option, and then click on the drive where the file is stored.

Work on 2 Docs: Run WordPad twice; open a doc in each WordPad Window

3. Double-click on the folder that contains the file. (To move up the directory tree, click on the folder icon with the arrow on it just to the right of the Look In drop-down list.)

4. Click on the name of the file you want to open in the list.

5. Click on the Open button. WordPad opens the file and displays it on-screen.

Select the drive and folder where the file is stored.

Click here to move up the folder tree.

Click on the file you want to open.

Beyond Survival

Inserting Pictures and Other Data

As you create a document, keep in mind that you can copy and paste text and pictures from other programs into it. For example, you can create a picture in Paint (see Chapter 16), copy it (or a portion of it), and then paste it into your document. Here's what you do:

1. Change to the program you need to open the file or enter the data you want to copy. (For example, to paste a picture from Paint, run Paint.)

2. Select the data you want to copy.

Ctrl+C = Copy
Ctrl+V = Paste

3. Open the Edit menu and choose Copy. The selected data is placed on the Windows Clipboard (see Chapter 17).

4. Switch back to WordPad, and open the document into which you want the copied data inserted.

5. Move the insertion point to where you want the copied data pasted.

6. Open the Edit menu and select one of the following options:

   Paste: Pastes the copied data from the Clipboard into the document.

   Paste Link: Pastes the copied data from the Clipbook into the document, and creates a link between the pasted data and the file that contains the data. If you change the file that contains the pasted data, the pasted data is updated automatically. For example, if you edit a picture that you created in Paint, those same changes appear on the pasted picture in your WordPad document.

   Paste Special: Lets you choose whether you want to Paste or Paste Link, and allows you to specify the format for the pasted data. For example, you can choose to paste a Paintbrush file as a Paint object, or in Bitmapped format. Make your selections, and then click on the OK button.

Whichever command you selected, the copied data is inserted into your document.

With Paste Special, you can Paste or Paste Link.

Another way to insert data into your document is to use the Edit/Insert Object command. This command lets you run a program that you can use to open a file or create an object. When you exit the program, the object you created is inserted in the WordPad document. For more information, refer to the end of Chapter 17, in the section called "Dynamic Data Sharing."

Cheat Sheet

Cutting, Copying, and Pasting Text

1. Drag over the text you want to copy or cut.
2. Open the Edit menu and select Cut or Copy.
3. Move the insertion point where you want the text inserted.
4. Open the Edit menu and select Paste.

Changing the Document Margins

1. Open the File menu and select Page Setup.
2. Tab to the margin setting you want to change.
3. Type the desired setting.
4. Repeat steps 2 and 3 for each margin setting you want to change.
5. Click on the OK button.

Aligning Text

1. Move the insertion point into the paragraph you want to align.
2. Open the Format menu and click on Paragraph.
3. Click on the arrow to the right of Alignment, and select Left, Center, or Right.
4. Click on the OK button.

Formatting Your Text

1. Drag over the text you want to format.
2. Open the Format menu and click on Font.
3. Select the desired type style, size, and enhancements.
4. Click on the OK button.

15

Editing and Formatting Your WordPad Document

In the previous chapter, you learned how to create and print a document, as well as how to save and open document files. In this chapter, you will learn how to cut and paste text into a document, as well as how to control the look and layout of your text. You'll learn how to change margins, make text bold and italic, change the text size, and change the tab settings.

Basic Survival

Selecting Text in a Document

Select word = double-click on it

Several tasks in this chapter require you to select text—for instance, to cut or copy text, you must first select it. To make a word or sentence bold, you must select it. The following list explains various ways to select text:

Select text	Move the mouse pointer to the first character you want in the selection; hold down the mouse button while dragging over additional text.
A single word	Double-click on the word.
A single line	Click inside the selection area (the blank space immediately to the left of the line) for the line you want to select.
Several lines	Move the mouse pointer into the selection area to the left of the first line you want to select; then hold down the mouse button while dragging up or down.
One paragraph	Double-click in the selection area to the left of the paragraph you want to select, or triple-click on any word in the sentence.

Several paragraphs

Double-click inside the selection area to the left of the first paragraph. On the second click, hold down the mouse button and drag the pointer up or down.

Range of text

Click in the selection area to the left of the first line in the desired range. Hold down the Shift key while clicking on the last line in that range.

Entire document

Hold down the Ctrl key while clicking anywhere inside the selection area.

When the mouse pointer is in the selection area, it reverses direction like this.

The selection area is the white strip to the left of the text.

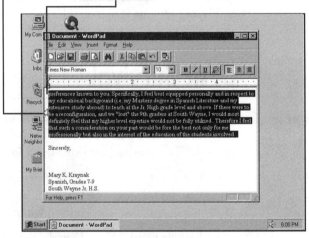

Cutting, Copying, and Pasting Text

As you edit your document, you may want to cut and paste the text you want to use (to move it), or copy and paste it into two or more places (for example, a list of numbers). To cut or copy and then paste text, do the following:

1. Select the text you want to cut or copy.

2. Open the Edit menu and select Cut or Copy. Cut removes the text and places it on the Clipboard so you can paste it somewhere else. Copy leaves the original text in place, and sticks a copy of it on the Clipboard.

Copy, Cut, and Paste are on the Edit menu.

3. Move the insertion point to where you want the text inserted.

4. Open the Edit menu and select Paste. The text is inserted.

Ctrl+C = Copy
Ctrl+X = Cut
Ctrl+V = Paste
Right-click on selected text to get shortcut menu

WordPad also allows you to cut, copy, and paste by dragging and dropping your text with the mouse. Select the text you want to copy or move, as explained earlier. Move the mouse pointer over any part of the selected text, and hold down the left mouse button (hold down the Ctrl key, if you want to copy the selection). Drag the selected text to the desired location. When you release the mouse button, the text is inserted at the mouse pointer.

For more details about cutting and pasting data using the Windows Clipboard and to learn about other ways to share data between applications, see Chapter 17, "Moving, Copying, and Sharing Information."

Setting Margins

The first thing you might want to do to format a document is to change the margins. The left and right margins are initially set at 1.25 inches. The top and bottom margins are set at 1 inch. To change the margins, here's what you do:

1. Open the File menu and select Page Setup. The Page Setup dialog box appears.

2. Tab to the margin setting you want to change.

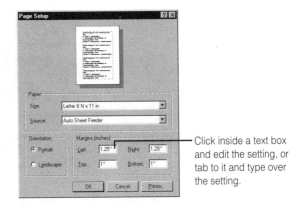

Click inside a text box and edit the setting, or tab to it and type over the setting.

3. Type the desired setting. When you start typing, the original setting is deleted.

4. Repeat steps 2 and 3 for each margin setting you want to change.

5. Click on the OK button.

Ctrl+Z = Undo

Beyond Survival

Changing the Look of Your Text

You can change the look of your text by changing its font (type style and size) or by adding an enhancement, such as bold or italic. Here's what you do:

1. Drag the mouse pointer over the text whose look you want to change.

2. Open the Format menu and select Font. The Font dialog box appears.

3. Enter your settings for the following options:

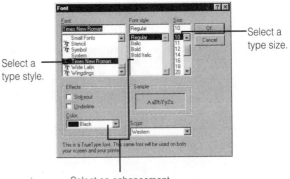

Select a type style.

Select a type size.

Select an enhancement.

Ctrl+B = Bold
Ctrl+U = Underlined
Ctrl+I = Italic

Font   Select the desired type style from the list. The **Sample** area shows what you'll get.

Font style   Select the desired enhancement (if any): bold or italic.

Size   Select the desired type size. Size is measured in points. There are about 72 points in an inch.

Effects   You can add underlining or strikethrough, or pick a color for the text (if you have a color printer).

4. Click on the OK button.

You may have noticed that some type styles in the Font list have a **TT** next to them. TT stands for TrueType fonts. These are special fonts that allow you to change the type size by a single point. Instead of selecting a type size from the Size list, you can type the precise size in the Size text box. Non-TrueType fonts usually allow you to select from a limited list of sizes.

Formatting Your Paragraphs

Ctrl+A selects whole document

You can apply paragraph formatting to any selected paragraphs to control their alignment (left, center, right) or to indent the paragraphs from the margins. Here's what you do:

1. Drag over all the paragraphs you want to format. (To change the formatting for the entire document, hold down the Ctrl key while clicking in the selection area—the area to the left of the paragraphs.)

2. Open the Format menu and click on Paragraph. The Paragraph dialog box appears.

3. To change the paragraph alignment, click on the arrow to the right of Alignment, and select one of the following options:

Left places the paragraph against the left margin.

Center centers the paragraph between the left and right margins.

Right shoves the right side of the paragraph against the right margin, leaving the left side of the paragraph uneven.

4. To indent the paragraphs from the left or right margins, type the desired indents (in inches) in the Indentation text boxes:

Left indents the left side of the paragraph from the left margin.

Right indents the right side of the paragraph from the right margin.

First Line indents the first line of the paragraph from the left margin, leaving remaining lines pressed against the left margin. To create a hanging indent (for a bulleted or numbered list), enter a positive number for the left indent and a negative number for the First line indent.

5. Click on the OK button.

Setting Tabs

WordPad is set up so that if you press the Tab key, the insertion point (and any text to the right of it) moves .5 inch to the right. This allows you to indent the first line of a paragraph or create columns of text. If you want to change the tab settings, perform the following steps:

1. Select all the paragraphs that you want the change in tab stops to affect.

2. Open the Format menu and select Tabs. The Tabs dialog box appears.

Type the desired settings here.

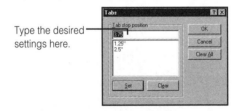

3. Type a tab stop position in inches, and then click on the Set button. (Repeat this step to set more tab stops.)

4. To clear a tab stop, click on it in the list, and then click on the Clear button (or click on Clear All to start over).

5. Click on the OK button.

Click inside Ruler to set tab stop; drag tab stop off Ruler to clear

Quick Formatting with the Toolbar and Ruler

Below the menu bar, WordPad has a couple of toolbars and a Ruler that can help you enter commands—and format your document—quickly. Use the Format Bar (as shown here) to enhance your text, change the paragraph alignment, or transform a series of paragraphs into a bulleted list.

Select text effects.

Select a paragraph alignment.

Select a font.

Select a type size.

Transform selected paragraphs into a bulleted list.

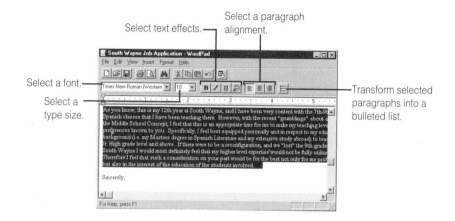

With the Ruler, you can quickly set tabs, and change paragraph indents, as shown here.

Click in the Ruler to set a tab stop, or drag a tab symbol off the Ruler to clear it.

Drag this triangle to indent the first line of the paragraph.

Drag this triangle to set the left margin.

Drag this box to move both the left margin and first line indent.

Drag this triangle to set the right margin.

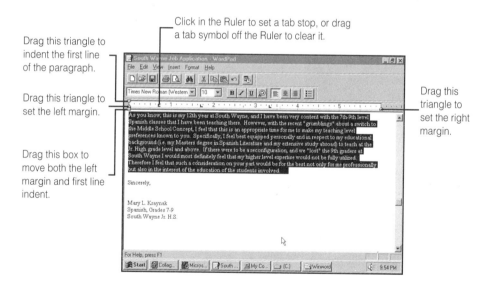

Cheat Sheet

Starting Paint

1. Click on the Start button.
2. Move the mouse pointer over Program, and then over Accessories.
3. Click on Paint.

Paint Tools

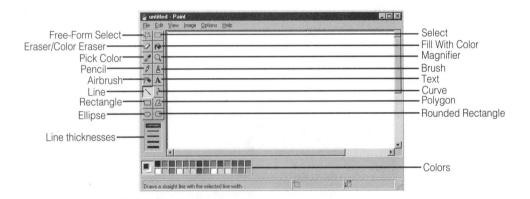

Drawing a Line or Shape

1. Click on the desired line thickness.
2. Click on the desired color or pattern.
3. Click on the shape you want to draw.
4. Move mouse pointer where you want one end of the object to appear.
5. Hold down the left mouse button and drag the mouse pointer to where you want the opposite end of the object to appear.
6. Release the mouse button.

Making Pictures with Paint

With Paint, you can create color or black-and-white drawings by "painting" your screen. Paint comes with a collection of basic shapes that you can assemble and fill to create simple or complex illustrations. Additional tools allow you to add text to your drawings; use others to cut, copy, and paste objects. You can even zoom in for detailed work. In this chapter, you'll learn how to use these tools to create and edit your own pictures.

Basic Survival

Starting Paint: What You'll See

You start Paint the same way you start any of Windows accessories. Take the following steps:

1. Click on the Start button. This opens the Start menu.

2. Move the mouse pointer over Program, and then over Accessories.

3. Click on Paint. The Paint program window appears.

Click on Maximize button for full-screen window

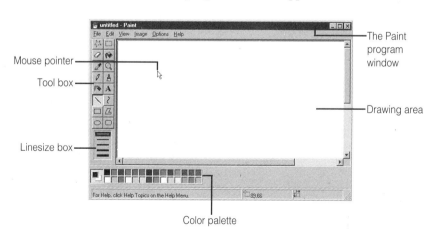

- The Paint program window
- Mouse pointer
- Tool box
- Drawing area
- Linesize box
- Color palette

Using the Paint Tools

The Paint tool box (on the left side of the screen), contains several tools that allow you to paint your screen, create basic lines and shapes, and edit your drawing. Following is a list of the tools and what they do:

Free-Form Select and Select   Click on the Free-form Select tool, and drag the mouse pointer around a section of the drawing to select it for cutting or copying. The Select tool allows you to select a rectangular area.

Eraser/Color Eraser   Click on the Eraser tool to wipe out areas of the picture. Click on a line-thickness button to make the eraser bigger or smaller. Drag the eraser over the area you want to remove. (To use the Color Eraser, right-click on a color in the palette to have the Eraser leave that color behind. To erase one color and replace it with another, left-click on the color you want to remove, and then right-click on the color you want to replace it with.)

Fill With Color   The Paint Roller lets you pour color or shading into an enclosed area. If you draw a box, you can click on Fill With Color, click on the desired color in the palette, and click inside the box to fill it with color. (To use two colors, left-click on one color in the palette, and right-click on the other. Then left-click to fill the object with the first color, or right-click to use the second color.)

Pick Color   The Pick Color tool lets you copy a color so you can use it on another object. Click on Pick Color, click on the color you want to use, and then draw or fill the object as you normally would. The color you picked up will behave just as if you had picked it in the color palette.

Magnifier   Click on the Magnifier and then click on an area on the screen you want to zoom in on for detailed work. Perform the same steps to zoom out.

Pencil   Use the Pencil to draw free-from lines, one pixel wide, across the screen. (You can't select a line thickness with this tool.)

Brush   The Brush lets you stroke color onto the screen. Unlike the Airbrush, the Brush puts down a uniform ribbon of color, no matter how fast you drag the mouse pointer.

Airbrush   Click on this tool and drag the mouse pointer across the screen to "spray-paint" your screen. Drag slowly to make the ribbon dark, or quickly to make it light.

A **Text**   Click on this tool, and then click where you want to type your text. Start typing. This method is useful for labeling a picture.

Line   The Line tool lets you drag a straight line on the screen.

Curve   This tool is tricky; you click on it and drag the mouse pointer to create a straight line. Then you drag the line you drew to one side or the other to make it curve.

Rectangle   The Rectangle tool creates a rectangle that has no color or shading inside. When you click on this tool, the line-thickness box displays three options: an outline, a filled rectangle, and a filled rectangle with no outline. The outline will appear in the foreground color; the fill will appear in the background color.

Polygon   The Polygon tools allow you to create an object made up of several straight lines. Select the tool, drag your first line segment, release the mouse button, and drag the next line. Continue until the object is complete, and then double-click where you want the last line to end.

Ellipse   The Ellipse tool lets you draw circles or ovals. To draw a perfect circle, hold down the Shift key while dragging the object into existence.

Rounded Rectangle   The Rounded Rectangle tool lets you create rectangles that have rounded corners.

Assemble shapes to create illustrations

Drawing Objects

Although each drawing tool creates a different type of object, the procedure for drawing objects is generally the same:

Right-click to cancel drawing

1. Click on the drawing tool you want to use.

2. In the Linesize box, click on the desired line thickness.

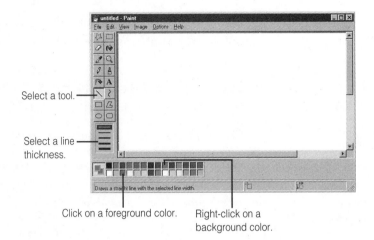

Select a tool.

Select a line thickness.

Click on a foreground color.

Right-click on a background color.

3. Click on the color you want to use as the object's foreground color (in the palette), and then right-click on the color you want to use as the background color. You can then use the left mouse button to draw with the foreground color, and the right mouse button to draw with the background color.

4. Move the mouse pointer where you want one end or corner of the object to appear.

5. Hold down the left or right mouse button, and drag to where you want the other end or corner of the object to appear.

To get straight line, perfect circle, or square: press Shift while dragging

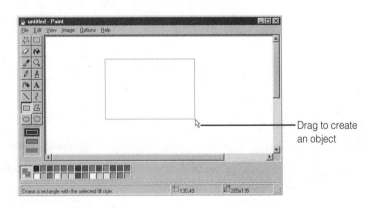

Drag to create an object

6. Release the mouse button.

Saving and Printing Your Work

To save your work, use the File/Save command. To print, select File/Print. To open a file you created and saved, use the File/Open command. These operations are the same in most Windows programs. Refer to Chapter 10, "Saving, Opening, and Printing Documents," for details.

Beyond Survival

Filling Objects with Color

You can fill an object with color or shading in two ways: draw a filled object, or use the Fill With Color tool to "pour" paint into the object. To draw a filled object (a rectangle or ellipse), make sure you select one of the fill options from the line thickness box. Left-click on the palette color you want to use for the object's outline, and right-click on the color you want to use to fill the object. When you draw the object, the right-click (background) color will appear inside the border.

If you already drew an unfilled object, you can fill an object with color by using the Fill With Color tool. Here's what you do:

1. Click on the Fill With Color tool in the tool box.

2. Click on the color you want to use on the Color Palette. (You can right-click to use a second color.)

3. Move tip of the mouse pointer (now a dribble from a paint can) into the object you want to fill.

Edit/Undo or Ctrl+Z to undo last move

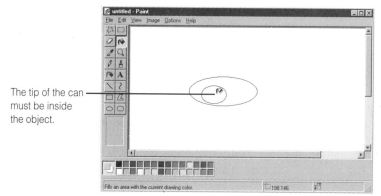

The tip of the can must be inside the object.

4. Click the left mouse button to use the foreground color, or the right mouse button to use the background color.

The Fill With Color tool pours color inside the boundaries or border of the object. If the border is broken or has a gap in it, the color pours out all over the screen, so make sure you pour color only inside closed boundaries.

Adding Text

If you want to add a label or title to your picture, you can do it with the Text tool. Here's what you do:

1. Click on the Text tool A in the tool box.

2. Drag the mouse pointer where you want the text to appear. A box appears, showing where the text will be positioned, and a Font dialog box appears, allowing you to select the type style you want.

3. If the Font dialog box does not appear, open the View menu and click on Text Toolbar.

4. In the Fonts dialog box, use the drop-down lists and buttons to select the type style and size you want to use—as well as any enhancements (such as Bold, Italic, and Underline).

Select a type style. Select a type size.

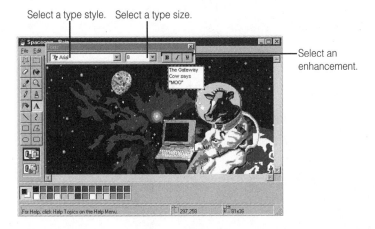

Select an enhancement.

5. To change the text color, click on the desired color in the palette.

6. Type your text; it will appear in the style, size, and color you selected in steps 3 and 4.

7. You can drag the border of the text box to move the text, or drag a *handle* (one of the tiny squares that surround the text box) to change the box's size or dimensions.

8. When you're done, click anywhere outside the text box to save your addition.

You can change fonts before you type or immediately after typing text. If you click outside the text box (or create a different object), however, you can't go back and style the text. In such a case, you have to cut the text (as explained next) and start over.

Cutting, Copying, and Pasting Selected Areas

In Paint, you cannot select text by dragging over it, or select an object (such as a circle or square) by clicking on it. Instead, you must use the *selection tool* to mark an area of the picture that might contain one or more objects. To cut or copy, and paste a selection, perform the following steps:

1. Click on the Free-Form Select or Select tool. Use Free-Form Select to select an irregular area. Use Select to mark a rectangular area.

2. Drag the mouse pointer to select the portion of the drawing you want to cut or copy.

3. Move the tip of the mouse pointer over any part of the selected area.

Right-click on a selection to view shortcut menu

4. Hold down the Ctrl key while performing the next step, if you want to copy the selection. If you want to move it, don't hold down the Ctrl key.

5. Drag the selection to where you want it, and then release the mouse button.

Cheat Sheet

Moving and Copying Selections

1. Mark the selection you want to copy or move.
2. Open the Edit menu and select Cut or Copy.
3. Move the insertion point to where you want the selection inserted.
4. Open the Edit menu and select Paste.

Viewing the Clipboard Contents

1. Click on the Start button.
2. Move the mouse pointer over Programs, and then over Accessories.
3. Click on Clipboard Viewer.

Dragging and Dropping

1. Mark the selection you want to copy or move.
2. Move the mouse pointer over any part of the selection.
3. Hold down the left mouse button (and the Ctrl key to copy), while dragging the selection to where you want it.

Copying and Moving with Shortcut Menus

1. Mark the selection you want to copy or move.
2. Right-click on the selection.
3. Click on Cut or Copy.
4. Right-click where you want the cut or copied selection inserted.
5. Click on Paste.

Moving, Copying, and Sharing Information

Windows owes much of its popularity to the fact that it allows you to work with several programs at the same time, and transfer information between programs. In this chapter, you'll learn how to copy and move information within (and between) documents, and how to use some of Windows' more advanced tools for sharing information between programs.

Basic Survival

Moving and Copying with the Clipboard

The Windows *Clipboard* is a temporary holding area that allows you to copy or move a selection within a document or from one document to another. Whenever you cut or copy a selection, it is placed on the Clipboard, replacing anything that was previously on the Clipboard. You can then paste the selection from the Clipboard into a document.

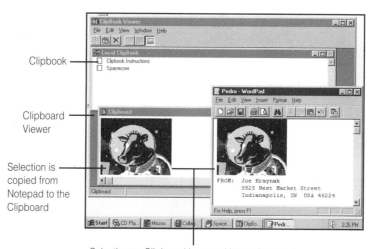

Clipbook

Clipboard Viewer

Selection is copied from Notepad to the Clipboard

Selection on Clipboard is pasted into a document

To transfer selections with the Clipboard, here's what you do:

Ctrl+C =
Copy
Ctrl+X =
Cut
Ctrl+V =
Paste
Right-click
on a
selection to
use a
shortcut
menu

1. Mark the selection you want to copy or move. To select text, drag over it. To select a picture, you can click on it or use the program's selection tool to drag a box around the picture.

2. Open the Edit menu and select Cut (to move an object) or Copy (to copy the selection). The selection is placed on the Clipboard.

3. Move the insertion point to where you want the selection inserted. (This can be in the same document, in a different document in the same program, or in a different document in a different program.)

4. Open the Edit menu and select Paste. A copy of the selection that's on the Clipboard is pasted into the selected location.

If you try to paste into a document created in another program, and Paste is dimmed (not available), the program cannot handle the format of the selection, and you cannot paste the Clipboard contents into this document.

Viewing the Clipboard Contents

The Clipboard works in the background, so you rarely see it (or need to see it). However, if you want to see what's on the Clipboard, here's what you do:

1. Click on the Start button.

2. Move the mouse pointer over Programs, and then over Accessories.

3. Click on Clipboard Viewer. The Clipboard Viewer window appears. The Clipboard window is minimized at the bottom of the Clipboard Viewer.

Pressing
Print Screen
puts picture
of screen on
Clipboard;
use
Alt+Print
Screen to
get current
window only

4. Click on the Clipboard's Maximize button.

A picture of the screen on the Clipboard

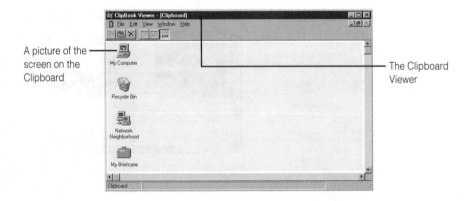

The Clipboard Viewer

Beyond Survival

Dragging and Dropping Selections

Some Windows programs allow you to bypass the Copy, Cut, and Paste commands by using a feature called *Drag and Drop*. If you have a program that offers Drag-and-Drop copying and moving, do the following to move or copy selections:

1. Mark the selection you want to copy or move. To select text, drag over it. To select a picture, you can click on it or use the program's selection tool to drag a box around the picture.

2. Move the mouse pointer over any part of the selection.

3. To copy the selection, hold down the Ctrl key while performing the following step. Otherwise the selection will be moved instead of copied.

4. Hold down the mouse button, and drag the selection to where you want it. (If you are copying a selection, a plus sign appears below the mouse pointer; if you are moving a selection, no plus sign appears.)

5. Release the mouse button. Windows inserts the selection at the mouse pointer.

Open two document windows and Drag and Drop

Dynamic Data Sharing with OLE

The Windows Clipboard allows you to share information dynamically, through a technology called OLE (short for *object linking and embedding*). With OLE (pronounced oh-LAY), you can insert objects created in other programs into a document in your current program. When you enter the command to insert an object, Windows runs the program you need to use to create the object. When you exit that program, the object you created is inserted into the current document. Whenever you want to edit the object, simply double-click on it to run the program you used to create it.

OLE gives you two options: *linking* and *embedding*. With linking, the object you insert is connected dynamically to its original file; if you modify the file, the object in your document is updated to reflect any changes. With embedding, you place a copy of the object in your document, breaking any link between the object and its file. If you modify the object's file, the changes do not appear in the object.

To embed copied or cut data from one document into another, simply use the Cut, Copy, and Paste commands, as explained earlier. Paste automatically embeds the data. When you double-click on the pasted selection, Windows runs the associated program, allowing you to edit the item.

Linking data is a little more complicated, as shown in the following steps:

1. Display the document that contains the selection you want to link, and then copy the selection. The selection is placed on the Clipboard.

2. Switch to the document into which you want to insert the copied selection.

3. Open the Edit menu and select Paste Special. A dialog box appears (like the one shown here), prompting you to select a format for the selection and whether you want the data linked.

4. Click on the format in which you want the selection pasted.

5. Click on Paste Link, and then click on the OK button. Windows inserts the selection as specified and creates a dynamic link to the original file. If you edit the original file, the edits will appear automatically in the pasted selection.

Use Edit/Paste Special to link a copied or cut selection.

You can also embed a selection or a new file by using the Insert Object command. This command runs a specified Windows program or *applet* (a small program that lets you create objects). To insert an object, perform the following steps:

1. Open the Insert menu and select Object (in some programs, you open the Edit menu and select Insert Object). A dialog box appears, showing the programs you can run to create an object.

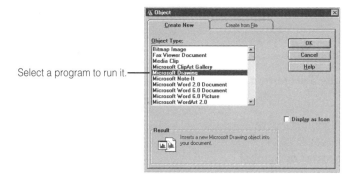

Select a program to run it.

2. Click on the desired program, and then click on OK. Windows runs the selected program.

3. Use the program to create the file you want to insert.

Alt+F4 to exit

4. Open the File menu and select Exit and Return To. A dialog box appears, asking whether you want to update the open embedded object.

5. Click on the Yes button. Windows inserts the object you just created into your document.

Whenever you want to edit the object, simply double-click on it, or click on it and choose a command from the Edit menu.

Cheat Sheet

Running Character Map

1. Click on the Start button.
2. Move the mouse pointer over Programs, and then over Accessories.
3. Click on Character Map.

Inserting a Character or Symbol

1. Open the Font list and click on a font.
2. Double-click on each character you want to insert.
3. Click on the Select button.
4. Click on the Copy button.
5. Switch to the application and document you want to paste the characters into.
6. Move the insertion point to where you want the characters.
7. Select the same font you selected in step 2.
8. Open the Edit menu and select Paste.

18

Inserting Characters and Symbols with the Character Map

Character Map allows you to insert special characters and symbols into your documents—characters and symbols that may or may not appear on your keyboard. With Character Map, you select the characters and/or symbols you want to insert, copy them to the Clipboard, and then paste them into your document. Keep in mind, however, that Character Map works only in Windows applications.

Basic Survival

Running Character Map

To run Character Map, perform the following steps:

1. Click on the Start button to open the Start menu.

2. Move the mouse pointer over Programs, and then over Accessories.

3. Click on Character Map. The Character Map program window appears.

Character Map contains several sets of special characters and symbols.

If you use Character Map often, keep it running. You may even want to make a shortcut for it so you can call it up quickly while you're working in another application. You can even assign a shortcut key to the shortcut; that way you can run it quickly by pressing a key combination: right-click on the shortcut, select Properties, click on the Shortcut tab, click inside the Shortcut

Key text box, and press the key combination you want to use (for example, Ctrl+Alt+C). Click on OK when you're done.

Inserting a Character or Symbol

You can use Character Map to insert symbols and characters that do not appear on your keyboard. Here's what you do:

1. Run Character Map.

2. Open the Font list and click on a font. A grid full of characters and symbols for the selected font appears.

3. Move the mouse pointer over a character or symbol and hold down the mouse button to see it more clearly.

Select a font for access to symbols and characters in that font.

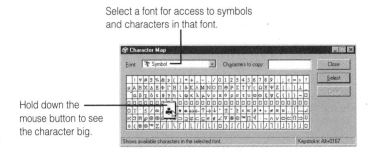

Hold down the mouse button to see the character big.

Use arrow keys to move from character to character

4. To add the character to the Characters to Copy text box, click on a character and click on the Select button. The characters in this text box will be copied to the Clipboard.

5. Repeat steps 3 and 4 to add more characters and symbols to the Characters to Copy text box. To remove a character, click to the right of it inside the text box, and then backspace over it.

Double-click on a character

6. Click on the Copy button. The characters in the Characters to Copy text box are placed on the Windows Clipboard.

7. Switch to the program and document you want to paste the characters into.

8. Move the insertion point to where you want the characters.

9. Select the same font you selected in step 2.

10. Open the Edit menu and select Paste. The characters from the Clipboard are pasted at the insertion point.

Cheat Sheet

Starting the Calculator

1. Click on the Start button.
2. Move the mouse pointer over Programs, and then over Accessories.
3. Click on Calculator.

Entering Calculations

1. Click on the number buttons to enter the first number.
2. Click on the operator you want to use:

    `+` to add the next number

    `-` to subtract the next number

    `*` to multiply by the next number

    `/` to divide by the next number

3. Click on the number buttons to enter the next number.
4. Repeat steps 2 and 3 until you have performed all your calculations.
5. Click on the equal button `=`.

Switching Calculators

1. Open the View menu.
2. Click on the calculator you want to use: Scientific or Standard.

19

Go Figure with the Calculator

Windows offers an on-screen calculator you can use just like a hand-held calculator. You key in the numbers and mathematical operators you want to use, and the Calculator performs the calculations for you. In this chapter, you'll learn how to use the two Windows calculators: Standard and Scientific.

Basic Survival

Starting the Calculator

You start the Calculator as you start any Windows accessory:

1. Click on the Start button.

2. Move the mouse pointer over Programs, and then over Accessories.

3. Click on Calculator.

4. To switch to the Scientific calculator, open the View menu and select Scientific. To switch back to the Standard calculator, open the View menu and select Standard.

Entering Calculations with the Standard Calculator

The Standard calculator works like a hand-held calculator. You simply click on the buttons to enter numbers and mathematical operators.

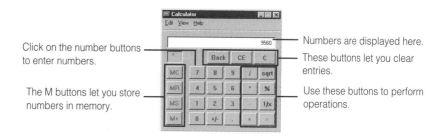

Click on the number buttons to enter numbers.

The M buttons let you store numbers in memory.

Numbers are displayed here.

These buttons let you clear entries.

Use these buttons to perform operations.

To enter a calculation, perform the following steps:

*Can also use
keyboard's
number keys
if NumLock
is on*

1. Click on the number buttons to enter the first number in the calculation. The number appears in the display area.

2. Click on the operator you want to use:

| + | to add the next number |

| - | to subtract the next number |

| * | to multiply by the next number |

| / | to divide by the next number |

3. Click on the number buttons to enter the next number.

4. Repeat steps 2 and 3 until you have performed all the calculations.

5. Click on the equal button | = |.

If you make a mistake while keying in a number, click on any of the following buttons:

| C | Clears all your work up to this point, so you can start over. |

| CE | Clears only the current entry, affecting no other entries. |

*Backspace =
Back button*

| Back | Deletes the digit you just typed. Keep clicking to remove additional digits. |

Beyond Survival

Using the Memory Functions

Sometimes you may want to store a value in memory while you perform other calculations. Say, for example, you want to total your last two paychecks, total the taxes, and then divide taxes by gross income to determine what percent is being taken for taxes; you'll want to store the gross pay total in memory until you need it at the end. To use the computer's memory in this way, use the following M buttons:

MS   Click on this button to store the displayed value in memory. An **M** appears below the area where values are displayed, to show that a value is stored in memory.

MR   Click on this button to display the value that's stored in memory.

MC   Click on this button to clear any value that is stored in memory. The **M** below the value display disappears.

M+   Click on this button to add the value currently displayed on-screen to the value that's stored in memory.

Calculating a Percentage

The Calculator's % key allows you to calculate sales percentages and perform similar calculations. Using the key, however, may not be the most intuitive operation. Here's what you do to determine a percentage:

1. Key in the number for which you want to calculate a percent. For example, if you want to determine 7% sales tax on $450, key in **450**.

2. Click on the division button / .

3. Key in the percentage (for example, **7** for 7%).

4. Click on the percentage button % .

Copying and Pasting the Results

Ctrl+C to Copy
Ctrl+V to Paste

If you performed the calculations to plug a number into a letter or other document, you can copy the result and then paste it into the document in the other application. Here's what you do:

1. Open the Edit menu and select Copy.

2. Switch to the document into which you want the result pasted.

3. Move the insertion point where you want the result.

4. Open the Edit menu and select Paste.

Cheat Sheet

Viewing the Time and Date

1. Look on the right side of the Taskbar to see the current time.

2. Rest the mouse pointer on the clock to view today's date.

3. Double-click on the time to view the Clock and Calendar.

Changing the Date or Time

1. Double-click on the time in the Taskbar.

2. To change the month, open the Month drop-down list, and click on a month.

3. To change the year, click on the up or down arrow to the right of the Year text box.

4. To change the day of month, click on it in the Calendar.

5. To change the time, click on the hour, minute, or seconds number, and then click on the up or down arrow to the right of the time.

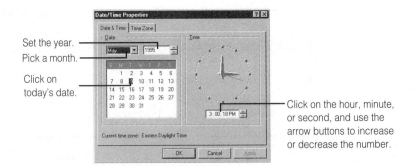

20

Tracking Time with the Clock

As you probably know, your computer has a built-in clock that keeps track of the date and time. Windows comes with a clock program that can display the system date and time on-screen. This clock also enables you to change the system date or time, which many programs can insert into your documents. In this chapter, you'll learn how to display the clock and change its settings.

Basic Survival

Turning the Clock On or Off

By default, the clock appears in the lower right corner of your screen, at the end of the Taskbar. You can view the date by resting the mouse pointer on the clock for a couple of seconds; a box pops up showing today's date (if it is set correctly). You can turn this clock off by performing the following steps:

Right-click on time in Taskbar; click on Properties

1. Right-click on the time (not on the speaker) in the Taskbar.

2. Click on Properties. The Taskbar Properties dialog box appears.

3. Click on Show Clock to hide the clock if it is displayed, or to display the clock if it is hidden. A check mark indicates that the clock will be displayed.

4. Click on the OK button. Windows displays or hides the clock according to your selection.

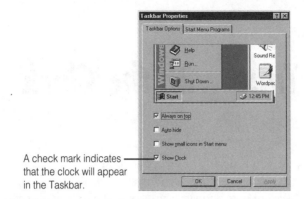

A check mark indicates that the clock will appear in the Taskbar.

If the clock is hidden, you can display it by clicking on the Start button, pointing to Settings, clicking on Taskbar, and then clicking on Show Clock.

Setting the Date or Time

As with any clock, your computer's clock may run a little fast or slow. In addition to causing you to be late for appointments and meetings, the wrong date or time can affect the date and time inserted in your documents. If you find that your clock is off, you can use the Windows clock to reset the time and date:

1. Double-click on the time in the Taskbar. (Make sure you double-click on the time, and not on the little speaker icon in the clock.) The Date/Time Properties dialog box appears.

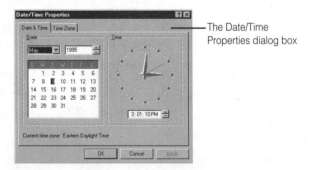

The Date/Time Properties dialog box

2. To change the month, click on the arrow to the right of the month, and then click on the current month.

3. To change the year, click on the up or down arrow to the right of the Year text box.

Double-click on
time in Taskbar
to set time
and date

4. To change the day of month, click on it in the Calendar.

5. To change the time, click on the hour, minute, or seconds number, and then click on the up or down arrow to the right of the time. (Repeat this step to change other digits or to change AM to PM or vice versa.)

Beyond Survival

Picking a Different Time Zone

If you travel or do business in various time zones, you can use the clock to keep track of the time zones and their relation to GMT (Greenwich Mean Time). In addition, you can make the clock automatically adjust itself for daylight savings time. Here's what you do:

1. Double-click on the time in the Taskbar. The Date/Time Properties dialog box appears.

2. Click on the Time Zone tab.

3. To pick a different time zone, open the time zone drop-down list and click on the desired time zone, or drag the highlighted band over the desired area on the globe.

4. To have the clock adjust itself for daylight savings time, click on Automatically Adjust Clock for Daylight Saving Changes to place a check mark next to the option.

5. Click on the OK button.

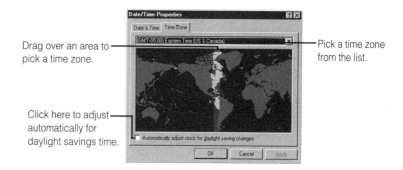

Drag over an area to pick a time zone.

Pick a time zone from the list.

Click here to adjust automatically for daylight savings time.

Cheat Sheet

Starting the Notepad

1. Click on the Start button.
2. Move the mouse pointer over Programs, and then over Accessories.
3. Click on Notepad.

Entering the Date and Time

1. Open the Edit menu.
2. Select Time/Date.

Turning Word Wrap On or Off

1. Open the Edit menu.
2. Select Word Wrap.

Undoing an Action

1. Open the Edit menu.
2. Select Undo.

Creating a Time Log

- *Time logs* are useful for keeping track of changes, time spent on a project, or a history of phone calls and contacts.
- Type **.LOG** at the top of the document.
- Whenever you open the document, Notepad inserts the current time and date.

21

Editing Text with Notepad

Notepad is useful for editing short text files; you might use these to enter settings for some of your DOS programs, or for writing brief messages you might send across the Internet or over your online service. Notepad creates pure text files, so the recipient will be able to open the file in just about any word processing program.

Notepad makes plain-text files

Notepad is also good for creating date-stamped documents. To have Notepad insert the current date and time whenever you open a file, you can enter the .LOG command in the document. In this chapter, you'll learn how to use Notepad to create and edit text files, and to stamp your documents with the date and time.

Basic Survival

Starting Notepad: What You'll See

To start Notepad, follow these steps:

1. Click on the Start button to open the Start menu.

2. Move the mouse pointer over Programs, and then over Accessories. The Accessories submenu appears.

3. Click on Notepad. The Notepad program window appears.

The Notepad window —

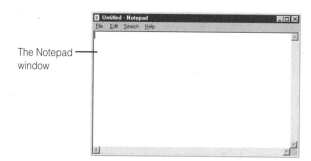

You can also start Notepad by double-clicking on any text file (files whose names end in .TXT) in Windows Explorer or My Computer. Other files you can double-click on to open them in Notepad have names that end in **.000**, **.INI**, **.DA0**, **.INF**, and **.DIC**, although you probably won't need to edit these file types. If you double-click on a file that's too large for Notepad, a dialog box will appear, asking whether you want to open the file in WordPad instead. You can then edit the document in WordPad and save it as a text file.

Typing in Notepad

Once you've started Notepad, you can start typing—or use the File/Open command to open a text file. You type just as you would in WordPad (see Chapter 14). The only difference between WordPad and Notepad is that Notepad does not wrap the text automatically from one line to the next; you have to press Enter at the end of each line. You can turn word wrap on, however, by performing the following steps:

Edit/Undo to cancel an action

1. Open the Edit menu.

2. Select Word Wrap.

You save, open, and print Notepad documents the same way you do in other Windows programs. For details, see Chapter 10, "Saving, Opening, and Printing Documents."

Beyond Survival

Inserting the Date and Time

Sometimes it's useful to insert the date and time into a file to keep track of notes and revisions. You could type the date as normal text, or have Notepad do it for you:

1. Open the Edit menu.

F5 = Time/ Date

2. Select Time/Date. Notepad inserts the time and date at the insertion point (for example **10:52 AM 10/15/95**).

Creating a Time Log

Suppose you need to keep track of phone calls and contacts (for legal or billing purposes), or if you need to keep track of the dates on which you entered changes to a file. You can use Notepad to create a *time log*: insert the current date and time at the bottom of the file whenever you open it, and position the insertion point below the date and time. To create a time log, type **.LOG** at the top of the document.

Notepad inserts the
date and time

Type your text here

Type .LOG here

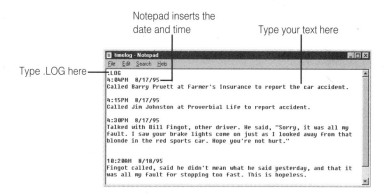

Creating a Batch File

A *batch file* contains a series of commands that execute automatically when you run it. The most famous batch file is AUTOEXEC.BAT, which runs whenever you boot your computer. You can use Notepad to create your own batch files. For example, say you often enter the command **c:\word5\ word.exe letter.doc** at the DOS prompt. The command starts runs Word and opens the document LETTER.DOC. You can create a batch file that enters the command for you. Here's how you do it:

1. Start Notepad.

2. Type the command or commands that you want the batch file to carry out. If you are entering two or more commands, press Enter at the end of each command line.

3. Open the File menu and select Save. The Save dialog box appears.

4. Type a name for the file (up to eight characters), type a period, and type **bat**. For example, type **letter.bat**.

5. From the Drives list, select c:.

6. In the Directories tree, double-click on the c:\ at the top of the tree.

7. Click on OK.

To run the batch file, type the file's name at the DOS prompt and press Enter. For example, to run a file named LETTER.BAT, you would type **letter** at the DOS prompt and press Enter.

Cheat Sheet

Playing an Audio CD

- Insert your audio CD into the CD-ROM drive and close it. Windows starts the CD Player and starts playing the CD.
- You can click on the CD Player's Minimize button, and the CD will continue to play.

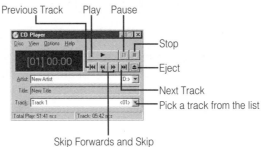

Previous Track   Play   Pause

Stop

Eject

Next Track

Pick a track from the list

Skip Forwards and Skip Backwards within a track

Repeating a Disc

1. Open the Options menu.
2. Click on Continuous Play.

Playing Selected Tracks

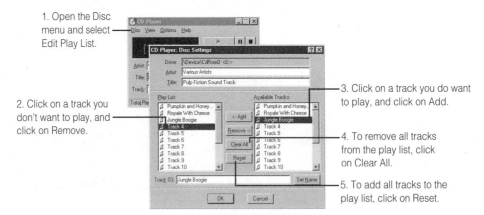

1. Open the Disc menu and select Edit Play List.

2. Click on a track you don't want to play, and click on Remove.

3. Click on a track you do want to play, and click on Add.

4. To remove all tracks from the play list, click on Clear All.

5. To add all tracks to the play list, click on Reset.

22

Playing Audio CDs

Just insert disc and Windows starts playing it

If you have a CD-ROM drive that can play audio CDs (some older CD-ROM drives do not have this capability), you can use Windows CD Player to play your favorite music CDs and other audio CDs. CD Player provides you with a control panel that looks and acts like one you might find on a real CD player. You simply click on the on-screen buttons to play, stop, pause, and eject your disc. CD Player also has some fancy features that allow you to select tracks, play them in a random order, and even change the volume and balance.

Basic Survival

Playing an Audio CD

Playing an audio CD in Windows 95 is a no-brainer. You stick the CD in the CD-ROM drive; Windows starts CD Player and plays the disc. You can then click on the CD Player's Minimize button, and the CD continues to play. To use CD Player's controls to stop, pause, restart, or eject the disc, take the following steps:

1. Click on CD Player in the Taskbar to switch to it.

2. To pause, click on the Pause button ⏸.

3. To restart the disc, click on the Play button ▶.

4. To stop playing, click on the Stop button ■.

5. To play the next track, click on the Next Track button ⏭.

6. To go back to the previous track, click on the Previous Track button ⏮.

7. To move forward or back in the current track (to hear your favorite drum solo), click on Skip Forwards or Skip Backwards ⏪ ⏩.

Click on Close
button to stop
playing and quit
CD Player

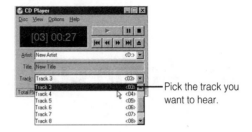

Pick the track you
want to hear.

8. To select a specific track, open the Track drop-down list, and click on the desired track.

Setting the Volume and Balance

The funny thing about most computers is that they have about four volume controls. There's usually one on the CD-ROM drive, one on the back of the sound card (assuming you have a sound card), and one or two on your speakers. In addition, if you have a sound card, its driver probably has a volume-control setting. If these controls can't crank the sound to the decibel level you want, you can use CD Player's volume control:

1. Open the View menu and select Volume Control. The Volume Control dialog box appears.

Adjust the
volume under
Volume Control
or CD

2. To adjust the volume, move the mouse pointer over the Volume slide bar and drag it up or down.

3. To change the balance, drag the Balance slide bar to the left or right.

Drag the Balance slider left or right.

Drag the Volume slider up or down.

You can also set the volume and balance here.

Beyond Survival

Making a Disc Play Continuously

You can set CD Player to play continuously by doing the following:

1. Open the Options menu.

2. Click on Continuous Play.

Playing Selected Tracks

If you have a CD that has certain tracks that you can't stand listening to, you can prevent CD Player from playing them. Here's what you do:

1. Open the Disc menu and select Edit Play List. The CD Player: Disc Settings dialog box appears.

To select more than one track in Play List, drag over tracks or Ctrl+click on each

2. To remove one track from the Play List, click on the track, and then click on Remove. The track is removed from the Play List, but still appears in the Available Tracks list, so you can add it later.

3. You can remove all tracks from the Play List by clicking on the Clear All button.

4. To add all the tracks from the Available Tracks list to the Play List, click on the Reset button.

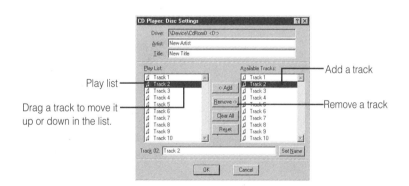

5. To add a single track to the Play List, click on the track in the Play List above which you want to insert the new track. Then click on the track you want to add (in the Available Tracks list), and click on the Add button. You can add the track more than once to have the song play several times.

6. To move a track in the Play List, click on it, drag it up or down in the list, and then release the mouse button.

7. Click on the OK button when you're done.

Once you've mastered the track numbers and Play List, you might want to replace the track numbers with actual song names. With song names displayed, editing the Play List becomes much more intuitive. Here's what you do:

1. Open the Disc menu and select Edit Play List. The CD Player: Disc Settings dialog box appears.

2. In the Artist text box, type the name of the group or artist.

3. Tab to the Title text box, and type the CD's title.

4. Click on Track 1 in the Available Tracks list.

5. Drag over Track 1 in the Track 01 text box, type the song or track name, and press Enter. CD Player highlights the next track number and lets you name it.

6. Type the name for the next track, and press Enter. Repeat this step to name all the tracks.

7. Click on the OK button. CD Player saves your changes for this CD.

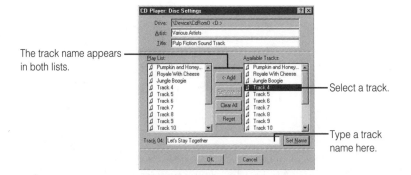

The track name appears in both lists.

Select a track.

Type a track name here.

Whenever you play this CD, the Play List for that CD will be in effect, complete with names instead of the track numbers. If you insert a new CD (one for which you did not enter track names), CD Player uses track numbers.

Playing Tracks in a Random Order

CD Player can play tracks in a random order to add some variety to a CD you frequently listen to. Take the following steps:

1. Open the Options menu.

2. Click on Random Order.

Setting the CD Player Preferences

You can set some preferences for the CD Player to determine whether it saves settings on exit, whether the CD continues to play after you exit, and so on. Here's what you do:

1. Open the Options menu and select Preferences. The Preferences dialog box appears.

2. Select any of the following options to turn it off if it is on, or on if it is off:

Stop CD Playing on Exit—When this option is on, the CD stops playing when you exit CD Player. If you turn this off, you can stop the CD by ejecting it from the CD-ROM drive.

Save Settings on Exit—When this option is on, CD Player saves any changes you may have made to it, including the volume and balance. If you're happy with your settings, and you want to prevent someone from changing them, turn off this option.

Show Tool Tips—If you turn this off, you won't see the pop-up button names when you rest your mouse on a button in CD Player.

3. To change the length of time a track plays for the intro, click on the arrows in the Intro Play Length spin box.

4. In the Display Font area, click on Small Font or Large Font to specify the size of text used for CD Player's track and time display.

5. Click on the OK button when you're done.

Enter CD Player preferences here.

Cheat Sheet

Recording Sounds with a Microphone

1. Click on the Start button and move the mouse pointer over Programs.

2. Move the mouse pointer over Accessories, and then over Multimedia.

3. Click on Sound Recorder.

4. Click on the Record button and start talking into the microphone.

5. Click on the Stop button.

6. Open the File menu and select Save.

7. Type a name for the file, and then click on the Save button.

Click on Record and start talking.

Click on Stop when you're done.

Attaching a Sound to an Event

1. Click on the Start button.

2. Move the mouse pointer over Settings, and then click on Control Panel.

3. Double-click on the Sounds icon.

4. In the Events list, click on the Windows event to which you want to assign a sound.

5. Open the Sound Name drop-down list, and click on the desired sound.

6. You can click on the Preview Play button to listen to the sound.

7. Click on the OK button.

23

Recording Sounds with the Sound Recorder

If you have a sound card (such as Sound Blaster) and a microphone or CD-ROM drive that plays audio CDs (through your sound board), you can use the Windows Sound Recorder to record music, your voice—or any other sound—and store them in files on disk. Then you can attach the sounds to certain events, and have Windows play the sounds whenever the events occur. For example, you can have a short piece of music play whenever you start Windows.

If you don't have a sound board, you can still perform some of the tasks in this chapter, such as attaching a sound to an event. The sound might not be of the highest quality, but you'll be able to hear it.

Basic Survival

Recording a Sound with a Microphone

The Sound Recorder lets you record a sound and save it in a .WAV file. To start the Sound Recorder and record a sound, here's what you do:

1. Click on the Start button and move the mouse pointer over Programs.

2. Move the mouse pointer over Accessories, and then over Multimedia.

3. Click on Sound Recorder. The Sound Recorder window appears.

3 submenus?!
Create a
shortcut for
Sound Recorder

Sound Recorder

Play button

Stop button

Record button

Put mouse pointer over Stop button so you can stop quickly

4. When you are ready to record, click on the Record button [●] and start talking, playing music, or making other sounds into the microphone.

5. When you're done talking, click on the Stop [■] button.

6. Open the File menu and select Save. The Save File dialog box appears.

7. Type a name for the file in the Name text box.

8. Select the drive and directory in which you want to save the file. (Windows stores its sound files in \WINDOWS\MEDIA. If you save your sound file there, it'll be easier to attach the sound to a Windows event.)

9. Click on the Save button.

Recording Sounds from an Audio CD

If you have a CD-ROM drive connected to your sound board, you can record portions of your favorite audio CDs and store them as sound files. Perform the steps just shown, but instead of talking or making noise into the microphone, play the CD with CD Player (as explained in Chapter 22). When CD Player starts playing the portion of the song you want to record, click on the Record button.

Once you've recorded a sound, you'll want to hear what you just recorded. Simply click on the Play button. If nothing happens, try clicking on the Seek to Start button, and then click on the Play button.

Adjusting the Recording and Playback Volume

If your microphone seems to record too softly, or if your speaker isn't cranking out your recordings at the right volume, you can change the volume. Take the following steps:

1. Run Sound Recorder.

2. Open the Edit menu and click on Audio Properties. The Audio Properties dialog box appears.

3. To change the volume at which recorded sounds play, drag the slider under Playback Volume to the right or left.

4. To change the volume at which sounds are recorded, drag the slider under Recording Volume to the left or right.

5. To change the quality at which sounds are recorded, click on the Customize button under Recording, open the Name drop-down list, and click on the desired recording quality (Radio, CD, or Telephone). Click on the OK button.

6. Click on the OK button to save your changes.

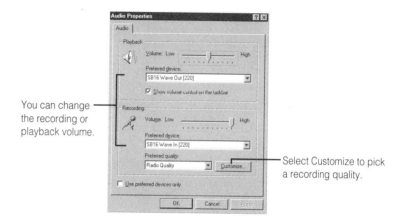

You can change the recording or playback volume.

Select Customize to pick a recording quality.

Beyond Survival

Adding Special Effects

Sound Recorder comes with a couple of tools that you can use to increase or decrease the volume of a sound, to add an echo, or to play the sound in reverse (useful for analyzing Led Zeppelin songs). To add any of these effects, open the Effects menu and select the desired effect:

To change volume for all sounds, right-click on speaker icon in Taskbar (next to the time)

Increase Volume: Increases the volume by 25%.

Decrease Volume: Decreases the volume by 25%.

Increase Speed: Plays the sound faster.

Decrease Speed: Plays the sound slower.

Add Echo: Adds an echo that reverbs your sound.

Reverse: Plays the sound backward.

Combining and Mixing Sounds

The Edit menu contains a couple of commands for inserting and mixing sounds. *Inserting* a sound sticks the sound from one file inside another. *Mixing* lays one sound over the other. To insert a sound, here's what you do:

1. Open the sound file into which you want the other sound inserted.

2. Use the Play and Stop buttons to go to the point at which you want the other sound inserted. (Use Seek to End to go to the end of the sound or Seek to Start to go to the beginning.)

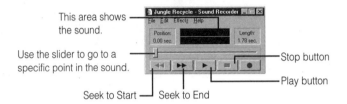

This area shows the sound.

Use the slider to go to a specific point in the sound.

Jungle Recycle - Sound Recorder
File Edit Effects Help
Position: 0.00 sec.
Length: 1.78 sec.

Stop button

Play button

Seek to Start — Seek to End

3. Open the Edit menu and select Insert File. The Insert File dialog box appears.

4. Select the drive, folder, and name of the file you want to insert.

5. Click on the Open button.

Attaching a Sound to an Event

In case you haven't noticed, Windows emits sounds when you start Windows and when you perform certain steps. For example, when you start Windows, it plays a phrase on the piano, and when you exit, Windows plays Tada! Windows has many such events to which you can assign sounds, and Windows comes with a wide selection of sounds to attach. In addition, you can attach the sounds and music you record (and save as .WAV files) to these events. Here's what you do:

1. Click on the Start button to open the Start menu.

2. Move the mouse pointer over Settings, and then click on Control Panel.

3. Double-click on the Sounds icon. The Sounds Properties dialog box appears.

4. In the Events list, click on the Windows event to which you want to assign a sound.

5. Open the Sound Name drop-down list, and click on the desired Windows sound. (Or click on the Browse button, change to the drive and folder where you saved your sound files, and click on one of your own sound files.)

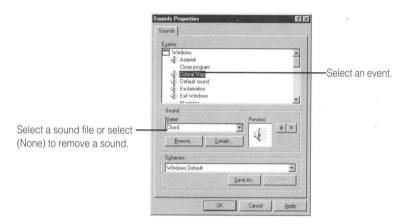

Select an event.

Select a sound file or select
(None) to remove a sound.

6. You can click on the Preview Play button to listen to the sound.

7. To save your sound configuration (*sound scheme*), click on the Save As dialog box, type a name for the sound scheme, and click on OK.

8. Click on the OK button. Windows activates your new sound configuration.

Sound Schemes
drop-down list
lets you turn
off sounds

At the bottom of the Sound dialog box is the Sound Schemes drop-down list. This list contains several collections of sound schemes from which to choose. For example, you can choose Windows Jungle Sound Scheme to hear wild animals, rattlesnakes, and other odd jungle sounds when you perform actions in Windows. To pick a sound scheme, open the drop-down list, and click on the desired scheme. You can create and use your own sound schemes by performing the steps given above, and then using the Save As button to save the scheme.

Cheat Sheet

Play the Media You Want

- Media Player plays sounds, video clips, audio CDs, and MIDI files. Many of these files are available on the Internet and on-line services.
- Windows comes with some sample media files you can play.
- You can play sound files that end in .WAV, video files that end in .AVI, and MIDI files that end in .MID or .RMI.

Playing Video Clips and Sound Files

1. Click on the Start button and move the mouse pointer over Programs.

2. Move the mouse pointer over Accessories, and then over Multimedia.

3. Click on Media Player.

4. Open the Device menu, and select the type of file you want to play: CD Audio, MIDI Sequencer, Sound, or Video for Windows.

5. Open the File menu and select Open.

6. Double-click on the file you want to play.

7. Click on the Play button.

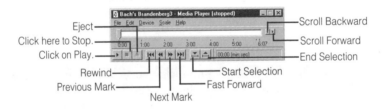

Simplifying Media Player's Controls

1. Open and start playing the media file.

2. Double-click on Media Player's title bar.

3. To restore the full control panel, double-click on the title bar again.

24

Going Multimedia with Media Player

Previous versions of Windows provided few tools for playing video clips and MIDI files (files recorded with a MIDI device such as a piano keyboard). You had to find special programs to make up for Windows shortcomings. Windows 95 includes Media Player, which fills this gap. With Media player, you can play the sound files you record, audio CDs (although CD Player does a better job), video clips (in .AVI format), and MIDI files (in .MID or .RMI format).

Where do you get the media files you want to play? Many programs now come with sample video clips and sound files. In addition, if you cruise the Internet or use an online service (such as CompuServe or America Online), you stumble across such files in your wanderings. After downloading the file (copying it to your computer), you can use Media Player to play it. In addition, Windows comes with its own sound files and MIDI files that you can try out.

Basic Survival

Playing Media Files

Media Player won't play MPEGs

Playing a media file is simple (though many Internet video clips come in MPEG format, and Media Player can't play these). You start Media Player, open the file, and click on the Play button. Here are the blow-by-blow instructions:

1. Click on the Start button and move the mouse pointer over Programs to open the Programs start menu.

2. Move the mouse pointer over Accessories, and then over Multimedia. The Multimedia submenu opens.

3. Click on Media Player. This starts Media Player.

Double-click on Media Player's title bar to simplify its controls

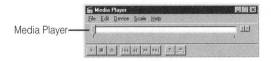

Media Player—

4. If you want to play an audio CD, insert it into the CD-ROM drive. (CD Player is a better tool for playing audio CDs; see Chapter 22.)

5. Open the Device menu, and select the type of file you want to play: CD Audio, MIDI Sequencer, Sound, or Video for Windows.

6. Open the File menu and select Open. The Open dialog box appears, showing the contents of the \WINDOWS\MEDIA folder. (Windows comes with some sample sound and MIDI files in the MEDIA folder. You can find sample video clips in the \WINDOWS\HELP folder, but they're not very exciting.)

The Media folder contains sample MIDI and sound files.

Click here to move up a directory.

7. Double-click on folder icons till you open the folder that contains the file you want to play. You can click on the Up One Level button to move up in the directory tree.

8. Double-click on the name of the file you want to play. The Open dialog box closes, and you're returned to Media Player.

9. Click on the Play button.

Once your media file starts to play, you can use the following buttons to fast forward, rewind, and play specific portions of the file:

▶ The Play button starts playing the clip.

■ Click here to stop playing.

▲ If you're playing an audio CD, click here to eject it.

|◀◀| To move to the beginning of the clip, click on the Rewind button.

|▶▶| To move to the end of the clip, click on the Fast Forward button.

Marking a Selection to Play

Some media files can be very long. The good news is that you don't have to play the entire file. You can specify where you want the clip to start and stop playing. Here's what you do:

1. Drag the slider on the scale to the point at which you want the clip to start playing.

2. Click on the Start Selection button. A triangle appears below the scale. You can pick a different point by repeating steps 1 and 2.

3. Drag the slider on the scale to the point at which you want the clip to stop playing.

4. Click on the End Selection button. Another triangle appears below the scale to show the end point. (Again, you can change this point by repeating steps 3 and 4.)

5. To clear the stop and end points (and play the entire clip), open the Edit menu, click on Selection, click on None, and click on the OK button.

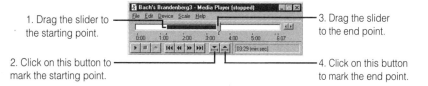

1. Drag the slider to the starting point.

2. Click on this button to mark the starting point.

3. Drag the slider to the end point.

4. Click on this button to mark the end point.

After you mark a start and end point, you can use the following buttons to move quickly forward or back to a marked point:

To set Auto Repeat or Rewind, select Edit/Options

|◀◀| Click here to go to the previous mark (the mark you added to specify where the clip should start or stop playing).

|▶▶| Click here to go to the next mark.

Cranking the Volume

You can adjust the volume using controls on your speakers or on your sound card. You can also adjust the volume from within Media Player. Here's what you do:

1. Open the Device menu and select Volume Control. The Volume Control dialog box appears.

2. Take a look at the dialog box. It offers several different volume controls that allow you to change the volume for the various file types you might play:

Volume Control changes the volume for all devices and file types (MIDI, Wave (sound files), CD, and Line In).

Wave changes the volume only for sound files (files that end in .WAV).

MIDI changes the volume only for MIDI files.

CD changes the volume only for audio CDs.

3. To adjust the volume, move the mouse pointer over the Volume slide bar and drag it up or down.

Drag the Balance slider left or right.

Drag the Volume slider up or down.

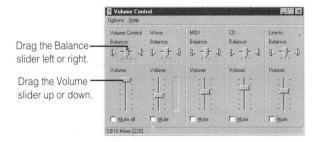

4. To change the balance, drag the Balance slide bar to the left or right.

Beyond Survival

Inserting a Media File into a Document

You can use Media player along with your favorite Windows word processor (or WordPad) to create your very own multimedia files, complete with icons that link to sounds, music clips, and video clips. Here's how you do it:

1. In Media Player, open the clip you want to insert into your document.

2. To copy a portion of the clip, use the Start Selection and End Selection buttons (as explained earlier) to mark the section you want to copy.

Press Ctrl+C to copy

3. Open the Edit menu and select Copy Object. Media Player copies the clip to the Windows Clipboard.

4. Switch to your word processing program; open the document into which you want to insert the clip.

5. Click inside the document to move the insertion point where you want the clip inserted.

6. Open the Edit menu and select Paste. The clip is inserted; an icon appears, representing the clip. (You can also use Paste Special to create a dynamic link between the clip and the copy; see Chapter 17 for details.)

7. To play the clip, double-click on its icon.

Double-click on the icon to play it.

An icon appears, representing the clip.

There's another way to insert a clip into a document. Use My Computer or Explorer (explained in Part 4) to open the folder that contains the clips you want to insert into the document. Then simply drag the clip's icon from the folder window into your document window. When you release the mouse button, Windows plops the clip into the document. You can then drag the clip's icon to where you want it.

PART 4

Managing Your Disks, Folders, and Files

If you normally perform your file, disk, and directory management at the DOS prompt—using commands like **MD** (make directory), **CD** (change directory), **COPY**, **DISKCOPY**, **FORMAT**, and so on—you know how clumsy the DOS prompt can be. In this section, you'll learn how to use My Computer and Explorer to perform those same tasks faster and more easily. You'll learn how to copy files by clicking and dragging, how to format a disk by selecting the Format command from a menu, and how to change to a directory (now called a *folder*) simply by double-clicking on its icon. Here's a complete rundown of what you're about to learn:

Cheat Sheet

Finding Stuff on Your Computer

1. Double-click on My Computer 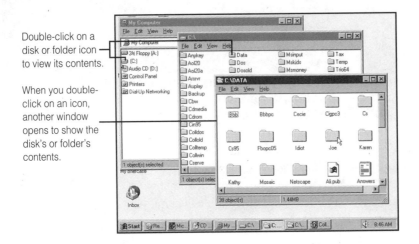.

2. Double-click on a disk icon or folder to open it and see its contents.

3. Keep double-clicking on folders till you find what you're looking for.

4. To back up through the open windows, press the Backspace key.

Double-click on a disk or folder icon to view its contents.

When you double-click on an icon, another window opens to show the disk's or folder's contents.

Displaying and Using the Toolbar

1. Open the View menu and click on Toolbar.

2. Use the drop-down list and buttons to enter commands quickly.

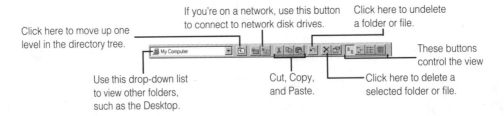

Click here to move up one level in the directory tree.

If you're on a network, use this button to connect to network disk drives.

Click here to undelete a folder or file.

Use this drop-down list to view other folders, such as the Desktop.

Cut, Copy, and Paste.

Click here to delete a selected folder or file.

These buttons control the view

25

Finding Out What's on Your Computer

Your computer has all sorts of devices attached to it and files stored on it. You need some way of keeping track of all this material. To help, Windows 95 features My Computer, a tiny program that gives you all the power you need to manage your disks, folders, files, printers, and other resources properly. In this chapter, you'll learn how to use My Computer to collect files in folders, run programs, copy files, create shortcuts, and perform most of your other file- and system-management tasks.

Basic Survival

Browsing Your Computer Contents

When you start Windows, the My Computer icon appears on the upper left corner of the desktop. Simply click on My Computer; a window appears, displaying icons for all the disks on your computer (along with icons for the Control Panel and Printers). To take a look at what you have, perform the following steps:

1. Double-click on My Computer ![icon]. The My Computer window appears, displaying icons for all your disk drives, for the Control Panel, and for any installed printers.

2. To view the contents of a floppy disk or CD, make sure the disk (or disc) is inserted in one of the disk drives.

3. Double-click on a disk icon or folder to open it and see its contents.

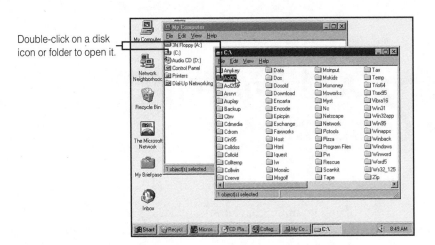

Double-click on a disk icon or folder to open it.

4. Keep double-clicking on folders till you find what you're looking for. Each time you click on a folder icon, a new window appears, showing the contents of that folder.

5. Press the Backspace key to move back to a previous window.

Managing Your Files and Folders

Okay, now that you've found a file or folder, what can you do with it? All sorts of things. For example, if you find a program file, you can run it by double-clicking on it. Following is a list of the most common tasks you'll perform in My Computer:

Select: Click on a file or folder to select it. Ctrl+click to select additional files or folders. Drag a box around a group of files or folders to select them.

To get shortcut menu: drag with right mouse button, release

Copy: Hold down the Ctrl key while dragging a file with the mouse to copy it to another window or to a disk or folder icon. (If you are copying the file to a disk in a different drive, you don't have to hold down the Ctrl key.)

Move: Hold down the Shift key while dragging a file with the mouse to move it to another window or to a disk or folder icon. (If you are moving the file to folder on the same disk, you don't have to hold down the Shift key.)

Delete: You can delete a selected file or folder using any of several techniques: Right-click on the file and select Delete; drag the file(s) over the Recycle Bin icon; open the File menu and select Delete, or click on the

Delete button in the toolbar (see the next section, "Working Fast with the My Computer Toolbar").

Rename: Rename a file, folder, or disk. Click on the name next to the icon, click on it again, and then type the new name. You can also open the File menu and select Rename, or right-click on the file or folder and select Rename.

Undo Actions: If you delete, move, copy, or rename an object by mistake, open the Edit menu and select Undo.

Run a Program: Double-click on the program's icon.

Open a Document: Double-click on the document's icon. If the document is associated with a program (see Chapter 37), My Computer runs the program and opens the document. If the document is not associated with a program, a dialog box appears, prompting you to select a program from the list.

Create a Shortcut: You can create a *shortcut* (an icon that points to the folder, program, or document) and drag it to the desktop. For instructions on how to create shortcuts, see Chapter 12.

Change a File's Properties: Right-click on an icon and select Properties to change the settings for a program, disk, file, or folder. Chapter 13 discusses properties in greater detail.

Format a Floppy Disk: My Computer offers a quick way to format floppy disks. Insert the floppy disk in the drive, and then double-click on the drive's icon in My Computer. Click on Yes to format the disk, and then follow the instructions. For details on formatting floppy disks, see Chapter 35.

Copy a Floppy Disk: To copy a floppy disk, insert the disk you want to copy in the floppy drive, right-click on the drive's icon, and click on Copy Disk. Follow the on-screen instructions to complete the process. Chapter 36 gives full instructions on how to copy disks.

Select View/ Refresh if window's contents don't change after deleting, moving, or copying

Copying, Moving, and Deleting Folders and Files

My Computer makes it easy to copy, move, and delete folders and files. The following list provides a brief overview of how you can manage files and folders with My Computer:

Selecting Files and Folders: You can select a file by clicking on it, and select additional files by holding down the Ctrl key while clicking on their names. For details on how to select files and folders, see Chapter 30, "Selecting Files and Folders."

Copying and Moving Files and Folders: You can copy selected files and folders by holding down the Ctrl key while dragging one of the selected files or folders over the drive or folder icon where you want the files or folders copied. To move selected files and folders, hold down the Shift key while dragging. For details, see Chapter 31, "Copying and Moving Files and Folders."

Deleting Files and Folders: You can quickly delete selected files and folders simply by dragging one of the selected items over the Recycle Bin icon and releasing the mouse button. For additional instructions on how to delete (and restore) files and folders, see Chapter 34, "Deleting and Undeleting Files and Folders."

Making New Folders: To make a new folder, right-click on a blank area inside the My Computer window, point to New, and click on Folder. For details on how to create new folders and name them, see Chapter 32, "Making New Folders."

Beyond the Basics

Working Fast with the My Computer Toolbar

My Computer has a toolbar that may or may not be displayed below the menu bar. This toolbar allows you to move quickly up one folder in the directory tree, delete and undelete files and folders, and browse around in other areas of your computer.

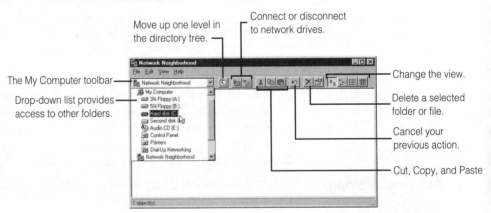

To turn the toolbar on and use it, take the following steps:

1. Open the View menu and click on Toolbar. (Each window you open by double-clicking on a folder icon has its own toolbar setting, on or off, so you must turn the toolbar on for each window you display.)

2. Open the toolbar's drop-down list and click on the desired system folder. The following folders are available:

> **Desktop** provides folders for all the icons on the Windows desktop, including My Computer, Recycle Bin, and any shortcuts you may have added.

> **My Computer** displays the icons that My Computer displays when you first run it.

> **Recycle Bin** displays all the folders, icons, and files you deleted (assuming you did not empty the Bin). For information about the Recycle Bin, see Chapter 7.

> **Network Neighborhood** appears if you are using a computer on a network. It allows you to tap into any files and resources on the network server.

> **My Briefcase** appears if you installed Windows 95 on a laptop computer. This briefcase allows you to quickly transfer files back and forth between your laptop and desktop computers.

3. Click on the Up One Level button (the button with the folder and the bent arrow on it) to move back to the previous window. For example, if you double-click on the drive C icon and then double-click on a folder, the Up One Level button takes you back to the contents of drive C.

4. Use the Cut, Copy, and Paste buttons to copy or move a file or folder. For details, see the next section, "Copying, Moving, and Deleting Folders and Files."

5. Use the Map Network Drive button if you're on a network, and one of the network server's drives does not appear in the My Computer window. This button displays a dialog box that lets you add a network drive. The Disconnect Net Drive lets you remove a network drive icon from My Computer.

6. Click on the Undo button to cancel your previous action (for example, if you deleted or moved a file or folder by mistake).

7. Click on the Delete button (the one with the big **X** on it) to delete a selected file, folder, or icon.

8. To turn off the toolbar, open the View menu and click on Toolbar.

Changing the Way My Computer Looks and Behaves

The most obvious way to change the look of a window in My Computer is to change the appearance of the icons in the window by using the options on the View menu. See Chapter 6, "Working with Icons," to learn what to do. You can make some more fundamental changes to a My Computer window by opening the View menu, selecting Options, and using the following tabs to set your preferences:

Use the Options dialog box to enter your preferences.

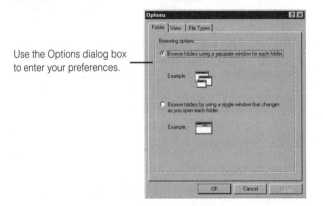

Folder: As you know, each time you double-click on a folder icon, a new window appears, cluttering your screen. To display only one window—whose contents change when you select a folder—click on the Browse Folders Using a Single Window That Changes as You Open Each Folder option.

View: This tab lets you hide certain file types and choose how you want file extensions displayed. By default, Windows prevents system files from appearing in file lists; that way you don't delete them and mess up your system by mistake. To include system files in the lists, click on Show All Files.

The Display Full MS-DOS Path in the Title Bar option shows a directory tree path to the current folder in the title bar. If you're in the Media folder under Windows, for example, this path will appear in the title bar: **C:\WINDOWS\MEDIA**.

The last option, Hide MS-DOS File Extensions for File Types That Are Registered, prevents the last part of a file's name (for example, .DOC or .TXT) from appearing. Windows 95 likes to rely more on icons to indicate file types, but if extensions help you determine a file type, turn this option off.

File Types: This tab allows you to specify which icons to use for various file types. Click on the file type whose icon you want to change, click on the Edit button, and then click on Change Icon. Click on the icon you want to use, and then click on the OK button to save your changes. For more details about the options in this dialog box, see Chapter 37, "Running Programs from Windows Explorer."

Cheat Sheet

Starting Windows Explorer

1. Click on the Start button.

2. Move the mouse pointer over Programs.

3. Click on Windows Explorer.

Browsing the Contents of Your Computer

Click on the plus sign next to a drive letter to view its contents.

Click on a folder to view its contents.

Click on the plus sign next to a folder to view a list of folders inside it.

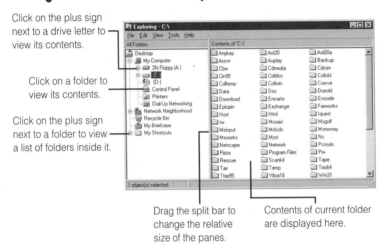

Drag the split bar to change the relative size of the panes.

Contents of current folder are displayed here.

Starting and Exiting Windows Explorer

Windows Explorer allows you to manage and keep track of your files, directories, and disks. You can use Windows Explorer to copy, move, and delete files; in addition, use it to format and copy disks, or create and delete folders on a disk. Before you can perform these tasks, however, you must run the Windows Explorer; in this chapter, you'll learn how to run Explorer, display a disk's or folder's contents, and exit when you're done. In later chapters, you'll learn how to use Windows Explorer to manage your disks and files.

Basic Survival

Starting Windows Explorer

To start Windows Explorer, perform the following steps:

1. Click on the Start button to open the Start menu.

2. Move the mouse pointer over Programs.

3. Click on Windows Explorer. The Windows Explorer window appears, showing the contents of drive C.

Add Windows Explorer to StartUp menu (Chapter 1), so it starts when you turn on computer

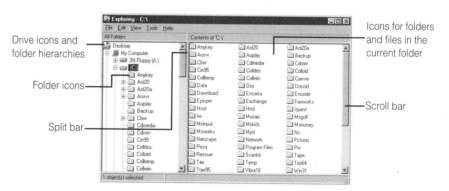

Drive icons and folder hierarchies

Folder icons

Split bar

Icons for folders and files in the current folder

Scroll bar

You can exit the Windows Explorer at any time by opening the File menu and selecting Exit. (Another way to exit: click on the Close button in the title bar.)

Browsing Through Disks and Folders

Windows Explorer is My Computer's fraternal twin. They look a little different, but you can use either one to perform the same tasks. One difference between the two is that Windows Explorer consists of a single window that gives you access to all the files and folders on your disks. To change to a different disk or folder, you do the following:

1. To change to a disk, make sure there's a disk in the disk drive, and then click on its icon.

2. To display the first level of folders on a disk, click on the plus sign that's next to the disk icon.

3. To display the folders that are inside a folder, click on the plus sign next to the folder's icon. A list of folders appears, and the plus sign turns into a minus sign (you can click on the minus sign to hide the folders).

4. To display the contents of a folder, click on its icon. The contents appear in the pane on the right.

Right-click on file or folder to see what you can do to it

Once you find the file or folder you're looking for, you can work with it. You can copy, move, or delete it, change its properties, create a shortcut for it, or perform other actions described later in this book.

Displaying and Using the Toolbar

Like My Computer, Windows Explorer comes with a toolbar that can save you some time by helping you bypass the menu system. To turn the toolbar on, open the View menu and select Toolbar. The toolbar appears, as shown here.

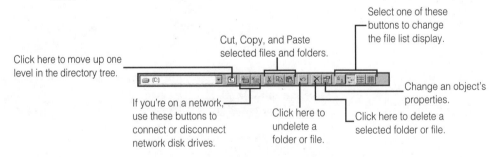

Select one of these buttons to change the file list display.

Cut, Copy, and Paste selected files and folders.

Click here to move up one level in the directory tree.

If you're on a network, use these buttons to connect or disconnect network disk drives.

Click here to undelete a folder or file.

Change an object's properties.

Click here to delete a selected folder or file.

Beyond Survival

Changing the File List Display

Initially, Windows Explorer shows only the names and icons of the files in the current directory. To see more information about the files (or change the way the files are listed and the icons are displayed), open the View menu and select one of these options:

Large Icons displays bigger icons.

Small Icons displays tiny icons and places folder icons at the top of the window, listing file icons at the bottom.

List displays columns of icons and file names—listing directories first, and then files, in alphabetical order. Unlike Small Icons view, List view displays the columns as in a newspaper, snaking from the bottom of one column to the top of the next.

Details shows more information about each file, including the file size, file type, and the date and time the file was last changed.

Arrange Icons opens a submenu that lets you list the icons by name, file type, size, or date.

Line Up Icons arranges the icons in such a way that they do not overlap, but doesn't necessarily make the best use of window space; in other words, it won't push the icons closer together so they take up less of the screen.

Change view options with buttons on right side of toolbar, or right-click on blank area in Explorer for shortcut menu

With Details on, Windows Explorer shows the date, time, file type, and size of folders and files.

Large Icons   Small Icons

Details
List

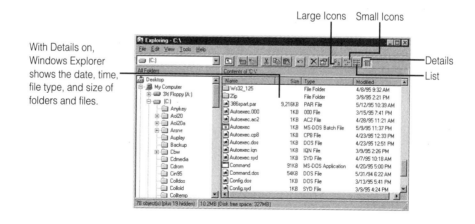

173

Cheat Sheet

Changing to a Drive

1. Make sure there is a formatted disk in the drive.

2. Click on the drive's icon.

3. To see a list of folders on the disk, click on the plus sign next to the disk's icon.

Changing to a Folder

1. Click on the folder's icon in the tree.

2. To see a list of folders within the folder, click on the plus sign next to the folder's icon.

Click on a drive icon to change to it.

Click on a folder icon to display its contents.

Contents window shows the folders and files on the selected drive and folder.

Opening Another Explorer Window

- It is often useful to display two windows on the desktop, so you can drag files from one window to another.

- To display another Explorer window, click on the Start button, move the mouse pointer over Programs, and click on Windows Explorer.

- To have both windows appear side by side, right-click on a blank area inside the Taskbar, and click on Tile Vertically.

27

Changing Drives and Folders

In order to work with the files on a disk or in a folder, you must first activate the drive and folder in which the files are stored. In this chapter, you'll learn how to change to a drive and folder, and how to work with the folder hierarchy.

Basic Survival

Changing to a Drive

At the top of the Folders window are drive icons that represent the drives installed on your system. These drives may include floppy disk drives, hard disk drives, network and CD-ROM drives, and RAM drives (if you set up part of your computer's memory to act as a disk drive). To change to a drive, perform the following steps:

1. Make sure there is a formatted disk in the drive.

2. Click on the drive's icon. The Contents window changes to display the folders and files on the current disk.

Click on a drive icon to see the folders and files it contains.

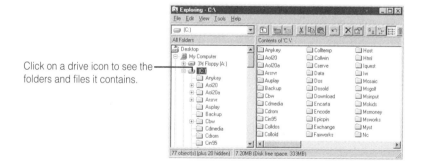

Changing to a Folder

All disks have at least one folder, which represents the *root directory*. Hard disks usually have additional folders and subfolders that relate files in groups. To change to a folder, do one of the following:

Down arrow =
Next folder
Up arrow =
Previous folder
Home = First
folder or
the desktop
End = Last
folder

- Click on a folder icon in the Folders list. The folder icon for the selected folder appears—opened—and the contents list displays the folders and files in that folder.

- To open a folder in the Contents list, double-click on its icon. The folder opens, and the Contents list changes to show what the folder contains.

- To display the contents of a disk or folder quickly, open the Tools menu, select Go To, type the path to the drive or folder (for example, type **a:** or **c:\windows\media**), and click on OK.

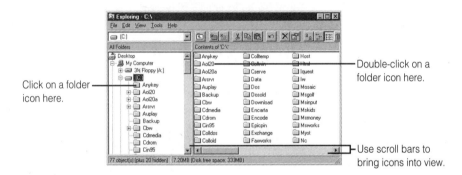

Click on a folder icon here.

Double-click on a folder icon here.

Use scroll bars to bring icons into view.

Beyond Survival

Expanding and Collapsing Folders

Folders may have other folders inside them, and these might also contain folders. Initially, Windows Explorer shows only the main folder of the current drive, and any folders under the main folder. Subfolders are hidden. To display the subfolders, perform the following steps:

Press NumLock
to turn on
numeric keypad,
use these keys:

[+] = Expand
one level
[*] = Expand
all
[−] = Collapse
branch

1. Click on the plus sign to the left of the folder icon (in the Folders, not in the Contents list). A list of folders appears under the current folder; a minus sign replaces the plus sign.

2. To hide the folders under the current folder, click on the minus sign next to the folder icon.

3. To view the contents of a folder quickly, double-click on the folder's icon in the Contents window. This displays the folders and files that are inside the selected folder in the Contents window.

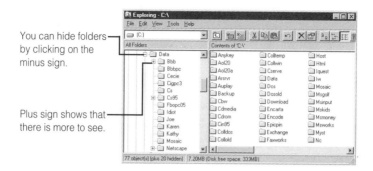

You can hide folders by clicking on the minus sign.

Plus sign shows that there is more to see.

Opening Another Window

Windows Explorer initially displays only one window. You can open additional windows to display the contents of another drive or folder. This can be useful if you are copying or moving files from one drive or folder to another.

One way to work with two windows is to run two sessions of Explorer, using the Start menu. There is, however, an easier way:

1. Right-click on the disk or folder icon for which you want to open another window. A shortcut menu appears.

2. Click on Open. Explorer opens a window for the selected drive or folder.

Whenever you open another window, the new window covers part or all of the original window. You can resize and move the windows to rearrange them, as explained in Chapter 5. You can also use right-click on a blank area of the Taskbar, and select one of the Windows arrangements to cascade or tile the windows.

Cheat Sheet

Sorting Files in the List

1. Open the View menu, and move the mouse pointer over Arrange Icons.
2. Click on one of the following options:

    By Name sorts files alphabetically by name.

    By Type sorts files alphabetically by extension. For example, all .BAT files will be listed, and then .COM files, and then .EXE files.

    By Size sorts files by file size, largest files first.

    By Date sorts files by date and time, the files most recently changed appear first in the list.

Changing the View Options

1. Open the View menu and select Options. (In My Computer, click on the View tab.)
2. Click on one of the following options:

    Show All Files to have all file names appear in your file lists.

    Hide Files of These Types to have Explorer hide any system files that could cause problems if you accidentally moved or deleted them.

3. Select any of the following options to turn it on or off (a check mark indicates that the option is on):

    Display the Full MS-DOS Path in Title Bar.

    Hide MS-DOS File Extensions for File Types That Are Registered.

    Include Description Bar for Left and Right Panes (in Explorer only).

4. Click on the OK button.

28

Changing the File Display

The Windows Explorer is initially set up to display folder and file names in alphabetical order, and to hide the names of any system files. You can, however, change the display to arrange the file names in a different order—or filter the files to display only files of a specific type. In this chapter, you'll learn how to take control of Explorer's file lists. (Most of the procedures in this chapter work in My Computer as well.)

Basic Survival

Sorting Files in the List

Initially, the Explorer Contents pane displays folder and file names in alphabetical order. You can sort the files and folders in a different order by selecting a sort order from the View/Arrange Icons submenu. These sort commands affect only the Contents area; they do not affect the Folders pane (on the left). To change the sort order, here's what you do (take the same steps to change the sort order in My Computer):

1. Change to the window whose contents you want to sort.

2. Open the View menu, and move the mouse pointer over Arrange Icons.

3. Select one of the following options:

Sort by date to find recently modified files

> By Name lists folders first and sorts files alphabetically by name. This is the default setting.

> By Type lists folders first and sorts files alphabetically by extension. For example, all .BAT files will be listed, and then .COM files, and then .EXE files.

> By Size lists folders first and sorts files by file size, listing the largest files first.

By Date sorts folders and files by date and time, listing the most recently changed files first.

(**Note:** In My Computer, when disk icons are displayed, the Arrange Icons submenu allows you to sort the icons By Drive Letter, By Type, By Size, and By Free Space.)

The sorting option you select affects only the current window and any new windows you create from it. You can select a different sorting order for two different windows.

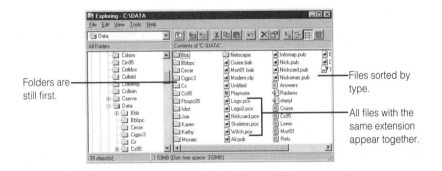

Folders are still first.

Files sorted by type.

All files with the same extension appear together.

Refreshing a Window's Contents

Normally Windows Explorer and My Computer perform much the same when refreshing a window. Each automatically updates the contents of its windows or panes whenever you enter a command, copy or move a file, or change disks or directories. If the list is not updated, perform the following steps:

1. Open the View menu.

2. Select Refresh.

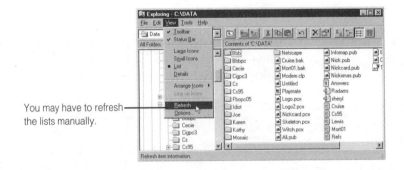

You may have to refresh the lists manually.

Beyond Survival

**Changing the
View Options**

The Explorer and My Computer windows are streamlined to prevent confu-
sion and to hide any system files that you should not delete or move. To take
control of the display, you can change the view options. Here's what you do:

1. Open the View menu and select Options. (If you're changing View
   options in My Computer, click on the View tab.)

2. Click on one of the following options:

   Show All Files to have all file names (including the names of
   system files) appear in your file lists.

   Hide Files of These Types to hide any system files that could cause
   problems if you accidentally moved or deleted them. A list of the
   hidden file types are listed below the option.

3. Select any of the following options to turn it on or off (a check mark
   indicates that the option is on):

   Display the Full MS-DOS Path in Title Bar displays the path to
   the current folder in the title bar. A path looks something like this:
   C:\WINDOWS\MEDIA, and it tells DOS where a folder or file is
   located.

   Hide MS-DOS File Extensions for File Types That Are Registered
   prevents the three-character file extension at the end of a file name
   from appearing in the file list. Windows 95 uses icons rather than
   extensions to indicate file types, but if extensions help you determine file types, turn this option off.

   Include Description Bar for Left and Right Panes (only available
   in Windows Explorer) displays a status bar at the bottom of each
   pane indicating the amount of storage space left on the disk, and
   the amount of space required by the selected files.

4. Click on the OK button.

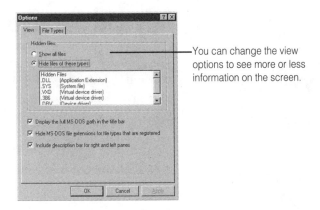

You can change the view options to see more or less information on the screen.

The View menu also contains options for changing the way files are listed. You can choose Large Icons or Small Icons to change the size of the folder and file icons. List displays a running list of the folders and icons; Details displays more information about each file and folder, including their sizes and the dates they were last modified. If you have the toolbar displayed, you can use the buttons on the right end of the toolbar to change these view options quickly.

Changing the Icon Used for a File Type

Explorer contains a file registry that assigns an icon to most common file types and associates common document files with the programs used to create and change them. (You'll learn more about file associations in Chapter 37.) For example, text files have an icon that looks like a piece of paper.

You can remove file types from this registry, so Explorer will display a generic icon for the file type, or you can edit the file type's registry entry to have Explorer treat the file type differently. To change a file type's registry entry, take the following steps:

1. Open the View menu and select Options.

2. Click on the File Types tab. A list of registered file types appears. Each file type is assigned a unique icon that represents the type.

3. Click on the file type whose icon you want to change.

4. Click on the Edit button, and then click on Change Icon. A list of available icons appears. (See Chapter 37 for instructions on how to use the more advanced options in this dialog box.)

You can change the
icon used for a
specific file type.

5. Click on the icon you want to use, and then click on the OK button.
You return to the Edit File Type dialog box, where the new icon
appears.

6. If you want to view a file's contents (by right-clicking on its name in a
file list, and then clicking on Quick View), make sure there is a check
mark next to Enable Quick View. (See Chapter 29 for details about the
Quick View feature.)

7. To have the extension for this file type displayed in all file lists, click on
Always Show Extension, to place a check mark next to the option.

8. Click on the Close button when you're done.

9. Click on Close to save your changes.

Cheat Sheet

Searching for a File in Explorer

1. Open the Tools menu, and move the mouse pointer over Find.
2. Click on Files or Folders.
3. Type the name of the file, or type a wildcard entry in the Named text box.
4. Open the Look In drop-down list; select the drive or folder you want to search, or click on the Browse button and select a drive and folder from the list.
5. Make sure there is a check mark in the Include Subfolders check box.
6. Click on the Find Now button.

Understanding Wildcard Entries

- Wildcard entries let you search for and select files that have similar names.
- Two wildcard characters are available, the asterisk (*) and the question mark (?). The asterisk stands in for two or more characters. The question mark stands in for a single character.
- **Example:** To find a group of files that have the extension .TXT, type ***.txt**.
- **Example:** To find a group of files that start with CHPT, have a two-digit number, and end in .TXT, type **chpt??.txt**. This would find CHPT01.TXT, CHPT02.TXT, and so on.

Looking at a File with Quick View

1. Right-click on the file you want to look at.
2. Click on Quick View.

29

Searching for Files and Folders

Sometimes you'll save a file without knowing which drive or folder you saved it to. You could sift through all the files in your folders to look for it, but that could take awhile. An easier way is to have Windows Explorer sniff out the file for you. In this chapter, you'll learn how to send the Windows Explorer on a search.

Basic Survival

Searching for a File or Folder

To search for a file or folder, you have to tell Windows Explorer where to search and what to search for. Here's how you do it:

1. To search a specific drive or folder, select it in Windows Explorer before you start the search.

2. Open the Tools menu, and move the mouse pointer over Find.

3. Click on Files or Folders. The Find: All Files dialog box appears. (You can also display this dialog box by clicking on the Start button, pointing to Find, and selecting Files or Folders.)

4. Type the name of the file, a partial name, or a wildcard entry in the Named text box. For more details on wildcard entries, skip to the next section.

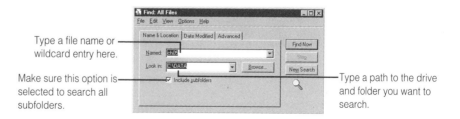

Type a file name or wildcard entry here.

Make sure this option is selected to search all subfolders.

Type a path to the drive and folder you want to search.

5. Open the Look In drop-down list; select the drive or folder you want to search, or click on the Browse button and select a drive and folder from the list. Following are examples of paths you might enter:

c:\searches the main folder of drive C. If the Include Subfolders option is on (see next step), Windows Explorer searches all the folders on drive C.

c:\DATA searches only the \DATA folder on drive C.

c:\DATA\LETTERS searches only the \DATA\LETTERS folder on drive C.

6. Make sure there is a check mark in the Include Subfolders check box. This tells Windows Explorer to search the folder and any subfolders of the folder you specified in step 5.

Search one folder = Turn off Include Subfolders

7. Click on the Find Now button. Windows Explorer performs the search and displays a list of all files that matched your search instructions. You can now select these files as explained in Chapter 30.

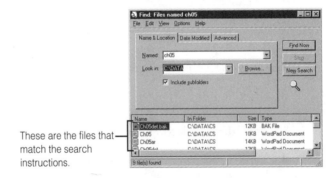

These are the files that match the search instructions.

If the list of files is too long, you can narrow the search by entering different search instructions. Explorer will search the list of files it found, and narrow the list according to the new instructions.

If you want to start all over, click on the New Search button. Otherwise Explorer will search only the list of files it found, not all the files on the drive or folder.

Understanding Wildcard Entries

A *wildcard character* is any character that takes the place of another character or a group of characters. Think of a wildcard character as a "wild card" in a game of poker. If the Joker is wild, you can use it in place of any card in the entire deck of cards. To search for (or select) a group of files, you can use two wildcard characters: a question mark (**?**) and an asterisk (*****). The question mark stands in for any single character. The asterisk stands in for any group of characters. Here are some examples:

. = all files

*.txt finds all files that have the .TXT extension—for example, CHAPTER.TXT, LETTER.TXT, SALES12.TXT.

Chapter.* finds all files named CHAPTER with any extension—for example, CHAPTER.TXT, CHAPTER.DOC, CHAPTER.BAK, CHAPTER.BK.

Sales??.xls finds all files that start with SALES and one or two additional char-acters, and have the extension .XLS—for example, SALES12.XLS, SALES01.XLS, SALES1.XLS.

S???.*finds all files whose file name starts with S and has four letters or fewer—for example, SORT.DOC, SAVE.TXT, SYS.INI.

Using Quick View to Look at a File's Contents

In File Manager (Windows' previous file-management program), you had to open a file to see what was in it. If you picked the wrong file, you had to go back to File Manager and start over. Windows Explorer offers a Quick View feature that lets you glance at a file's contents before you open the file. Here's what you do:

1. Click on the file whose contents you want to view.

2. Open Explorer's File menu and select Quick View. The Quick View window appears, displaying the file's contents.

Can't read text? Click on Quick View window's Maximize button

3. You can use the Increase Font Size or Decrease Font Size button to change the type size used for the display.

4. If the document file has more than one page, click on the arrows in the upper-right corner of the page to flip back or forward through the document.

5. To open the file, click on the Open File for Editing button.

6. To display a different file in the Quick View window, you can drag the file's icon (from Explorer) into the Quick View window.

7. To exit Quick View, click on the Close button, or open the File menu and select Exit.

Beyond Survival

Finding Files That Contain Specific Text

In the steps given at the beginning of this chapter, you performed a simple file name search. But what if you forgot the file's name? Or what if you named all the files something like Letter01, Letter02, and so on, and you don't know which letter file you want to open? In that case, you can have Explorer search the contents of the file. Here's how:

1. To search a specific drive or folder, select it in Windows Explorer before you start the search.

2. Open the Tools menu, and move the mouse pointer over Find.

3. Click on Files or Folders. The Find: All Files dialog box appears.

4. (Optional) You can type a file name or wildcard entry, and select a drive and folder to search, as explained earlier.

5. Click on the Advanced tab.

6. To search for a specific file type, open the Of Type drop-down list, and click on a file type. (For example, you can search for only those files created in WordPad.)

7. Tab to the Containing Text text box, and type the entry you want to search for. For example, if you know that the document you're looking for contains a reference to Arizona, type **Arizona** in the text box.

Search for unique text in document file

Type some unique text that the file contains.

8. (Optional) If you know the size of the file you're looking for, you can use the Size Is drop-down list and spin box to specify a size that is At Least or At Most a certain number of kilobytes.

9. Click on the Find Now button. Windows Explorer performs the search and displays a list of all files that contain the specified text.

Finding Files and Folders by Date

If you can't remember the name of the file or any unique text it might contain, but you can remember the date or month when you last changed the file, you can have Explorer search for the file by date. Take the following steps:

1. To search a specific drive or folder, select it in Windows Explorer before you start the search.

2. Open the Tools menu, and move the mouse pointer over Find.

3. Click on Files or Folders. The Find: All Files dialog box appears.

4. (Optional) You can type a file name or wildcard entry, and select a drive and folder to search, as explained earlier.

5. Click on the Date Modified tab.

6. Click on Find All Files Created or Modified: to select files created or modified during a certain time period.

7. Select one of the following options:

Between _____ and _____ Select this one and type two dates in the text boxes to specify the range of dates when you think the file was created or modified.

During the Previous _____ Month(s) Select this one and use the spin box arrows to set the number of months during which you believe the file was created or edited.

During the Previous _____ Day(s) Select this one and use the spin box arrows to set the number of days ago you think the file was created or edited.

8. Click on the Find Now button. Windows Explorer performs the search, displaying a list of all files that were created or modified during the specified period.

Cheat Sheet

Selecting a Single File or Folder

1. Change to the drive and folder containing the subfolder or file you want to select.
2. Click on the desired folder or file in the contents list.

Selecting a Group of Neighboring Items

1. Click on the first folder or file in the group, and then hold down the Shift key while clicking on the last folder or file in the group.
2. Move the mouse pointer above and to the left of the first item in the group, and then hold down the mouse button while dragging down and to the right. Release the mouse button.

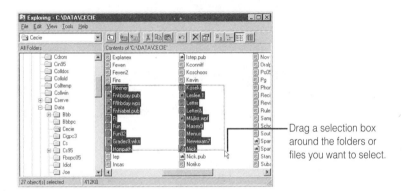

Drag a selection box around the folders or files you want to select.

Selecting Non-Neighboring Items

1. Click on the first folder or file in the group.
2. Hold down the Ctrl key while clicking on additional items.

Selecting Files with the Edit Menu

1. Change to the drive and folder containing the files you want to select.
2. To select all files, open the Edit menu and click on Select All.
3. To select most of the files, click on the files you do not want selected, and then open the Edit menu and click on Invert Selection.

30

Selecting Files and Folders

In order to copy, move, rename, or delete files or folders, you must first select them. In this chapter, you will learn how to select individual and multiple files and folders in Explorer and My Computer. In later chapters, you'll learn how to copy, move, rename, and delete selected items.

Basic Survival

Selecting Individual Files and Folders

If you want to perform some action on a single file or folder, perform the following steps to select it.

1. Change to the drive and folder that contains the folder or file you want to select. (Chapter 27 explains how to change to a drive or folder.)

Tab to contents list and use arrow keys

2. Click on the desired folder or file in the contents list.

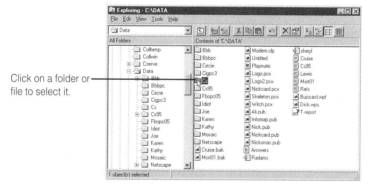

Click on a folder or file to select it.

Dragging to Select

If the group of files or folders you want to select appear next to each other in the list, you can drag a box around those files. Simply move the mouse pointer to the upper left of the area you want to select, hold down the left mouse button, and drag down and to the right. As you drag, a box appears, surrounding all the files that will be selected; the icon for each selected file or folder appears highlighted. Release the mouse button.

You can select another group of files by holding down the Ctrl key while dragging a box around them.

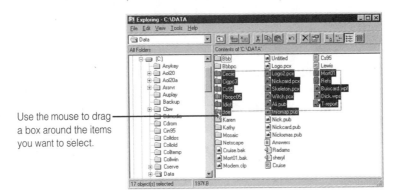

Use the mouse to drag a box around the items you want to select.

Selecting Non-Neighboring Items

If you want to work with a group of files or folders that are not next to each other in the list, perform the following steps to select them:

1. Click on the first folder or file in the group. This item appears highlighted.

2. Hold down the Ctrl key while clicking on additional items. Each item you Ctrl+click on appears highlighted.

3. To deselect a selected item, Ctrl+click on it again.

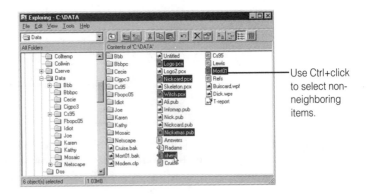

Use Ctrl+click to select non-neighboring items.

Selecting All Files and Subfolders in a Folder

Sometimes you'll want to select all (or most) of the files and subfolder a folder. To select all files and subfolders, take the following steps:

1. Change to the drive and folder containing the folders and files yo to select.

2. Open the Edit menu and click on Select All. All the folder and file in the contents list are highlighted.

Ctrl+A = Select All.

3. To deselect files or folders, hold down the Ctrl key while clicking on them.

Beyond Survival

Selecting a Group of Neighboring Items

If you want to copy or move several files or folders, you don't want to have to do it one by one. If the files or folders are listed next to each other in the contents area, perform the following steps to select them:

1. Click on the first folder or file in the group. A group can include all files, all folders, or a mix of files and folders.

2. Hold down the Shift key while clicking on the last folder or file in the group. The first and last items you clicked on and all items in between are selected and appear highlighted.

Note: This procedure works differently depending on which icon arrangement you're using. If icons are displayed in List or Details view, you select columns of files. In Small or Large Icon view, files are selected by rows.

Shift + arrow keys = Extend selection

Deselecting Individual Files

To deselect a selected file, hold down the Ctrl key and click on the file again. To deselect all the selected files, click on any file in the contents area.

Deselect = Ctrl + click

Cheat Sheet

s in

or Move

file(s) or folder(s) to copy or move.

want

e the destination (drive icon, folder icon, or folder window) is visible.

cons

he mouse pointer over any of the selected files.

down the Shift key to move files or the Ctrl key to copy files while performing
next step.

old down the mouse button while dragging the pointer over the destination icon
window.

Release the mouse button, and then release the key you were holding down.

. Click on the Yes button.

Copying and Pasting Files and Folders

1. Select the files or folders you want to copy.
2. Open the Edit menu and select Copy.
3. Change to the drive and folder in which you want the copies placed.
4. Open the Edit menu and select Paste.

Moving Files by Cutting and Pasting

1. Select the files or folders you want to move.
2. Open the Edit menu and select Cut.
3. Change to the drive and folder in which you want the cut files or folders placed.
4. Open the Edit menu and select Paste.

Copying and Moving Files and Folders

You may want to move files from one drive or folder to another to reorganize your files. You may also want to copy files from your hard drive to a floppy drive (or vice versa) to exchange files with other users. You might need to create a copy of a file on the same drive so you can edit the file without changing the original. Whatever the reason, this chapter will teach you how to copy and move files with Windows Explorer.

Basic Survival

Copying Files with the Mouse

The easiest way to copy or move files and folders is to use the mouse to drag the selected files or folders from one drive or folder to another. To copy files or folders, here's what you do:

1. Select the files or folders you want to copy. (Refer to Chapter 30 for details.)

2. Make sure the source and destination are visible. The *source* is the folder window that contains the selected files or folders. The *destination* can be any of the following:

   Drive icon: You can drag the files up to a drive icon in the pane on the left. The files will be copied to the current folder on that drive. (Using a drive icon is good if you are copying files to a floppy disk. If you're copying them to a hard disk, you won't know which folder you're copying them to.)

   Folder icon: To copy files to a specific folder, make sure the folder's icon is visible. You may have to open another window or scroll down the Folders list to see the icon.

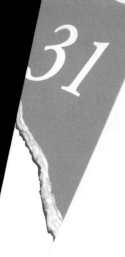

Folder window: You can drag files into the contents area of another window. Just make sure the desired folder is selected. Chapter 27 has instructions for opening additional windows.

Windows desktop: You can drag files onto the Windows desktop to provide convenient access to the file. (To create a shortcut for the file, drag with the right mouse button, and then click on Create Shortcut(s) Here.)

Drive icon ——

Folder icon ——

Source

Folder window

No Ctrl if copying to different drive

3. Move the mouse pointer over any of the selected files.

4. Hold down the Ctrl key and the left mouse button while dragging the pointer over the destination icon or window. As you drag, a plus sign (+) appears below the mouse pointer. This means the files will be copied. If the plus sign does not appear, try again, making sure you're holding down the Ctrl key.

Files will be copied to the disk in drive A. ——

As you drag, a plus sign appears. ——

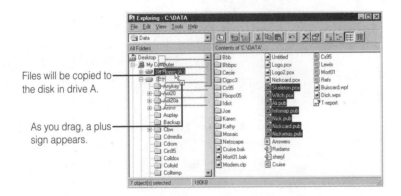

Drag with right mouse button to view a shortcut menu

5. Release the mouse button, and then release the Ctrl key. A dia
appears, showing sheets of paper flying from one folder to anot
display the copy operation.

If the destination contains a file that has the same name and extension
of the files you are copying, you'll get a warning box that asks whether
want to overwrite the existing file. Click on No to skip this file and con
copying the other files, or click on Yes to overwrite the existing file with
copy. The Yes to All button replaces all existing files that have the same n
with the copies.

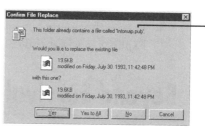

If you try to copy one fi
over another of the sam
name, Windows Explore
warns you.

Moving Files with the Mouse

You can move files or folders by dragging them from one drive or folder to
another. Here's what you do:

1. Select the files or folders you want to move. (Refer to Chapter 30 for
details.)

2. Make sure the source and destination are visible. The *source* is the folder
window that contains the selected files or folders. The *destination* can be
a drive icon, folder icon, or folder window.

No Shift if moving on the same drive

3. Move the mouse pointer over any of the selected files.

4. Hold down the Shift key and the left mouse button while dragging the
pointer over the destination icon or window. If there's a plus sign below
the mouse pointer, the files will be copied (not moved); hold down the
Shift key.

and Folders

g box
er to

will be moved to
Data folder.

is one
ou
inue
he
me

drag to move files,
us sign should appear
ow the mouse pointer.

use

o use

menu

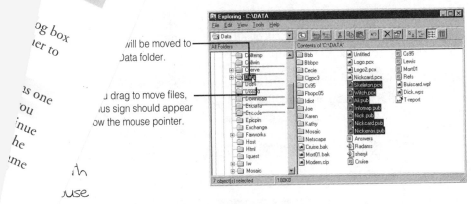

5. Release the mouse button, and then release the Shift key. Windows Explorer moves the files.

Beyond Survival

ring, Copying,
d Pasting Files
and Folders

When copying or moving files, dragging is definitely the easiest way to go. However, if you prefer using menus, perform the following steps to copy or move files:

1. Select the files or folders you want to copy or move.

2. Open the File menu, or right-click on one of the selected files to display a shortcut menu.

Ctrl + C for
Copy
Ctrl + X for
Cut

3. Click on Cut (to move the files or folders) or click on Copy (to copy them). If you select Cut, the selected icons appear grayed to show that they will be removed from this folder when you paste them into another folder.

4. Change to the drive and folder into which you want to copy or move the selected items.

5. Open the File menu or right-click on a blank area inside the window (or on the folder into which you want the items placed).

6. Click on Paste. The cut or copied items are inserted into the specified folder. If you cut the selected items, they are removed from their original folder.

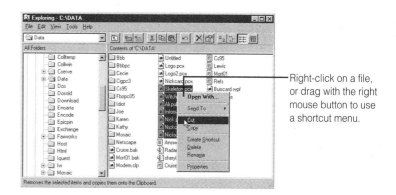

Right-click on a file, or drag with the right mouse button to use a shortcut menu.

If toolbar is visible, use Cut, Copy, and Paste buttons

If you're moving file(s) or folder(s) from your hard disk to a floppy, you can use the Send To command. Simply right-click on one of the selected files, move the mouse pointer over Send To, and then click on the floppy drive to which you want the files sent.

Pasting Items as Shortcuts

In Chapter 12, you learned how to create shortcuts for folders, programs, and documents. You can quickly create shortcuts from Windows Explorer by copying a file or folder and then pasting it as a shortcut. Here's a quick way to do it with the right mouse button:

1. Select the file(s) or folder(s) for which you want to create shortcuts.

2. Make sure the source and destination are visible. The *source* is the folder window that contains the selected files or folders. The *destination* can be the Windows desktop, a folder or disk icon, an open window, or another shortcut icon on the desktop.

3. Move the mouse pointer over any one of the selected items.

4. Hold down the *right* mouse button, and drag the selected items over the destination window or icon (or onto the Windows desktop).

5. Release the mouse button. A shortcut menu appears.

6. Select Create Shortcut(s) Here. Explorer creates the shortcut icons, and plops them down in the destination (window, icon, or desktop).

Cheat Sheet

Making a Folder in Explorer

1. In the All Folders list, click on the folder or disk icon under which you want the new folder to appear.

2. Open the File menu and move the mouse pointer over New.

3. Click on Folder.

4. Type a name for the folder.

5. Press Enter.

Making a Folder on the Desktop

1. Right-click on a blank area on the Windows desktop.

2. Move the mouse pointer over New.

3. Click on Folder.

4. Type a name for the folder.

5. Click anywhere outside the folder icon.

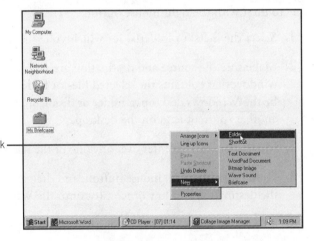

Right-click on a blank area of the desktop, select New, and select Folder.

Making New Folders

Don't bury folders any more than four deep

Hard disks can store thousands of files. To keep those files from getting lost, you should organize them using *folders*—logical divisions that keep related files together. For example, you might create a \DATA folder to store all the files you create, and create a subfolder called \PERSONAL for all your personal letters and diaries. In this chapter, you'll learn how to create folders in Windows Explorer, My Computer, and on the Windows desktop.

Basic Survival

Making a Folder

All disks have at least one folder, the *main folder*, that you cannot name or change. You can, however, add folders under the main folder, and under any existing folders. Here's how you do it:

1. Run Windows Explorer (Start, Programs, Windows Explorer).

2. In the All Folders list, click on the drive icon or folder icon under which you want the new folder to appear. (Or click inside the Contents window to create the folder in that window.)

Click on a drive icon to place the folder one level below the drive.

Select a folder to make a subfolder under it.

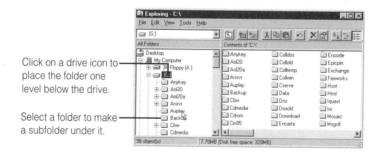

3. Open the File menu and move the mouse pointer over New.

4. Click on Folder. Explorer creates a new folder called New Folder, and places it at the end of the Contents list.

5. Type a name for the folder (up to 255 characters), and press Enter.

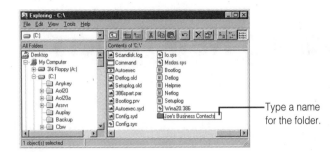

Type a name
for the folder.

Right-click on a blank area in a window, point to New, and click on Folder.

You can also create folders in My Computer. Simply display a window for the drive or folder in which you want the new folder placed. Then open the File menu, point to New, and click on Folder. Type a name for the folder and press Enter.

If the new folder does not appear in the folder tree immediately, open the View menu and select Refresh. Windows Explorer (or My Computer) rereads the disk and updates the All Folders and Contents lists.

Beyond Survival

Creating a Folder on the Windows Desktop

If your Windows desktop becomes cluttered with shortcut icons, you can clean it up by creating one or more folders for those icons. You can then drag your shortcut icons into the folders to keep them out of the way. To create a folder on the Windows desktop, here's what you do:

1. Right-click on a blank space on the Windows desktop. A shortcut menu appears.

2. Move the mouse pointer over New, and then click on Folder. Windows places a New Folder icon on the desktop.

3. Type a name for the folder to replace "New Folder" with something more descriptive.

4. Press Enter or click anywhere outside the folder icon.

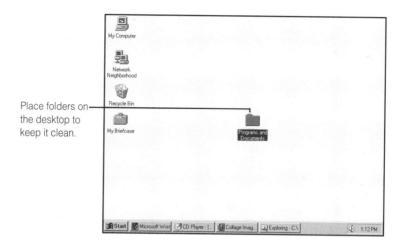

Place folders on the desktop to keep it clean.

Once you've created a folder on the Windows desktop, you can double-click on the folder to see what's inside it. You can also drag icons from the desktop, Windows Explorer, and My Computer over the new folder icon to store shortcuts and copies of files in the folder. This provides quick access to the documents and programs you use the most.

Cheat Sheet

Renaming a File or Folder

1. Click on the icon for the file or folder you want to rename.

2. Click on the name of the selected file or folder.

3. Type a new name for the file or folder.

4. Press Enter or click on a blank area in the window.

Renaming with the Right Mouse Button

1. Right-click on the file or folder you want to rename.

2. Select Rename.

3. Type a new name for the folder.

4. Press Enter or click on a blank area in the window.

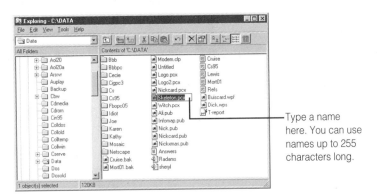

Type a name here. You can use names up to 255 characters long.

Renaming with File/Rename

1. Click on the file or folder you want to rename.

2. Open the File menu and select Rename.

3. Type a new name for the folder.

4. Press Enter or click on a blank area in the window.

33

Renaming Files and Folders

As you accumulate more and more files and folders on your hard disk, you may have to rename files to make the names more descriptive, or to use other versions of names used previously for other files. In this chapter, you will learn how to rename files and folders.

Before you start renaming files, here's a word of caution: Rename only the files you create, or the data files that someone gives you. Do not rename system files or program files. If you rename program files, the program may not run. If you rename system files, your computer or Windows 95 may not run. Okay, now you're ready to start renaming files and folders.

Basic Survival

Renaming a File or Folder

You can rename a file or folder in Explorer or My Computer; the procedures are basically the same. As you name files and folders, keep in mind that in Windows 95, you can use long names (up to 255 characters), and you can use spaces, but you *cannot* use any of the following characters:

\ ? : * " < > |

Also, you can't use a name that is already being used by a file or a folder that occupies the folder you're working in. Here's the quickest way to rename an item:

Right-click on file or folder; click on Rename

1. Click on the icon for the file or folder you want to rename. The selected item appears highlighted.

2. Open the File menu and select Rename. A text box appears around the current name, and the name appears highlighted.

3. Take one of the following steps to replace or edit the name:

     To replace the name, simply type the new name over the old one.

To edit the name, use the left arrow key to move the insertion point, use Del or Backspace to delete existing characters, and then type your changes.

Type the new name here.

4. Press Enter or click on a blank area inside the window.

If you try to use a name that is already in use by a file in this folder, Windows Explorer displays a dialog box warning you that the name is already being used. Select OK, and then repeat the steps using a different name.

You cannot use a name that is already in use by another file in this folder.

Beyond Survival

Bypassing the File/Rename Command

Now that you've learned the long way to rename files and folders, I'll explain the quick and easy way. Simply click on the icon belonging to the file or folder, and then click on its name. A text box appears around the selected item. Type a new name for the item; then press Enter.

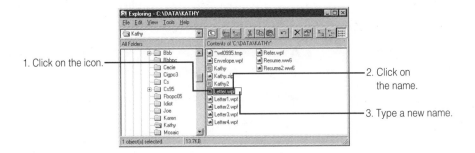

1. Click on the icon.

2. Click on the name.

3. Type a new name.

Cheat Sheet

Deleting Files and Folders

1. Select the file(s) or folder(s) you want to delete.

2. Open the File menu, and select Delete.

3. Select Yes.

Undeleting Files and Folders

1. Double-click on the Recycle Bin icon 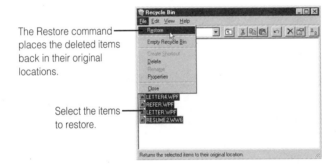.

2. Click on the item you want to restore (Ctrl+click on additional items, if desired).

3. Open the File menu and select Restore.

The Restore command places the deleted items back in their original locations.

Select the items to restore.

34

Deleting and Undeleting Files and Folders

To keep disks from getting cluttered with obsolete programs and with data files that you no longer need, you should back up these old files (or copy them), and then delete them from your hard disk. In this chapter, you'll learn how to delete files from disks and folders. You'll also learn how to restore accidentally deleted files in the event of a mishap.

Basic Survival

Deleting Files and Folders

Before you delete files, make sure you will never *ever* need the files again, or at least make sure you have a copy of the files on floppy disks in a safe storage area. (See Chapter 51 for instructions on how to back up files and folders.) Once you've done that, take the following steps to delete one or more items:

1. Select the file(s) and folder(s) you want to delete.

Del Key = Delete file

2. Open the File menu and select Delete. A dialog box appears, asking you to confirm the deletion.

3. Click on the Yes button. A dialog box appears, showing you the progress of the operation. Windows places the file(s) and folder(s) in the Recycle Bin.

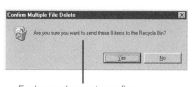

Explorer asks you to confirm.

The steps just shown provide the standard procedure for deleting files and folders. You do, however, have a couple of time-saving alternatives:

- Right-click on a selected file or folder, and then click on Delete.

- If the toolbar is displayed, click on the Delete button ⊠.

- Press the Delete key on your keyboard.

Beyond Survival

Undeleting Files and Folders

Whenever you delete a file or folder, Windows Explorer places the item in the Recycle Bin. As long as you haven't emptied the Bin or exceeded its storage capacity, you can restore deleted files and folders to their original locations. Here's how you do it:

1. Double-click on the Recycle Bin icon 🗑 .

2. Click the item you want to restore. To select additional files or folders, hold down the Ctrl key while clicking on them.

3. Open the File menu and select Restore. The Recycle Bin undeletes the selected file(s) or folder(s) and restores them to the folder from which they were deleted.

4. If the restored files do not appear in the contents area, open the View menu and select Refresh. Sometimes Explorer cannot immediately update information that has changed on a disk.

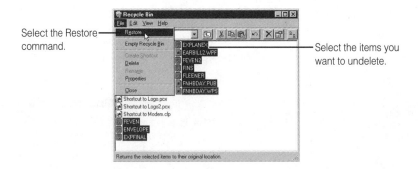

Select the Restore command.

Select the items you want to undelete.

Right-click on selected file or folder; select Restore

For more details about using the Recycle Bin to delete and restore files and folders, refer to Chapter 7.

Cheat Sheet

Formatting a Floppy Disk in Explorer

1. Insert a blank disk in drive A or B, and close the drive door, if necessary.

2. Click on My Computer in the Folders list.

3. Click on the icon (in the contents list) for the disk you want to format.

4. Open the File menu and select Format.

5. Open the Capacity drop-down list, and select the capacity of the disk.

6. Click on the Start button.

7. Wait until the formatting is complete, then click on the Close button.

8. Click on the Close button.

Making a Bootable Disk

- If the disk is formatted, follow the instructions just given, but click on Copy System Files Only in the Format dialog box.

- If the disk is not formatted, follow the instructions just given; then click on Copy System Files in the Format dialog box.

Labeling a Disk

1. Make sure the formatted disk you want to label is in the drive.

2. Click on the drive icon for the disk you want to label.

3. Open the File menu and select Properties.

4. Type a label for the disk.

5. Click on the OK button.

35

Formatting Floppy Disks

Before you can use a floppy disk to store files, the disk must be formatted. Formatting divides a disk into small storage areas and creates a *File Allocation Table* (FAT) on the disk that acts as a map, telling your computer the location of all its storage areas. Whenever you save a file to disk, it is saved in one or more of these storage areas. In this chapter, you will learn how to format a floppy disk, label disks, and make a disk you can use to start your computer.

Basic Survival

Disk and Drive Capacities

High-density = High-capacity

Although the procedure for formatting floppy disks is fairly simple, understanding the drive and disk capacities can be confusing. The problem is that the disk's manufacturer, the drive's manufacturer, and Windows Explorer may all use different terms to describe *capacities*. For example, the disk label may describe the disk as 3.5-inch high-density, and Windows Explorer will ask whether the disk is 1.44MB or 720KB. Use the following table to translate:

Disk Size	Density	Capacity
3.5-inch	High-Density (HD)	1.44MB (High)
3.5-inch	Double-Density (DD)	720KB (Low)
5.25-inch	High-Density (HD)	1.2MB (High)
5.25-inch	Double-Density (DD)	360KB (Low)

No high-capacity disks in low-capacity drives

You should also know that floppy disk *drives* come in high-capacity and low-capacity models, as well. If you have a high-capacity disk drive (1.44MB or 1.2MB), you don't have to worry—you can format both high-density and double-density disks. If you have a low-capacity drive, you will be able to

213

format only double-density disks (360KB or 720KB). (However, low-density drives are fairly obsolete; if you purchased your computer in the last 4 years, you probably have a high-density floppy drive.)

Formatting a Floppy Disk

In general, you format a disk only once—when it is brand new. If you format a disk that has already been formatted, you risk destroying any files that may already be on the disk. It's better to just delete the files (see Chapter 35). If you have a new disk or one that is old and needs to be reformatted, perform the following steps to format the disk:

Format only blank disks

1. Insert a blank disk in drive A or B; close the drive door if necessary.

2. Click on My Computer in the Folders list. The contents list changes to show the available disk drives on your computer.

3. Click on the icon for the drive you're using to format the disk: A or B. (DO NOT double-click on the drive icon; Explorer cannot format a disk whose contents are displayed.)

Click on My Computer.

Click on the drive that contains the blank disk.

4. Open the File menu and select Format. The Format dialog box appears.

5. Open the Capacity drop-down list, and select the capacity of the disk. For a high-capacity, 3.5-inch disk, for example, you would select 1.44MB (3.5").

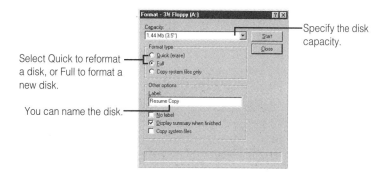

Specify the disk capacity.

Select Quick to reformat a disk, or Full to format a new disk.

You can name the disk.

6. If you are formatting an unformatted disk, click on Full under Format Type. If you are reformatting a formatted disk (to refresh it), click on Quick (Erase).

7. (Optional) Click inside the Label text box, and then type a label for the disk (up to 11 characters). If you add a disk label, the label will appear next to the drive's icon in Explorer and in My Computer.

8. (Optional) Click on any of the following options to turn them on:

No Label tells Explorer not to add a label to this disk.

Display Summary When Finished displays a dialog box at the end of the format operation, indicating how much storage space is available on the disk (and whether the disk has any defects).

Copy System Files makes the floppy disk *bootable*. That is, you can stick it in drive A and start your computer with it.

9. Click on the Start button. Explorer displays a dialog box that shows the format's progress. If you turned on Display Summary When Finished, a dialog box appears when the formatting is complete.

10. Wait until the formatting is complete, and then click on the Close button. You're returned to the Format dialog box, where you can format another floppy disk.

11. Click on the Close button.

Easy way to
format: insert
unformatted
disk and
double-click on
its icon

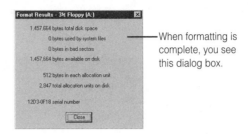

When formatting is
complete, you see
this dialog box.

Beyond Survival

Making a Formatted Disk Bootable

You should always have at least one *bootable* floppy disk on hand in case your system crashes and you can't boot from your hard disk. You can stick the bootable floppy disk in drive A, reboot, and at least call up your files and programs.

When you installed Windows 95, you were given the option of creating a floppy *startup disk*, which is a bootable floppy disk that contains additional files for helping you recover data and nudge Windows 95 into starting up. If you did not create such a disk, see "Making a Floppy Startup Disk" at the end of Chapter 1.

Create a
Windows 95
startup disk
to help you
boot Windows
95 when
you can't boot
from your
hard drive

To make a bootable floppy disk that does *not* contain the Windows 95 startup and recovery files, you can perform the following steps on a formatted floppy disk:

1. Insert a blank, formatted disk in drive A. You can boot a computer only from a disk in drive A.

2. Click on My Computer in the Folders list. The Contents list changes to show the available disk drives on your computer.

3. Right-click on the icon for the drive you're using to format the disk: A or B. A shortcut menu appears.

4. Click on Format. The Format dialog box appears.

5. Click on Copy System Files Only.

6. Click on the Start button. Windows Explorer copies the files IO.SYS, MSDOS.SYS, DRVSPACE.BIN, and COMMAND.COM from the hard disk to the floppy.

You may also want to copy the files AUTOEXEC.BAT and CONFIG.SYS from the root directory of drive C to the floppy disk. Then *write-protect* the disk (place a write-protect sticker over the write-protect notch on a 5.25-inch disk, or slide the write-protect tab so you can see through the window of a 3.5-inch disk). This ensures that nothing will happen to the files on the disk.

Adding or Editing a Disk Label

The best way to label a disk is to write a description of the disk's contents on a stick-on label, and put it on the disk. You can, however, label a disk electronically as well, which will make this label appear next to the disk's icon. You can add a label when you format a disk (as explained earlier), or you can add or edit it later by performing the following steps:

Right-click on disk icon and select Properties

1. Make sure there is a formatted disk in the drive. You can label floppy disks or your hard disks.

2. Click on the drive icon for the drive that contains the disk you want to label.

3. Open the File menu and select Properties. The Properties dialog box appears; the insertion point is in the Label text box.

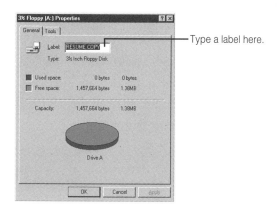

Type a label here.

4. Type a label for the disk (up to 11 characters).

5. Click on the OK button.

Cheat Sheet

Copying Disks Using One Disk Drive

1. Insert the disk you want to copy into one of the floppy disk drives.
2. Click on My Computer in the Folders list.
3. In the Contents list, click on the icon for the drive that contains the disk.
4. Open the File menu and select Copy Disk.
5. Click on the same drive letter in the Copy From and Copy To lists.
6. Click on the Start button.
7. Wait until a message appears that tells you to insert the destination disk.
8. Remove the original disk and insert the destination disk.
9. Click on the OK button.

Copying Disks Using Two Drives of the Same Capacity

1. Insert the disk you want to copy into drive A; put the disk you want to copy it to in drive B.
2. Click on My Computer in the Folders list.
3. In the Contents list, click on the icon for the drive that contains the disk you want to copy.
4. Open the File menu and select Copy Disk.
5. In the Copy From list, click on drive A (the drive that contains the original disk).
6. In the Copy To list, click on drive B (the drive that contains the blank disk).
7. Click on the Start button.

36

Copying Disks

Whenever you get a new program on floppy disks, you should write-protect the original floppy disks, and then copy them. You should use the copies, rather than the originals, to install and use the program. This method prevents accidental damage to the original disks. In this chapter, you'll learn how to copy floppy disks with Windows Explorer.

Basic Survival

Disk Copying Rules and Regulations

If you've copied disks before, you know the rules you need to follow. If you're new to all this, here are the rules:

- You can copy a disk only to a disk of the same size and capacity. You can't copy a 5.25-inch disk to a 3.5-inch disk, or a 360K disk to a 1.2MB disk. You can copy a 3.5-inch, 1.44MB disk only to a 3.5-inch, 1.44MB disk.

- If you have two disk drives of the same size and capacity, you can copy the disk in one drive (the source) to the disk in the other drive (the destination).

Source = Original disk Destination = Blank disk

- If you do not have two disk drives of the same size and capacity, you must use the same drive for both the source and the destination. You'll have to swap disks into and out of the drive during the process.

- The destination disk (the blank one) does not have to be formatted. The copy operation will format the disk for you. If the disk contains files, those files will be lost during the copy operation.

Copying Disks Using One Disk Drive

If you have only one floppy drive that is the size and type you need to copy your disks, perform the following steps:

1. Write-protect the original disk (not the blank disk). This prevents the disk from being ruined if you try to copy the destination disk over the source disk accidentally.

2. Insert the disk you want to copy into one of the floppy disk drives.

3. Click on My Computer in the Folders list.

4. In the Contents list, click on the icon for the drive that contains the disk.

Click on My Computer.

Click on the icon for the drive you want to use.

Right-click on floppy-disk icon in Folders or Contents list; click on Copy Disk

5. Open the File menu and select Copy Disk. The Copy Disk dialog box appears, showing you which drive will be used for copying the disk.

6. Click on the same drive letter in the Copy From and Copy To lists. (If you have only one floppy disk drive, you'll have only one drive letter in both lists, as shown in the figure.)

If you have only one floppy drive, you have no choices here.

7. Click on the Start button. Windows Explorer copies the disk to memory, and then displays a message telling you to insert the destination disk.

8. Wait until a message appears that tells you to insert the destination disk.

9. Remove the original disk and insert the destination disk.

10. Click on the OK button. Windows Explorer writes the data it copied from the original disk to the blank disk.

Beyond Survival

Copying Disks Using Two Drives of the Same Capacity

Drive A for Source
Drive B for Destination

If you have two drives of the same size and capacity (say two 3.5-inch, 1.44MB drives), you can copy a disk without swapping the source and destination disks in the drive. Here's what you do:

1. Write-protect the original disk (not the blank disk). This prevents your original from being ruined if you try to copy the destination disk over the source disk accidentally.

2. Insert the disk you want to copy into drive A; put the disk you want to copy it to in drive B.

3. Click on My Computer in the Folders list. The Contents list shows the icons for all the drives on your computer.

4. In the Contents list, click on the icon for the drive that contains the disk you want to copy.

5. Open the File menu and select Copy Disk. The Copy Disk dialog box appears, prompting you to specify which drives you want to use for the source and destination disks.

6. In the Copy From list, click on drive A (the drive that contains the original disk).

7. In the Copy To list, click on drive B (the drive that contains the blank disk).

8. Click on the Start button. Explorer copies the data from the disk in drive A to the disk in drive B.

Cheat Sheet

Running a Program from Explorer

1. Change to the drive and folder that contains the program's files.
2. Double-click on the icon for the file that runs the program.

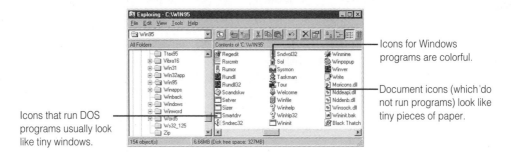

Icons for Windows programs are colorful.

Document icons (which do not run programs) look like tiny pieces of paper.

Icons that run DOS programs usually look like tiny windows.

Opening a Document in a Program

1. Open two folder windows (see Chapter 27).
2. In one window, display the name of the document file you want to open.
3. In the other window, display the icon for the program in which you want to open the document.
4. Drag the document icon over the program icon.
5. Release the mouse button.

Associating a Document with a Program

1. Run Windows Explorer or double-click on My Computer.
2. Open the View menu, and select Options.
3. Click on the File Types tab.
4. In the Registered File Types list, click on the file type you want to associate with a program.
5. Click on the Edit button.
6. Click on Open in the Actions list, and then click on the Edit button.
7. Click on the Browse button, and use the dialog box that appears to select the program in which you want to open the specified document type.
8. Click on the Open button, and then on OK, on Close, and on OK again to save your changes.

37

Running Programs from Windows Explorer

As explained in Chapter 3, you typically run a program by clicking on the Start button, pointing to Programs, and then clicking on the program you want to run. Windows Explorer and My Computer provide another, sometimes faster, method. With either of these resource management tools, you can double-click on a program file to run the program, or double-click on a document file (which runs the program you used to create the document *and* opens the document in that program). In this chapter, you'll learn how to do all this.

Basic Survival

Running a Program from Windows Explorer

Every program has an *executable program file* that starts the program. In almost all cases, the file ends in .BAT, .EXE, or .COM. But remember that Windows 95 doesn't display file extensions for these files unless you tell it to (as explained in Chapter 28). Instead, Windows 95 displays icons that indicate the type of file you're dealing with. As you look for the files that run your programs, use the following list as a guide:

DOS program icons look like tiny windows. You can usually double-click on one of these icons to run a DOS program.

Windows program icons are usually colorful pictures that represent the programs.

Document icons usually look like a piece of paper with one corner folded over. You can't "run" documents, but if you double-click on a document icon that's *associated* with a program, Windows will run the program and open the document in it.

Many document icons include a piece of paper in the background, with a picture of the program that opens the document in the foreground. Normally this image means the document is associated with a specific program.

The point of all this is that you can run programs from Explorer or from My Computer by double-clicking on an icon for an executable program file. The following steps show you how:

1. Run Windows Explorer or double-click on My Computer [icon].

2. Change to the drive and folder containing the program's files.

3. Click on the file that runs the program.

4. Open the File menu and select Open. Windows runs the program.

Bypass menu = Double-click on program file

The name of the executable file

If you have a hard time sifting through the file lists to find executable program files, open the View menu, move the mouse pointer over Arrange Icons, and click on By Type. This clumps together all the .BAT files in one group, .COM files in another, and .EXE files in a third group. You can then locate the files more easily.

If you arrange files by type, you can easily spot groups of executable files.

Opening a Document in a Program

Drag & Drop to open document

If you want to run a program and open a document file automatically, you can drag the document's icon over the program icon. Here's how you do it:

1. Open two folder windows. (You need two so you can see both the document and program icons.)

2. In one window, display the name of the document file you want to open.

3. In the other window, display the name of the program file that runs the program.

4. Drag the document-file icon over the program-file icon.

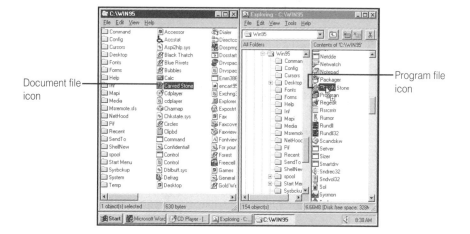

Document file icon

Program file icon

5. Release the mouse button. Windows Explorer runs the program and automatically opens the selected document file.

Dragging and dropping document icons onto program icons is effective, but shuffling the windows around requires some dexterity. To help out, Windows offers a couple of options for opening document files more quickly:

- Right-click on the document file you want to open. If you see an Open command at the top of the menu, the document is associated with a program. Click on Open to run the associated program and open the document file in it.

- Right-click on the document file you want to open. If the file is not associated to a program, **Open With...** appears at the top of the menu. Click on Open With..., and then use the dialog box that appears to select the program in which you want to open the document.

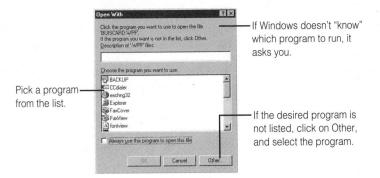

Pick a program from the list.

If Windows doesn't "know" which program to run, it asks you.

If the desired program is not listed, click on Other, and select the program.

Beyond Survival

Associating a Document with a Program

In the previous section, you learned how to open a document file in a program by dragging the document icon over the program icon. There's an easier way. You can *associate* a type of document file with a particular program (for example, you can associate all files that have the extension .DOC with Word for Windows). Once you've set up the file association, just double-click on a document-file icon to run the associated program and open the document. To create an association, here's what you do:

1. Run Windows Explorer or double-click on My Computer .

2. Open the View menu and select Options. The Options dialog box appears.

3. Click on the File Types tab. A list of registered file types appears.

4. In the Registered File Types list, click on the document file type you want to associate with a program. If the file type you want to associate is not in the list, skip ahead to "Adding a File Type to the Register," later in this chapter.

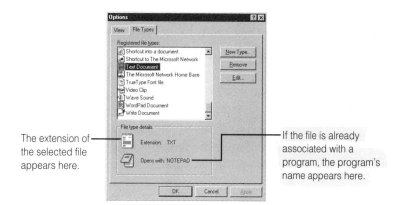

The extension of the selected file appears here.

If the file is already associated with a program, the program's name appears here.

5. Click on the Edit button. The Edit File Type dialog box appears.

6. In the Actions list, click on Open, and then click on the Edit button. A dialog box appears, prompting you to select the program you want to use to open the document file.

7. Click on the Browse button; when a dialog box appears, use it to select the drive, folder, and file name of the program you want to run with this document. Click on the Open button.

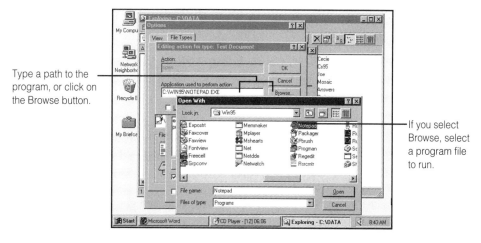

Type a path to the program, or click on the Browse button.

If you select Browse, select a program file to run.

Associate document type to only one program

8. Click on OK, then on Close, and then on Close to save your changes.

Opening an Associated Document File

Once a document file is associated with a program, you can open the document in the program simply by double-clicking on the document file you want to open.

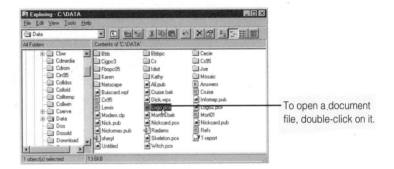

To open a document file, double-click on it.

Adding a File Type to the Register

If you're trying to associate a particular document file type with a program but the file type is not registered, you can add it to the register. Take the following steps:

1. Run Windows Explorer or double-click on My Computer .

2. Open the View menu and select Options. The Options dialog box appears.

3. Click on the File Types tab. A list of registered file types appears.

4. Click on the New Type button. The Add New File Type dialog box appears.

5. Click on the Change Icon button; when a dialog box appears, use it to pick an icon for the document file, and then click on OK. The selected icon appears next to the Change Icon button.

6. Click in the Description of Type text box, and type a description of the document file type.

7. Click in the Associated Extension text box, and type the file-name extension for this file type (for example, **DOC**, **GIF**, **PCX**).

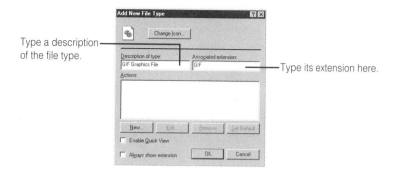

Type a description of the file type.

Type its extension here.

8. Under Actions, click on the New button. The New Action dialog box appears.

9. In the Action text box, type **open**.

10. Click on the Browse button; when a dialog box appears, use it to select the drive, folder, and name of the program you want to use to open this new document file type. Click on Open.

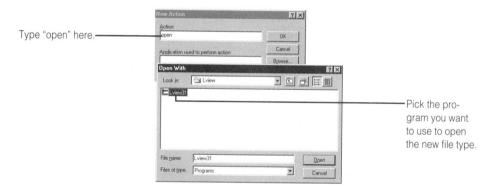

Type "open" here.

Pick the program you want to use to open the new file type.

11. Click on the OK button to return to the Add New File Type dialog box.

12. (Optional) Click on one or both of the following options to turn them on:

Enable Quick View lets you use Windows 95's new Quick View feature to look at the file's contents from Explorer or My Computer.

Always Show Extension displays the file name extensions for files of this type in Explorer and in My Computer.

13. Click on the Close button. This file type now appears in the Registered File Types list.

PART 5

Using the Windows Control Panel

The Windows Control Panel allows you to change the appearance and function of several Windows features. You can use the Control Panel to change the screen colors, control how fast the mouse pointer moves across the screen, set up your printer, set the date and time on your computer, and much more. In this section, you'll learn what you can do with the Control Panel—and how to customize Windows to suit your needs. Specifically, you'll learn how to perform the following tasks:

Cheat Sheet

Starting the Control Panel

1. Click on the Start button.
2. Move the mouse pointer over Settings, and then click on Control Panel.

The Control Panel Icons

Double-click here if you have special needs.

If you connected a new device to your system, run the Add New Hardware Wizard.

Double-click on this icon to install a new program.

Change the system date and time.

Change the screen resolution and colors.

Add or remove fonts from your system.

Configure your joystick, if you have one.

Set the cursor speed and key repeat rate.

Enter settings for e-mail and faxes.

If your computer is on a network, set up your post office here.

Install and set up your modem.

Change the speed of your mouse.

Enter settings for sound and video devices.

Set up network connections and printers.

Enter passwords to protect your computer against unauthorized use.

Install and set up printers.

Set date, time, and currency format for various countries.

Link sounds to system events.

Assign system resources to applications.

38

Seeing What's in the Control Panel

The Control Panel allows you to enter settings for many Windows features. In this chapter, you will learn how to start the Control Panel, and you will learn about the various Control Panel icons that let you enter settings. In later chapters in this section, you'll get specific instructions on how to use most of these icons.

Basic Survival

Starting the Control Panel

Before you can use the Control Panel, you have to start it. Here's how:

1. Click on the Start button.

2. Move the mouse pointer over Settings, and then click on Control Panel. The Control Panel window appears, displaying the icons you can use to configure your system.

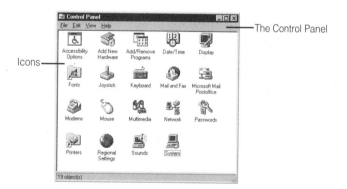

Icons —

The Control Panel

Beyond Survival

The Control Panel Icons

To change a system setting using the Control Panel, double-click on an icon in the Control Panel. Following is a list of the icons and a description of each:

Accessibility Options: If you have some hearing loss, vision impairment, or have difficulty moving the mouse or using the keyboard, double-click on this icon. You can then select a high-contrast display, choose to use sounds for various system events, use your numeric keypad instead of the mouse (to move the mouse pointer), and more.

Add New Hardware: If you connected a new device to your system, run the Add New Hardware Wizard. The Wizard leads you step-by-step through the process of setting up the new device. See Chapter 48 for details.

Add/Remove Programs: Double-click on this icon to install a new program. For details, see Chapter 9.

Date/Time: Double-click on this icon to change the system date and time. (It's easier to change the date and time by right-clicking on the time in the Taskbar, and selecting Adjust Date/Time, although this icon does the same thing. See Chapter 20 for more information.)

Windows has screen saver

Display: If you double-click on this icon, you get a dialog box with several tabs. You can change the background color or design, turn on a screen saver, change the colors that Windows uses, or change the resolution for your monitor. See Chapter 39 for details.

Font = type style and size

Fonts: This icon opens a dialog box that allows you to add or remove fonts (type styles and sizes) from your computer.

Joystick: If you have a joystick connected to your computer, this icon lets you set up, configure, calibrate, and test the joystick. See Chapter 48 for details.

Keyboard: Double-click on this icon to set the speed at which characters (or spaces) repeat when you hold down a key, and to set the amount of time you have to hold down a key before it starts repeating. See Chapter 41 for details.

Mail and Fax: If you send and receive e-mail (electronic mail) or faxes using a modem or over a network connection, you can use this icon to set up the programs you'll use to exchange e-mail and faxes.

Microsoft Mail Postoffice: If you use Microsoft Mail and you're on a network, you can create a workgroup post office for sending and receiving e-mail.

Modems: If you have a modem, you can double-click on this icon to set it up and change any modem settings that might be giving you problems. See Chapter 55 for details.

Mouse: Change the speed that your mouse pointer travels across the screen, and control how fast you have to click twice for a double-click. You can also set your mouse up to swap the functions of the left and right mouse buttons. See Chapter 41 for details.

Multimedia: This icon displays a dialog box that lets you enter settings for the audio, visual, MIDI, and CD devices installed on your system. Chapter 42 offers complete instructions.

Network: If you're on a network, use this icon to connect to a network printer or server.

Passwords: To prevent unauthorized use of your computer, double-click on this icon and enter a password. To add or change a password, refer to Chapter 43.

Printers: This icon displays a dialog box that lets you select the printer you want to use and enter settings to specify how you want the printer to operate. Chapter 46 explains how to use this icon to install or select a printer.

Regional Settings: Set date, time, and currency format for various countries. These settings will control any Windows applications that support international settings for sorting or managing information. This does not change the language used for Windows commands and options. See Chapter 44 for details.

Sounds: You can have Windows emit sounds when you perform specific tasks. Windows comes with several sound configurations, including a collection of jungle sounds. Chapter 23 explains how to attach sounds to Windows events.

System: This icon gives you a peek at what's on your system, and allows you to change system settings—such as the one that tells Windows how much disk space to use as memory (virtual memory). (See Chapter 45 for details on how to configure virtual memory.)

Virtual memory = disk space used as RAM (random-access memory)

235

Cheat Sheet

Changing the Windows Background

1. Right-click on a blank area of the Windows desktop, and then click on Properties.
2. From the Pattern list, click on the desired background pattern.
3. From the Wallpaper list, click on the desired wallpaper design.
4. Select Tile to have the wallpaper design fill the screen, or Center to have one section of the design placed in the middle of the screen.
5. Click on the OK button.

Turning on a Screen Saver

1. Right-click on a blank area of the Windows desktop, and then click on Properties.
2. Click on the Screen Saver tab.
3. Open the Screen Saver drop-down list; click on the desired screen saver.
4. Click on the OK button.

Picking a Windows Color Scheme

1. Right-click on a blank area of the Windows desktop, and then click on Properties.
2. Click on the Appearance tab.
3. Open the Scheme drop-down list, and click on the desired Windows color scheme.
4. Click on the OK button.

Selecting a Monitor Resolution

1. Right-click on a blank area of the Windows desktop, and then click on Properties.
2. Click on the Settings tab.
3. Open the Color Palette drop-down list, and select the number of colors you want your monitor to display.
4. Drag the slider under Desktop Area to the right to increase the screen resolution, or to the left to decrease it.
5. Click on the OK button.

39

Changing the Display Settings

You may think that you're stuck with the standard Windows look, the plain green background that sits behind your shortcuts and windows. Not true. You can use the Display Settings icon in the Control Panel to select an interesting Windows background and to turn on a screen saver that just might keep your monitor from going south. In this chapter, you'll learn how you can take control of your display.

Basic Survival

Changing the Windows Background

The Windows background is the desktop on which your shortcuts and windows appear. When you first start Windows, the background is a uniform color, having no design or pattern. You can select a pattern for the background and/or pick a wallpaper—a design that lies on top of the background. Here's what you do:

1. Click on the Start button.

Right-click on desktop and pick Properties

2. Move the mouse pointer over Settings, and then click on Control Panel. The Windows Control Panel appears.

3. Double-click on the Display icon 🖥. The Display Properties dialog box appears. (A quicker way to display this dialog box is to right-click on a blank area of the Windows desktop, and then click on Properties.)

4. From the Pattern list, click on the desired background pattern. A pattern gives some texture to the background, such as bricks or pillars. (If you installed Windows 95 over a previous version of Windows and you had a special pattern selected, that pattern appears in the list.)

5. From the Wallpaper list, click on the desired wallpaper design. Wallpaper is any graphic that lies on top of the desktop; Windows comes with several wallpaper designs from which you can select, or you can create your own wallpaper, as explained in Chapter 66, "10 Cool Tricks."

6. Select Tile to have the wallpaper design fill the screen, or Center to have one section of the design placed in the middle of the screen.

7. Either click on the OK button to save your changes, or move on to the next section to change another display property.

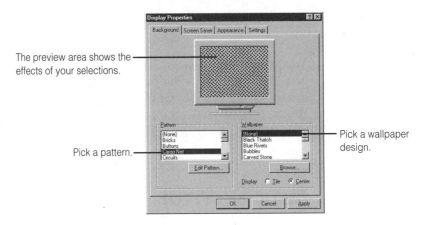

The preview area shows the effects of your selections.

Pick a pattern.

Pick a wallpaper design.

Giving Your Desktop New Colors

Windows uses a default color scheme that is easy on your eyes. If you want a color scheme that's a little wild (or at least more interesting), you can select one of Windows' other color schemes or design your own. Take the following steps to pick a Windows color scheme:

1. Right-click on a blank area of the Windows desktop, and then click on Properties. The Display Properties dialog box appears.

2. Click on the Appearance tab. The preview area shows the current color scheme in action.

3. Open the Scheme drop-down list, and click on a color scheme. The preview area changes to show the effects of the new color scheme.

4. To change the look of an item in the preview area (and modify the color scheme), click on the item in the preview area. The Item drop-down list shows the name of the selected item, allowing you to change its look.

5. To change the size of the selected item, click on the arrows to the right of the Size spin box.

6. To change the color of the selected item, open the Color drop-down list, and click on the desired color.

7. If the selected item has text in it (as in a title bar or menu), you can use the Font, Size, and Color drop-down lists to control the appearance of the text.

8. To save your settings as a new color scheme, click on the Save As button, type a name for the new color scheme, and then click on OK.

9. Click on the OK button, or skip ahead to the next section to enter additional display properties.

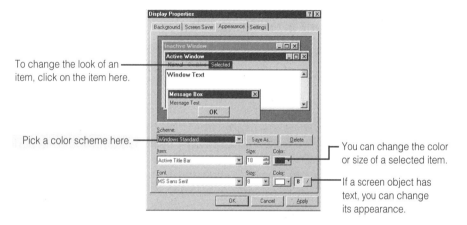

To change the look of an item, click on the item here.

Pick a color scheme here.

You can change the color or size of a selected item.

If a screen object has text, you can change its appearance.

Beyond Survival

Using a Windows Screen Saver

If you leave one image on your screen for an extended period, the image can burn into an older monitor's screen, permanently damaging it. You'll see evidence of burn-in at automatic teller machines and on video games in arcades. To prevent it from happening to your computer, you should use a screen saver.

Screen savers typically blank the screen or display images that move across the screen. The screen saver starts when the computer is inactive for a certain amount of time. Windows contains several screen savers; you can turn them on by performing the following steps:

1. Double-click on the Display icon 🖥️ in the Control Panel, or right-click on a blank area of the Windows desktop, and click on Properties.

2. Click on the Screen Saver tab. The Screen Saver options appear.

3. Open the Screen Saver drop-down list; click on the desired screen saver.

4. To change the settings for the selected screen saver, click on the Settings button and enter your preferences. (Preferences vary depending on the screen saver; if you turn on Flying Windows, for example, you can specify the number of flying windows and the speed at which they fly.)

5. Click on the arrows next to the Wait _____ Minutes spin box to specify how long your computer should be inactive before the screen saver kicks in.

6. To use the screen saver to protect your computer from unauthorized use, click on the Password Protected option. Then click on the Change button, type your password in the New Password and Confirm New Password text boxes, and click on OK.

7. If you have a monitor and video card that support Advanced Power Management (APM), you can pick one of the following options to have Windows power-down the monitor during periods of inactivity:

Low-Power Standby triggers the monitor's power-saving feature. The monitor remains on. Use the Minutes spin box to specify how long the computer must remain inactive before the power saver kicks in.

Shut Off Monitor turns the monitor off after a specified number of minutes (use the Minutes spin box).

8. Click on the OK button.

Password-protect your system with the screen saver

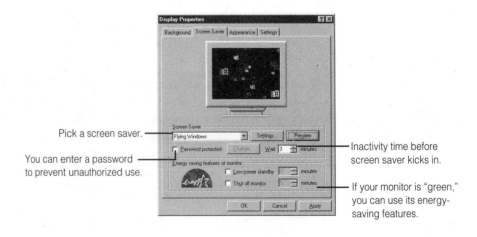

Pick a screen saver.

You can enter a password to prevent unauthorized use.

Inactivity time before screen saver kicks in.

If your monitor is "green," you can use its energy-saving features.

Changing the Resolution for Your Monitor

256 colors and 640-by-480 pixels work well

Depending on your monitor and display adapter (the circuit board into which you plug your monitor), you may be able to change the number of colors your monitor displays—as well as the size of the items displayed on the monitor. If you have an SVGA monitor with a video card, for example, you can increase its resolution to display more information (smaller) on your screen. Here's what you do:

1. Double-click on the Display icon 🖥️ in the Control Panel, or right-click on a blank area of the Windows desktop, and click on Properties.

2. Click on the Settings tab. The color and resolution settings appear.

3. Open the Color Palette drop-down list, and select the number of colors you want your monitor to display. (If you plan to play video clips, view pictures, or play computer games, pick at least 256 colors; otherwise the display will look horrid.)

4. Drag the slider under Desktop Area to the right to increase the screen resolution, or to the left to decrease it. Higher resolutions (for example, 1024-by-768) display more information on the screen, but display smaller objects than do lower resolutions (such as 640-by-480).

5. If you picked a higher resolution, you can use the Font Size drop-down list to select a large or small font for the display. (You might want to pick a larger font size so you can read the type.) If you prefer to pick a scaling percentage for the fonts, click on the Custom button.

6. Click on the OK button to save your settings.

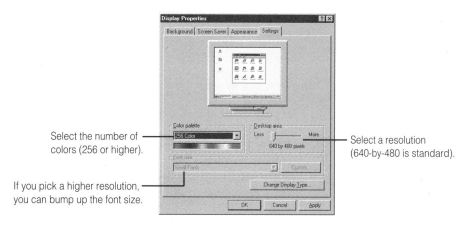

Select the number of colors (256 or higher).

Select a resolution (640-by-480 is standard).

If you pick a higher resolution, you can bump up the font size.

Consult
monitor's
documentation
for correct
settings

If you have a high-quality monitor, and the Display Properties dialog box doesn't seem to offer you all the options that you know your monitor supports, Windows 95 might not be set up to use your monitor. In such a case, you should pick a different display type. First, however, check the documentation that came with your monitor and display adapter to determine the display type; if you pick the wrong display type, you may run into problems after making the change. Once you've determined the display type, take the following steps:

1. Click on the Settings tab in the Display Properties dialog box, and then click on the Change Display Type button. This opens the Change Display Type dialog box, which allows you to pick a display adapter.

2. Under Adapter Type, click on the Change button. A dialog box appears, showing a list of the display adapters that are compatible with the selected monitor.

3. Take one of the following steps:

   If your display adapter is listed, click on it, and then click on OK.

   If your display adapter is not listed, click on Show All Devices, and then click on the adapter type installed on your system. (If your adapter type does not appear on the list, and you have a disk from the adapter manufacturer, insert the disk, and click on Have Disk. Follow the instructions to install the device driver.)

4. If Windows prompts you to insert one of the Windows 95 installation disks, insert the disk and click on OK. Windows copies the necessary display adapter driver from the disk to your hard disk.

5. Under Monitor Type click on the Change button. A dialog box appears, showing a list of the available monitor types.

6. Take one of the following steps:

   If your monitor type is listed, click on it, and then click on OK.

   If your monitor type is not listed, click on Show All Devices, and then click on the correct monitor type. (If your monitor type does not appear in the list, and you have a disk from the monitor manufacturer, insert the disk, and click on Have Disk. Follow the instructions to install the device driver.)

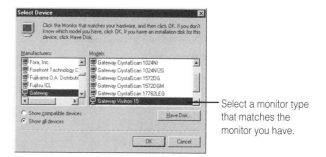

Select a monitor type that matches the monitor you have.

7. Click on the Close button to close the Change Display Type dialog box and return to the Display Properties dialog box.

8. Click on the OK button. In most cases, a message appears, asking whether you want to restart your computer to load the new display drivers. Click on the Yes button.

Windows restarts your computer, and loads the new display adapter and monitor drivers. If Windows runs into a problem with the devices you selected, it shuts down your computer automatically, and then restarts it with the previous settings. For now, just sit back and watch what happens. If Windows starts okay, you're in business. If Windows has a problem, you'll have to follow the steps again and try different settings.

Cheat Sheet

Viewing a Font Sample

1. Click on the Start button.
2. Move the mouse pointer over Settings, and then click on Control Panel.
3. Double-click on the Fonts icon.
4. Double-click on the icon for the font you want to view.

Adding Soft Fonts

1. Click on the Start button.
2. Move the mouse pointer over Settings, and then click on Control Panel.
3. Double-click on the Fonts icon.
4. Open the File menu and click on Install New Font.
5. Insert the disk that contains the fonts you want to install.
6. Change to the drive and directory that contains the fonts.
7. Hold down the Ctrl key while clicking on each font you want to install.
8. Make sure Copy Fonts to Fonts Folder has a check mark next to it.
9. Click on the OK button.

Removing Fonts

1. Click on the Start button.
2. Move the mouse pointer over Settings, and then click on Control Panel.
3. Double-click on the Fonts icon.
4. Hold down the Ctrl key while clicking on each font you want to remove.
5. Open the File menu and select Delete.
6. Click on Yes.

40

Working with Fonts

Windows comes with several fonts (type styles and sizes) that are installed automatically when you set up Windows for the first time. You can remove some of these fonts to free up computer memory and disk space, and you can reinstall them to make them available on font lists in your Windows applications. In addition, you can purchase and install more fonts. In this chapter, you'll learn how to add and remove fonts in Windows.

Basic Survival

Understanding Fonts

Printer fonts installed when you select a printer

A *font* is any text that has the same type style and size. For example, Courier 12-point is a font. Courier is the type style, and 12-point is the size. Fonts come from different sources, depending on the type of font. Here's a list of the most common font types:

- *Printer fonts* are built into the printer. When you select a printer (see Chapter 46), the printer setup installs the screen fonts (used to display the selected fonts on-screen) and the printer fonts (used to create the fonts on paper). You don't need any of the information in this chapter to install printer fonts.

- *Cartridge fonts* are additional fonts you can plug into some printers (usually laser or dot-matrix printers). They act as additional printer fonts.

- *Screen fonts* are fonts Windows uses to display options and messages on-screen. Screen fonts may also be included with printers, cartridges, and soft fonts to make the type appear on-screen as it will in print. If Windows does not have a screen font that matches the selected printer or cartridge font, Windows uses a screen font that most closely matches the selected font. Most cartridges and soft fonts come with an installation program that installs the screen fonts for you. If no setup program exists, you can follow the instructions in this chapter to install the fonts.

- *Soft fonts*, such as Adobe fonts, come on disk. Most of these fonts come with their own installation program and include both the screen and printer fonts. If no installation program exists, you can follow the instructions in this chapter to install the fonts.

- *TrueType fonts* are soft fonts designed especially for Windows. TrueType fonts act as both printer and screen fonts. Unlike other fonts that come in a fixed number of sizes, TrueType fonts allow you to select any size and rotate the text. Follow the instructions in the next section to install TrueType fonts.

TrueType fonts = TT in font lists

Viewing the Fonts You Have

Most people see the fonts they have only when they try to use them to style text in one of their documents. However, when you want to clear your system of the fonts you use, you might want to take peek at a font before you decide to delete it. To see a sample of a font that's on your system, take the following steps:

1. Click on the Start button.

2. Move the mouse pointer over Settings, and then click on Control Panel.

To view a font, double-click on its icon

3. Double-click on the Fonts icon 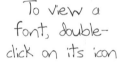. A window appears, showing icons for the fonts that are installed on your computer.

4. Double-click on the icon for the font you want to view. A window appears, showing sample text styled with the selected font.

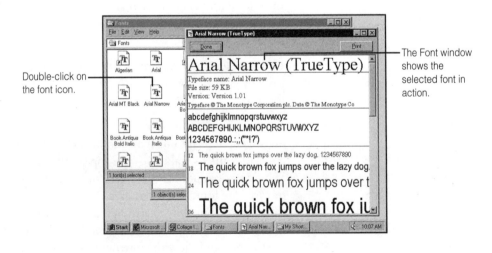

Double-click on the font icon.

The Font window shows the selected font in action.

5. To print the sample page for the font, make sure your printer is turned on, and then click on the Print button.

6. When you're done viewing the sample, click on the Done button to close the window.

Installing Screen Fonts and TrueType Fonts

You'll need to use the Windows Font installation program if the fonts you want to install did not come with an installation program, or if you want to add previously installed fonts back into your fonts lists (provided you've removed them, as explained later in this chapter). To install fonts using the Installation program, here's what you do:

1. Click on the Start button.

2. Move the mouse pointer over Settings, and then click on Control Panel. The Control Panel window appears.

3. Double-click on the Fonts icon 🖾 . The Fonts dialog box appears, showing all the fonts installed in the WINDOWS\FONTS directory.

4. Open the File menu and click on Install New Font. The Add Fonts dialog box appears, prompting you to specify the location of the fonts you want to add.

5. Insert the disk that contains the fonts you want to install.

6. Open the Drives drop-down list; click on the drive that contains the disk with the fonts.

7. If the disk contains folders, double-click on the Fonts folder in the Folders list. Windows reads the disk, and displays the names of the fonts under List of Fonts.

8. Click on the font you want to add. Hold down the Ctrl key while clicking on each additional font you want to install. (Or click on the Select All button to install all the fonts.)

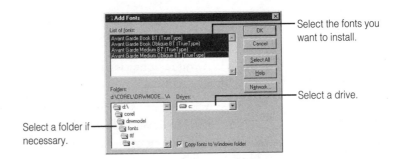

Select the fonts you want to install.

Select a drive.

Select a folder if necessary.

9. If you want to make the fonts permanently available, make sure Copy Fonts to Windows Folder has a check mark next to it. (If this box is not checked, you'll be able to use the fonts from the original disk only; they will not be copied to your hard disk. If you are installing from a folder on your hard disk or from a CD that you always keep in your drive, you may want to turn this option off.)

10. Click on the OK button. Windows copies the fonts files to the WINDOWS\FONTS folder. You can now use these fonts in your other Windows programs.

You can view a font in the Fonts window by double-clicking on its icon. A window appears, showing the selected font in different sizes so you can see what it looks like. Also, you can clean up the Fonts window by hiding variations of a font; for example, you can hide the icons for bold and italic versions of a font, so that only the icon for the plain font is visible. To hide variations of fonts, open the View menu and select Hide Variations.

In case you're wondering, the Fonts window does not contain icons for printer fonts. Even so, your printer fonts will appear in your program font lists (for example, in WordPad or Excel).

Beyond Survival

Removing Soft Fonts

Fonts take up disk space and memory. If you never use a font, it's a good idea to remove it. There's one exception. Do not remove the font called MS Sans Serif. Windows uses this font (which is easy to read) to display text in its windows, menus, and dialog boxes. If you remove this font, you may not be able to read all the on-screen text.

More fonts slow down system

To remove a font, here's what you do:

1. Click on the Start button.

2. Move the mouse pointer over Settings, and then click on Control Panel. The Control Panel window appears.

3. Double-click on the Fonts icon ⊞. The Fonts window appears.

4. Select each font you want to remove:

> **Single font:** Click on it.

> **Group of neighboring fonts:** Click on the first one in the group, and then hold down the Shift key while clicking on the last font in the group.

> **Group of non-neighboring fonts:** Hold down the Ctrl key while clicking on each font you want to remove.

5. Open the File menu and select Delete, or simply press the Del key. A dialog box appears, prompting you to confirm the deletion.

6. Click on Yes. Windows deletes the selected fonts files.

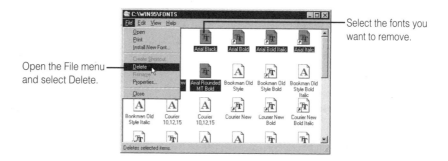

Open the File menu and select Delete.

Select the fonts you want to remove.

Cheat Sheet

Changing Your Mouse Settings

Click on this tab to control the mouse pointer's appearance.

Select left- or right-handed mouse use.

Drag to change speed at which you have to click twice for a double-click.

Click on General to select a different mouse driver.

Use the Motion tab to set the speed of the mouse pointer.

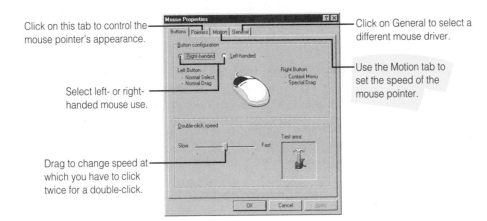

Changing Your Keyboard Settings

Test the repeat rate here.

Drag to control how long you have to hold down a key to start repeating the character.

Drag to control how fast the character repeats.

Drag to set how fast the insertion point blinks.

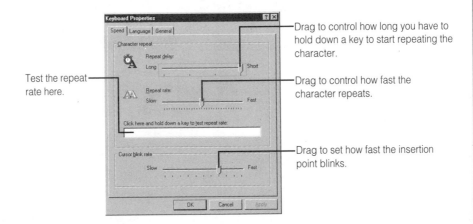

41

Controlling Your Mouse and Keyboard

Have you ever wished your mouse pointer would travel faster or slower across the screen, or that you didn't have to click so fast to enter a double-click? With the Control Panel, you can change the mouse settings to make your mouse behave the way you want it to. In addition, you can change the keyboard settings so you don't have to hold down a key so long to have it repeat a character. In this chapter, you'll learn how to change your mouse and keyboard settings.

Basic Survival

Changing Your Mouse Settings

A mouse that operates too fast or too slow can be frustrating. Fortunately, you can change the way your mouse behaves. Here's what you do:

1. Click on the Start button.

2. Move the mouse pointer over Settings, and then click on Control Panel.

3. Double-click on the Mouse icon ![Mouse icon]. The Mouse dialog box appears.

Give your mouse pointers a new look.

Control the speed of the mouse pointer.

The Buttons tab lets you pick left- or right-handed use.

Pick a different mouse driver.

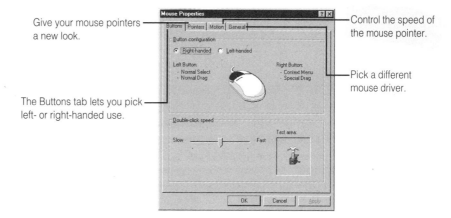

Cheap system security—Swap mouse buttons before going home

Double-click on the jack-in-the-box to test

4. Under Button Configuration, click on Right-Handed or Left-Handed. Left-Handed swaps the functions of the left and right mouse buttons so that the left button brings up shortcut menus and the right button selects items.

5. To change the speed at which you must click twice for Windows to acknowledge a double-click, drag the Double-Click Speed slider to the left or right. (You can double-click on the jack-in-the-box animation to test the speed.)

6. Click on the Pointers tab. This displays several variations for displaying the mouse pointer.

7. Open the Scheme drop-down list; click on the desired mouse-pointer scheme. The list of mouse pointers changes to display the various mouse pointers in this scheme. (You can change the look of a pointer by clicking on it, clicking on the Browse button, and then selecting a pointer.)

8. Click on the Motion tab to set the speed at which the mouse pointer travels across the screen.

9. Drag the Pointer Speed slider to the left or right to change the speed of the pointer.

10. To have the mouse leave a trail as it travels across the screen, click on Show Pointer Trails, and then use the slider to set the length of the pointer tail. (Roll your mouse around to test the effects of your change.)

11. If you have a special mouse and it's not working well, click on the General tab, click on the Change button, and select your mouse type from the list. Click on the OK button when you're done. (As a rule, you should avoid the General tab if your mouse is working okay.)

12. Click on the OK button.

Changing Your Keyboard Settings

Whenever you hold down a key on your keyboard, it starts to repeat its character. The Keyboard option lets you control how long you have to hold a key down before it starts repeating, and how fast the character repeats once it starts. To change these settings, perform the following steps:

1. Click on the Start button.

2. Move the mouse pointer over Settings, and then click on Control Panel.

3. Double-click on the Keyboard icon ⌨.

4. To change how long you have to hold down a key before it starts repeating, drag the Repeat Delay slider to the left (so you have to hold down the key longer) or to the right (so the character will start repeating right away).

Click inside test repeat rate box, hold down key

5. To change how fast the character repeats when it starts repeating, drag the Repeat Rate slider to the left (to repeat slowly) or to the right (for a more frenetic pace).

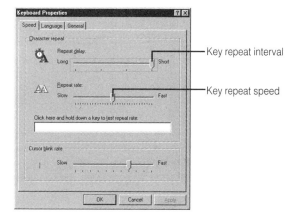

6. To change the speed at which the insertion point blinks, drag the Cursor Blink Rate slider to the left or right.

7. If you're working with a keyboard in a language other than English, click on the Language tab, click on the Add button, select the desired language from the drop-down list, and click on OK.

8. If you have a special make or model of keyboard, click on the General tab, and then select the correct make and model from the list. (If you have a standard keyboard, you can usually ignore the General tab.)

9. Click on the OK button. Your changes are saved, and your keyboard will start acting as instructed.

Cheat Sheet

Accessing Your Multimedia Settings

1. Click on the Start button.
2. Rest the mouse pointer on Settings, and then click on Control Panel.
3. Double-click on the Multimedia icon .

Changing Sound Board Settings

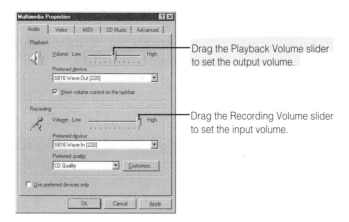

Drag the Playback Volume slider to set the output volume.

Drag the Recording Volume slider to set the input volume.

Changing Video Settings

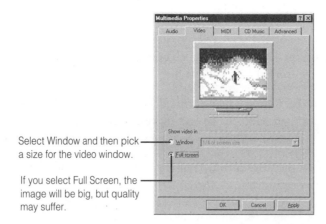

Select Window and then pick a size for the video window.

If you select Full Screen, the image will be big, but quality may suffer.

42

Entering Multimedia Settings

With multimedia washing over you as the latest wave in technology, you need some way to control your multimedia devices: your sound board, CD-ROM drive, video, and MIDI device (for example, a synthesizer). The Control Panel gives you control over these devices through the Multimedia Properties dialog box. In this chapter, you'll learn how to use this dialog box to control your multimedia devices.

Basic Survival

Changing Sound Board Settings

In Chapter 23, "Recording Sounds with the Sound Recorder," you learned one way to control the recording and playback volume for your sound board. You can enter the same settings through the Multimedia Properties dialog box. Here's what you do:

1. Click on the Start button.

2. Rest the mouse pointer on Settings, and then click on Control Panel. The Control Panel window appears.

3. Double-click on the Multimedia icon . The Multimedia Properties dialog box appears, with the Audio tab up front.

Double-click on speaker icon in Taskbar to set volume

4. Under Playback, you can change any of the following:

    Volume: Drag the slider to increase or decrease the volume at which sounds are played back.

    Preferred Device: If you have two sound cards in your computer, you can select the sound card you want to use for playing back sounds.

Show Volume Control on Taskbar: This turns the speaker icon (next to the clock on the Taskbar) on or off. When this is on, you can double-click on the speaker icon to display a dialog box that lets you set the volume for various sound devices.

5. Under Recording, you can change any of the following:

Volume: Drag the slider to increase or decrease the volume at which sounds are recorded. This also affects the volume at which recorded sounds are played back.

Preferred Device: If you have two sound cards installed on your computer, you can pick the one you want to use to record sounds.

Preferred Quality: You can pick a sound quality for recording from the drop-down list, or click on Customize to pick from a more extensive list. Files for high-quality recordings are much larger than those for low-quality recordings.

6. If you have two or more sound cards installed in your system, and you have a program that can use only the devices selected in the Preferred Devices boxes, click on Use Preferred Devices Only. If your audio programs or games can use any of the sound cards on your system, clear this check box.

7. Click on OK to save your changes, or move on to the next section to set the display size for video clips.

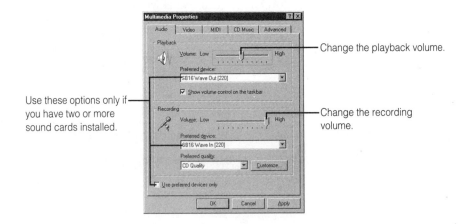

Change the playback volume.

Use these options only if you have two or more sound cards installed.

Change the recording volume.

Controlling the Video Clip Size

If you've ever played computerized video clips, you know that they usually take up a mere corner of your screen, sort of like those TV sets that let you watch five programs at the same time. The problem is that a full-screen, high-resolution clip takes up a lot of disk space and requires enormous amounts of computer power. You can, however, increase the size of the window in which you play your favorite flicks. Here's how:

1. Double-click on the Multimedia icon 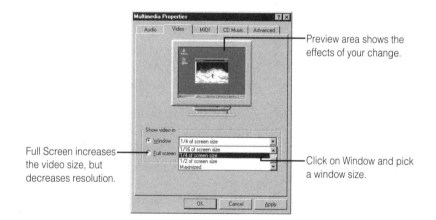 in the Control Panel. The Multimedia Properties dialog box appears.

2. Click on the Video tab. The video display options appear.

3. Select one of the following options to set the video display size:

Click on Window and then select a window size from the drop-down list. Note that as you pick larger window sizes, the image becomes more blocky. That's what's going to happen to the video clips you play.

Click on Full Screen to have the video clips take up the entire screen.

4. Click on OK to save your changes, or move on to the next section to set the volume for your audio CD output.

Preview area shows the effects of your change.

Full Screen increases the video size, but decreases resolution.

Click on Window and pick a window size.

Beyond Survival

MIDI (pronounced "MID-dee") stands for Musical Instrument Digital Inter-face, a technology that allows you to record various instruments on different tracks or channels. This allows you (or someone who knows what they're doing) to control the volume, tempo, pitch, and other qualities of each instrument separately. If you have one or more MIDI devices (such as a piano keyboard) and a MIDI port (usually on your sound card), you can use the MIDI options to install the instrument and select it. Take the following steps:

1. Plug the MIDI device into the MIDI port on the back of your com-puter. (Most sound cards include a MIDI port.)

2. Double-click on the Multimedia icon in the Control Panel. The Multimedia Properties dialog box appears.

3. Click on the MIDI tab. The MIDI output options appear.

4. Click on the Add New Instrument button. This starts the MIDI Instrument Installation Wizard.

5. If you have more than one MIDI port on your computer, click on the port into which you plugged the instrument, and then click on the Next button. The Wizard prompts you to select a type of instrument.

6. Click on the type of instrument you connected in Step 1, and then click on the Next button. (If you're not sure, click on General MIDI Instru-ment.) The Wizard prompts you to type a name for the instrument.

7. Type a name for the instrument (for example, **Piano**), and click on the Finish button. The Wizard returns you to the Multimedia Properties dialog box, and inserts the name of the new instrument in the list of available instruments.

8. Click on Single Instrument, and click on the name of the new instrument.

9. Click on the OK button to save your change.

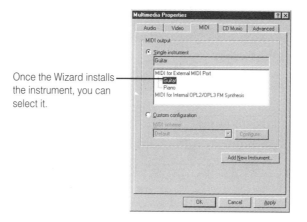

Once the Wizard installs the instrument, you can select it.

If you have several musical instruments connected to your computer, you can assign them to different recording tracks (or channels). First, follow the instructions just given to add all the instruments to the list. Then click on the Custom Configuration option; follow up by clicking on the Configure button. This brings up a dialog box that lets you assign each instrument to its own channel. Simply click on the channel, click on the Change button, and pick the desired instrument from the Instrument drop-down list. Then click on the OK button. Repeat the steps for each instrument.

Meeting Your Multimedia Drivers Face to Face

If you want to disable a multimedia device (prevent it from loading when you start Windows), or if you want to change the device's settings directly, you can click on the Advanced tab in the Multimedia Properties dialog box. This displays a list of all the multimedia drivers installed on your system. Double-click on a device to display a dialog box that lets you change the driver settings. (These driver settings vary depending on the driver.)

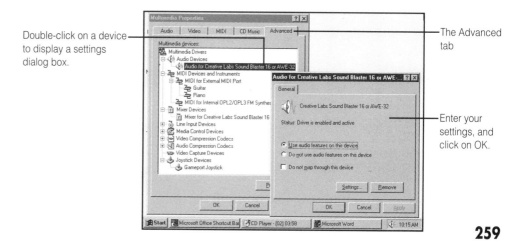

Double-click on a device to display a settings dialog box.

The Advanced tab

Enter your settings, and click on OK.

Cheat Sheet

Entering a Windows Password

1. Click on the Start button.
2. Rest the mouse pointer on Settings, and then click on Control Panel.
3. Double-click on the Passwords icon.
4. Click on the Change Windows Password button.
5. Tab to the New Password text box; type your password. (Whatever you type appears as asterisks.)
6. Tab to the Confirm New Password text box; retype your password.
7. Click on the OK button.
8. Click on the OK button.
9. Click on the Close button.

Setting Up Windows for Multiple Users

1. Click on the Start button.
2. Rest the mouse pointer on Settings, and then click on Control Panel.
3. Double-click on the Passwords icon.
4. Click on the User Profiles tab.
5. Click on Users Can Customize Their Preferences and Desktop Settings…
6. To prevent other users from changing your Start menu or program groups, click on Include Start Menu and Program Groups in User Settings.
7. Click on the OK button.

43

Adding and Changing Passwords

In Chapter 39, you learned how to protect your system by turning on a screen saver and adding a password to it. The screen saver provides an excellent way to prevent unauthorized use of your computer. If several people use your computer, however, the screen-saver password is not very practical, because it prevents other users from gaining access.

Windows offers another password feature that allows each user to type a different password and *log on* to the system. Although these types of passwords do not prevent unauthorized access to files and folders, they do prevent a user from changing another user's Windows settings. For example, multiple user passwords prevent other users from deleting your shortcuts, rearranging your shortcuts, or messing with your display settings.

Use passwords to prevent others from changing Windows settings

In this chapter, you'll learn how to enter a Windows password and set up your system for multiple users.

Basic Survival

Protecting Your System with a Password

The password you are about to enter does not prevent other users from turning on your computer and using it, peeking at your documents, and using your programs. So what good is it? This password can prevent other users from changing your Windows desktop and any other Windows settings you may have entered. To add or change your password, take the following steps:

1. Click on the Start button.

2. Rest the mouse pointer on Settings, and then click on Control Panel. The Control Panel window appears.

3. Double-click on the Passwords icon. The Passwords Properties dialog box appears with the Change Passwords tab up front.

4. Click on the Change Windows Password button. The Change Windows Password dialog box appears, prompting you to type your old password and your new password.

If you have an old pass-word, type it here.

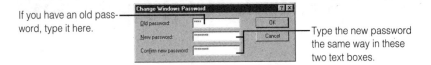

Type the new password the same way in these two text boxes.

5. If you have an old password, type it in the Old Password text box. If you don't have a password, skip this step.

6. Tab to the New Password text box and type your password. (Whatever you type appears as asterisks, so nobody can peek over your shoulder and see what you're typing.)

7. Tab to the Confirm New Password text box; retype your password *exactly* as you typed it in step 6.

8. Click on the OK button. A dialog box appears, informing you that the password has been successfully changed.

9. Click on the OK button. You are returned to the Passwords Properties dialog box.

10. Click on the Close button.

To remove a password, perform the same steps. In the Old Password text box, type the password that you're currently using. Then leave the New Password and Confirm New Password text boxes blank.

Use password you'll never forget and no one else will guess

Logging On with Your Password

To try out your new password, restart Windows: click on Start, and then on Shut Down, Restart the Computer, and Yes. When Windows starts, it displays a dialog box that prompts you to type your *log-on name* (also known as a *username*) and password. If the log-on name is correct, simply type your password and click on the OK button. If the log-on name is incorrect, drag over it in the text box, type your user name, tab to the Password text box, type your password, and then click on the OK button.

When you log on with a new password, a dialog box informs you that you have not logged on to this computer before, and asks whether you want any system changes you make during this session to be saved for next session. Click on Yes to have your changes saved, or No to retain the original settings.

If you forget your password, or you're a new user who hasn't logged on before, you can still get into Windows. Simply type your name in the User Name text box and click on OK. If you want to add a password at this time, type your password in the New Password and Confirm New Password text boxes, and then click on OK. However, you don't have to enter a password; you can click on the OK button and get right to work in Windows.

Beyond Survival

Using Passwords for Multiple Users

If you have your computer at home where your kids, your roommates, or others might use it—or if several people use the same computer at work—you can make Windows save separate system settings for each user. That way your shortcuts, screen colors, and other system settings remain in effect no matter how Junior chooses to set up his desktop. To allow for multiple users, take the following steps:

1. Click on the Start button.

2. Rest the mouse pointer on Settings, and then click on Control Panel.

3. Double-click on the Passwords icon.

4. Click on the User Profiles tab. The User Profiles options appear, allowing you to use the same Windows settings for all users, or let each user set individual preferences.

5. Click on Users Can Customize Their Preferences and Desktop Settings… With this option on, Windows creates a customized settings file for each user, and saves any changes the user makes to Windows in this file.

6. To prevent other users from changing your Start menu or program groups, click on Include Start Menu and Program Groups in User Settings to place a check mark next to this option.

7. Click on the OK button.

Cheat Sheet

What Are Regional Settings?

- Regional settings control the default date, time, currency, and number formats (for programs that support these settings).
- Any regional settings you enter in your programs will override the settings you enter here.
- If you use Windows in English in the U.S., you don't have to worry about these settings, but you may want to change the date or time format or the measuring system.
- Regional settings do not change the language of Windows title bars or menus; they merely change measurement standards.

Accessing the Regional Settings

1. Click on the Start button.
2. Move the mouse pointer over Settings, and then click on Control Panel.
3. Double-click on the Regional Settings icon .

Selecting a Country

- Click on the Regional Settings tab, open the drop-down list, and click on the desired country.
- Click on a country in the map below the drop-down list.

Changing a Format

1. Click on the tab for the format you want to change: Number, Currency, Time, or Date.
2. Use the drop-down lists to select your preferences.
3. Click on the OK button.

44

Changing the Regional Settings

Windows is set up to work in English. If you need to work in another language, you can use enter *regional settings* for the country and language you intend to use. These settings will control the following features in all of your Windows programs that support regional settings:

Measurement System: Windows measures format settings (such as tab stops and indents) in inches. If you prefer measuring in centimeters, you can choose the metric option.

Date and Time Formats: Some programs can insert the date and time from your computer's clock into a document. The date and time will appear in the format most appropriate for the selected country. You can change the format if you want.

Currency and Number Formats: Currencies vary from country to country. America uses dollars, France uses francs, and Germany uses the deutschmark. Windows lets you select a currency format and then fine-tune it.

Sort Order: If a language uses accented characters, the sort order for a list can get thrown off. To ensure that a list is correctly sorted, you must choose the right language.

If you use Windows in the United States and in English, you don't have to worry about the regional settings; the defaults should work fine. You might still want to use the regional settings to change a format, however, such as the date or time format.

Basic Survival

Changing the Regional Settings

The Control Panel contains an icon for changing the regional settings. You simply double-click on the icon and enter your preferences. Here's how you do it:

1. Click on the Start button.

2. Move the mouse pointer over Settings, and then click on Control Panel.

3. Double-click on the Regional Settings icon 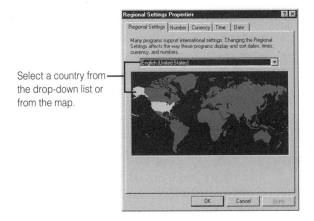. The Regional dialog box appears.

4. Open the drop-down list, and click on the desired country and language, or click on the country in the map. The Date, Time, Currency, and Number formats change to reflect the default settings for the selected country.

Select a country from the drop-down list or from the map.

5. To change a specific format (for example, currency or time), click on the tab for that format, and use the drop-down lists to select your preferences. For more details, refer to the sections at the end of this chapter.

6. Click on the OK button. A dialog box appears, informing you that your changes won't be put into effect until you restart your computer.

7. Click on Yes to restart your computer or No to keep Windows running. If you click on No, the changes won't be activated till you restart Windows.

Each tab lets you change a set of formats.

Beyond Survival

Changing the Date Format

The Regional Settings Properties dialog box has four tabs for changing the date, time, currency, and number formats. You can change a format by clicking on its tab. The following steps explain how to change the date format. When changing the date format, you have to pick a format from a drop-down list, or type a format. The following table provides a quick overview of date formats. Use **M** for month, **d** for day, and **y** for year.

Type	Sample	To Display
d, y, M	**M/d/y**	Single digits with no leading zeros for single-digit days or months (for example, 2/5/96)
dd, yy, MM	**MM/dd/yy**	Single digits with leading zeros for single-digit days or months (for example, 02/05/96)
dd, yy, MMM	**dd, MMM, yy**	Three-letter abbreviation for the day, and month (for example, Tue, May, 1996)
dddd, yyyy, MMMM	**dddd, MMMM dd, yyyy**	Full name for the day, month and date, and year (for example, Tuesday, May 12, 1996)

You can mix and match the date formats in the table. For example, you can type **dd MMMM yyyy** to enter a date such as 25 February 1996. To change the date format, perform the following steps:

1. Double-click on the Regional Settings icon ▣ in the Control Panel.

2. Click on the Date tab. The date format options appear.

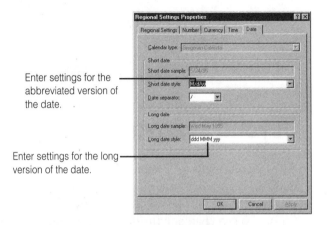

Enter settings for the abbreviated version of the date.

Enter settings for the long version of the date.

To see date format work, click on Apply button

3. Open the Short Date Style drop-down list; then click on the desired format, or double-click inside the text box and type the desired format (for example, **MM-DD-YY**). The Short date sample area shows today's date in the specified format.

4. Open the Date Separator drop-down list, and select the symbol you want to use to separate the month, day, and year (a dash or a forward slash).

Alt + ↓ to open drop-down list

5. Open the Long Date Style drop-down list; then click on the desired long date format, or double-click inside the text box and type your own format (for example, **MMMM, dd, yyyy**).

6. Click on the OK button.

Changing the Time Format

Depending on the country that's selected, the time may be set up on a 12- or 24-hour clock. To change the time format, here's what you do:

1. Display the Regional Settings Properties dialog box.

2. Click on the Time tab. The Time formats appear.

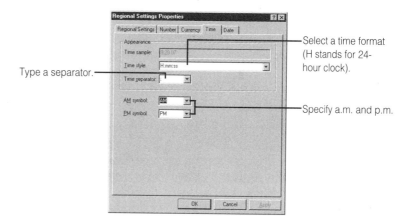

Type a separator.

Select a time format (H stands for 24-hour clock).

Specify a.m. and p.m.

3. Open the Time Style drop-down list, and then click on the desired time format. Uppercase H represents 24-hour (military) time. Lowercase h represents standard 12-hour time.

4. Click inside the Time Separator text box; type the character you want to appear between hours and minutes, and between minutes and seconds. If you type a period, for example, the time will appear as **2.40** instead of 2:40.

5. If you want something to appear after the time (such as **AM** or **PM**), type the desired entry in the AM Symbol or PM Symbol text box:

   12-Hour Format: Type **AM** (or **am** or **a.m.**) in the top text box and **PM** (or **pm** or **p.m.**) in the bottom text box.

   24-Hour Format: Type **PST** for Pacific Standard Time, or some other entry to designate the time zone.

6. Click on the OK button.

Changing the Currency Format

You can change the currency format to use a different currency symbol, control its position in relation to the number, specify how you want negative values displayed, and to control the number of digits that appear after a decimal point. To change the currency options, take the following steps:

1. Display the Regional Settings Properties dialog box.

2. Click on the Currency tab. The currency formats appear.

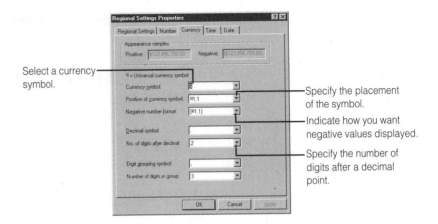

Select a currency symbol.

Specify the placement of the symbol.

Indicate how you want negative values displayed.

Specify the number of digits after a decimal point.

3. Click inside the Currency Symbol text box, and type the symbol you want to use to represent money.

4. To change the position of the symbol in relation to the value, open the Position of Currency Symbol drop-down list, and select the desired placement.

5. To display negative values in a different way, open the Negative Number Format drop-down list and select an option. (Accountants prefer displaying negative numbers in parentheses, for example.)

6. To specify a set number of digits to display to the right of a decimal point, No. of Digits After Decimal drop-down list, and select a number of digits.

7. Click on the OK button to return to the Regional dialog box.

Changing the Number Format

To format non-currency values, you can change the number format. This allows you to specify a character to mark the thousand's place and decimal place. It also allows you to specify the number of digits you want to appear after a decimal point. To change the Number format, here's what you do:

1. Display the Regional Settings Properties dialog box.

2. Click on the Number tab. The number formats appear.

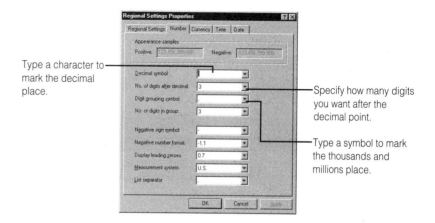

Type a character to mark the decimal place.

Specify how many digits you want after the decimal point.

Type a symbol to mark the thousands and millions place.

3. To change the character used to mark a decimal place, tab to the Decimal Symbol text box and type the desired character. For example, type a period.

4. To specify a set number of digits to display to the right of a decimal point, tab to the No. of Digits After Decimal text box, and type the number of digits.

5. To change the character used to mark the thousand's place, type the desired character in the Digit Grouping Symbol text box. For example, type a comma.

Right-click on option; click on What's this? to learn about it

6. Enter any other changes as desired. (Remember, if you have a question about a setting, click on the question mark in the upper-right corner of the dialog box, and then click on the setting's name. A help box will appear, explaining the option.)

7. Click on the OK button to return to the Regional dialog box.

Cheat Sheet

What Are System Settings?

- System settings tell Windows how to use the devices and resources on your computer.
- In most cases, you do not have to change system settings; Windows 95 manages most of your system resources automatically.
- If a device that's connected to your computer does not operate in Windows 95, you may have to change a setting for that device.
- Device settings can also help you optimize the performance of a device or use system resources more efficiently.

Accessing System Settings

1. Click on the Start button.
2. Move the mouse pointer over Settings; click on Control Panel.
3. Double-click on the System icon.

Optimizing Windows for a 2X, 3X, or 4X CD-ROM Drive

1. In the System Properties dialog box, click on the Performance tab.
2. Click on the File System button.
3. Click on the CD-ROM tab; under Settings, open the Optimize access pattern for the drop-down list, and click on the speed of your CD-ROM drive.
4. Click on the OK button, and then on Close.
5. Click on Yes to restart your computer.

Letting Windows Manage Virtual Memory

- Virtual memory is disk space that Windows uses as if it were RAM.
- Windows automatically manages the virtual memory most efficiently; it is best to allow Windows to continue doing so.
- If you want to increase or decrease the amount of virtual memory, display the System Properties dialog box, click on the Performance tab, and click on the Virtual Memory button.

45

Changing Your System Settings

Windows 95 prides itself on its ability to handle all the technology issues behind the scenes, freeing you to do your work. You may, however, have to intervene at times to help Windows acknowledge a particular device or help it resolve a conflict. In such a case, you can access the System Properties dialog box through the Windows Control Panel.

In this chapter, we'll look first at a couple of quick ways you can optimize the performance of your system: specifying the speed of your CD-ROM drive, and selecting the amount of disk space you want to use as memory (*virtual memory*). Then we'll take a look at some more advanced tools (which you should be able to avoid having to use).

Basic Survival

Optimizing CD-ROM Performance

When you installed Windows 95, the installation program recognized most of your devices—your sound card, CD-ROM drive, printer, modem, and so on. One thing it may have overlooked, however, is the speed of your CD-ROM drive. If you have a double-, triple-, or quad-speed CD-ROM drive (or faster), you may be able to optimize its performance in Windows by assigning it a bigger memory cache.

A *cache* (pronounced "cash") acts as a buffer area between Windows and your CD-ROM drive. The CD-ROM drive reads data off the disc into the cache; Windows then reads the information from the cache. The cache supplies a steady flow of information to Windows, so Windows doesn't have to wait for the CD-ROM drive. By increasing the cache size for a CD-ROM drive, you ensure that Windows has a steady flow of information to work with at one time. To change the cache size, take the following steps:

1. Click on the Start button.

2. Move the mouse pointer over Settings, and then click on Control Panel. The Windows Control Panel appears.

3. Double-click on the System icon 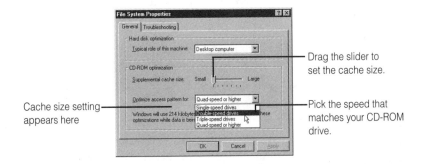. The System Properties dialog box appears.

4. Click on the Performance tab. This tab contains options for optimizing the performance of CD-ROM drives, graphics, and *virtual memory* (disk space used as if it were memory). (This tab may also offer suggestions on how you can optimize your system's performance.)

5. Click on the File System button. The CD-ROM optimization options appear.

6. Click on the CD-ROM tab; under Settings, open the Optimize Access Pattern For drop-down list, and click on the speed setting that matches the capabilities of your CD-ROM drive. (Check your CD-ROM drive documentation or look on the front of the drive.)

Cache size setting appears here

Drag the slider to set the cache size.

Pick the speed that matches your CD-ROM drive.

Try 726 cache for 4X CD-ROM drive

7. Drag the Supplemental Cache Size slider to set the cache size for the CD-ROM drive. If you use your CD-ROM drive a great deal, and your computer has 8MB or more of RAM, increase the cache size (to 576 for a 1X drive or 726 for a 4X drive). If you don't make frequent use of the CD-ROM drive, keep the slider at the low end, so more system memory will be available for other work.

8. Click on the OK button to return to the System Properties dialog box.

9. Click on the Close button to save your changes, or keep the dialog box open to enter additional changes later in this chapter. If you click on Close, a dialog box appears, informing you that your changes won't become effective till you restart your computer. (Click on Yes to restart or No to continue working.)

Letting Windows 95 Manage Virtual Memory

Windows can use disk space as memory (virtual memory). Windows creates a *swap file* on the disk, trading data back and forth between RAM and the swap file as you work. The extra memory allows you to run more programs (and more complex programs). The downside: because of all the swapping required, virtual memory is slower than RAM. If you need more memory, however, slow memory is better than no memory.

Unlike previous versions of Windows, Windows 95 does an excellent job of managing virtual memory for you. As long as you have some free disk space, Windows 95 can automatically adjust how much disk space it uses for virtual memory. If your software requires less memory, Windows uses less. If it requires more, Windows fetches it. In short, I strongly recommend that you allow Windows to control the virtual memory settings. To make sure Windows is on the job, take the following steps:

1. Click on the Start button.

2. Move the mouse pointer over Settings, and then click on Control Panel. The Windows Control Panel appears.

3. Double-click on the System icon 🖳. The System Properties dialog box appears.

4. Click on the Performance tab. This tab contains options for optimizing the performance of CD-ROM drives, graphics, and virtual memory (disk space used as memory).

Let Windows control the amount of virtual memory

5. Click on the Virtual Memory button. The Virtual Memory dialog box appears.

6. Make sure Let Windows Manage My Virtual Memory Settings is selected, so Windows will control your computer's virtual memory.

Click here to let Windows control virtual memory.

If you insist on controlling virtual memory, enter settings here.

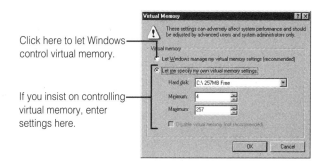

7. Click on the OK button to return to the System Properties dialog box.

8. Click on the Close button to save your changes, or keep the dialog box open to enter additional changes later in this chapter. If you click on Close, a dialog box appears, informing you that your changes won't become effective till you restart your computer. (Click on Yes to restart, or No to continue working.)

Beyond Survival

Using Device Manager to Check Hardware Settings

Device Manager contains a list of all the hardware devices installed on your system, including printers, disk drives, joysticks, and sound cards. If a device is giving you problems, or if you just received an updated *driver* for the device (a program that tells Windows how to use the device), you can use Device Manager to solve the problem or install the new driver. Here's what you do:

1. Click on the Start button.

2. Move the mouse pointer over Settings, and then click on Control Panel. The Windows Control Panel appears.

3. Double-click on the System icon 🖥. The System Properties dialog box appears.

4. Click on the Device Manager tab. Device Manager displays a tree of all the hardware installed on your computer.

5. To check the settings of a device, click on the plus sign to the left of the device type, and then double-click on the name of the device. A dialog box appears, displaying general information about the device.

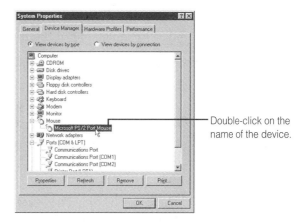

Double-click on the name of the device.

6. To change the driver for a device (if you obtained a new driver from the manufacturer), click on the Driver tab, click on the Change Driver button, and then follow the trail of dialog boxes to complete the change.

7. To determine whether this device is using settings that conflict with those of another device, click on the Resources tab. The Resources page lists the card's settings; it also indicates whether they conflict with those of another device.

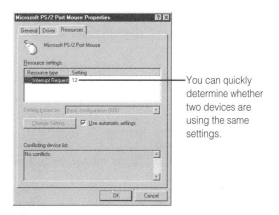

You can quickly determine whether two devices are using the same settings.

8. To change a setting, typically you have to make a physical change to the device itself first (with a sound card, for example, you might have to flip a jumper switch on the card). Refer to the device's documentation to determine how to change the setting. Then click on Use Automatic

Settings (to turn it off), and then use the Change Setting button under Resources to pick a setting that matches the setting of the device.

9. Click on the OK button to save any changes you may have entered.

Sorting Out Device Conflicts

As you'll see in Chapter 48, Windows 95 can help you set up a joystick, sound card, printer, scanner, CD-ROM drive, and other devices on your computer. You can usually avoid the complicated tasks of figuring out why a device you installed doesn't work or why it prevented another device from working.

There may be times, however, when two devices you installed conflict; they try to use the same settings, and one or both devices will not operate. In such a case, Device Manager can help you sort out the problem:

1. Click on the Start button.

2. Move the mouse pointer over Settings, and then click on Control Panel. The Windows Control Panel appears.

3. Double-click on the System icon ⊞ . The System Properties dialog box appears.

4. Click on the Device Manager tab. Device Manager displays a tree of all the hardware installed on your computer.

5. Click on Computer at the top of the tree, and then click on the Properties button. The Computer Properties dialog box appears, listing all the devices on your system organized by the settings they use. With this display, you can quickly see if two devices are trying to use the same settings.

6. Select one of the following options to check for conflicts:

Interrupt Request (IRQ) is a number that allows the device to request the computer's attention. If two devices are set up to use the same interrupt, they can demand system resources at the same time, causing one or both devices to operate incorrectly.

Direct Memory Access (DMA) is a memory channel that the device uses to communicate with your system's RAM. Again, if two devices are set up to use the same DMA, conflicts can occur that render one or both devices inoperable.

Input/Output (I/O) like IRQ and DMA is a number that specifies the input and output path the device will use. If two devices are set to use the same I/O, check the documentation for one of the devices to see whether it can be set to use a different I/O.

Memory specifies the memory addresses assigned to the device driver (the program that tells Windows how to use this device). Because Windows manages the device drivers, you should have little trouble with memory conflicts.

7. Click on the OK button when you're done.

8. Click on Close to save your changes.

Listing devices by their interrupt or DMA numbers can quickly show any hardware conflicts.

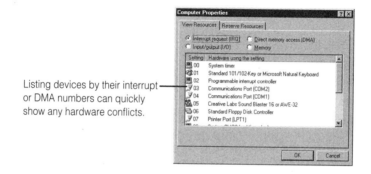

Cheat Sheet

Adding a Printer

1. Double-click on My Computer .
2. Double-click on Printers .
3. Double-click on Add Printer .
4. Click on the Next button.
5. Make sure Local Printer is selected, and then click on the Next button.
6. Click on the brand name of the printer in the Manufacturers list.
7. Click on the make and model of the printer in the Printers list.
8. Click on the Next button.
9. Click on the port into which you plugged the printer (usually LPT1), then click on the Next button.
10. To have this printer act as your full-time printer for all your Windows programs, click on Yes, and then click on the Next button.
11. Click on the Finish button.
12. If prompted to insert a disk, insert the disk, and click on the OK button.

Selecting a Default Printer

1. Double-click on My Computer .
2. Double-click on Printers .
3. Right-click on the icon for the printer you want to use in all your Windows programs, and click on Set As Default.

46

Setting Up and Selecting a Printer

Printer settings
= paper size,
print quality,
graphics
resolution

Before Windows came along, each program had its own printer driver (a file that tells the program how to communicate with the printer). For each program, you had to install a new printer driver and play with it till you got your printer working. With Windows, you install the printer driver only once. All Windows programs then use the Windows printer driver to control the printer. In this chapter, you'll learn how to install a printer driver in Windows, and how to change the settings for your printer.

Basic Survival

Adding a Printer

When you installed Windows, the installation program prompted you to select a printer. If you selected a printer, you can probably skip this section. If you did not select a printer, however (or if you obtained a new printer since installing Windows), you can perform the following steps to add a printer to Windows:

1. Click on the Start button.

2. Move the mouse pointer over Settings, and then click on Control Panel.

Use My
Computer and
double-click on
Printers

3. Double-click on the Printers icon 🖨. The Printers window appears, showing icons for all the printers installed on your computer.

4. Double-click on the Add Printer icon 🖨. The Add Printer Wizard appears; it will lead you through the process of installing a printer driver.

5. Click on the Next button. A dialog box appears, asking whether you want to install a local printer (connected directly to your system) or a network printer (which will be available to other computers on the network).

6. Make sure Local Printer is selected, and then click on the Next button. A dialog box appears, asking you to specify the manufacturer and model of your printer.

7. Do one of the following:

If your printer isn't listed, pick a model that's close

- Click on the brand name of the printer in the Manufacturers list; then click on the make and model of your printer in the Printers list.

- If the printer came with its own printer driver on a disk, click on the Have Disk button, insert the disk into drive A or B, select the drive from the Copy Manufacturer's Files From drop-down list, and click on OK.

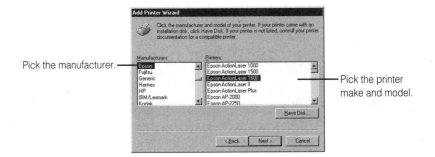

Pick the manufacturer.

Pick the printer make and model.

8. Click on the Next button. A list of printer ports appears. Most printers connect to the parallel printer port (LPT1). If in doubt, pick LPT1.

9. Click on the port into which you plugged the printer (usually LPT1), then click on the Next button. The Wizard asks whether you want to use this printer as the default printer for your Windows programs.

10. To have this printer act as your full-time printer for all your Windows programs, click on Yes, and then click on the Next button. If you select No, you'll have to select this printer in your program's printer setup in order to use it.

11. Click on the Finish button. If the files for the selected printer are on your hard disk, the Wizard installs the printer and adds an icon for it in the Printers window. If the files are not available, the Wizard prompts you to insert a Windows disk (or the disk on which the files for the printer are available).

12. If prompted to insert a disk, insert the disk, and click on the OK button.

If your printer did not appear on the list of printers, you have several options:

- Select a printer that is like the one you have. If (for example) an older model of your printer's brand is listed, select the older model. You may not be able to use the advanced features of the newer model.

- Select Generic/Text Only to print plain text. You won't be able to print fancy fonts or enhancements.

- Call the printer manufacturer or Microsoft Corporation; ask them to send you an updated Windows print driver for your printer.

Selecting a Default Printer

If you use two or more printers (say, a color and a black-and-white printer), you can select one to use as the default printer by doing the following:

1. Click on the Start button.

2. Move the mouse pointer over Settings, and then click on Control Panel.

3. Double-click on the Printers icon ⊞. The Printers window appears, showing icons for all the printers installed on your computer.

4. Right-click on the icon for the printer you want to use in all your Windows programs, and click on Set As Default. This printer will be used by most programs unless you specify in that program to use a different installed printer.

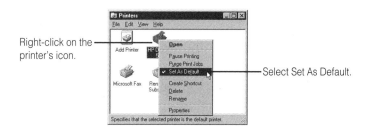

Right-click on the printer's icon.

Select Set As Default.

In Program, select File/Print Setup

Most programs contain a Print Setup option—usually on the File menu, or as a button in the dialog box that appears when you try to print a document. If you select this option, usually you get a dialog box that lets you select a specific printer for this work session. This is an easy way to select a printer without making it the default printer.

283

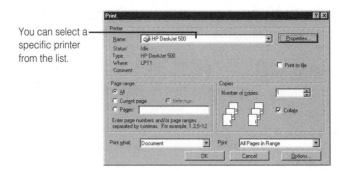

You can select a specific printer from the list.

Beyond Survival

Changing the Printer Settings

Most printers are initially set up to print on 8.5-by-11-inch paper, in portrait orientation, using a certain print quality. You can, however, change these settings if your printer is using a different setup, as explained in the following steps. As you work through the steps, please note that not all printers have the same settings. If you have a PostScript laser printer, for example, the Properties dialog box for your printer will have a PostScript tab. If you encounter an option not included in the steps, right-click on the option and click on What's This?, for information about the option.

To change your printer's settings, here's what you do:

1. Click on the Start button.

2. Move the mouse pointer over Settings, and then click on Control Panel.

3. Double-click on the Printers icon 🖥️. The Printers windows appears, showing icons for all the printers installed on your computer.

4. Click on the icon for the printer whose settings you want to change.

Right-click on printer icon; select Properties

5. Open the File menu and select Properties. The Properties dialog box for the selected printer appears. Each tab lets you control a different aspect of printing. Your dialog box may look different, depending on the type of printer you have.

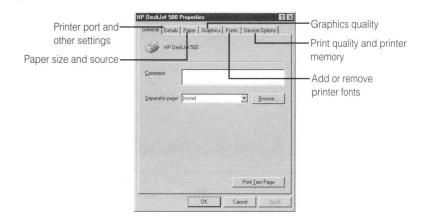

Printer port and other settings

Paper size and source

Graphics quality

Print quality and printer memory

Add or remove printer fonts

6. Click on the General tab and select any of the following options:

> Comment: If you share this printer with other users, you can type a comment here to let other users know of printer settings or problems.

> To insert a page between documents (so you know where a document begins and ends), select an option from the Separator Page drop-down list.

7. Click on the Details tab, and select any of the following options:

> If you have installed a printer and it doesn't respond, try selecting a different port from the Print to the Following Port drop-down list.

> You can choose a different printer driver for this printer from the Print Using the Following Driver drop-down list, but you're better off installing the new driver as explained earlier in this chapter.

> The Capture Printer Port and End Capture buttons allow you to map the printer port to a network drive (if your computer is on a network), and disconnect the printer from the network drive.

> The Timeout Settings specify how long Windows should wait before reporting a printer error (for example, you forgot to turn on the printer, or it ran out of paper). If you have trouble printing large documents, you might want to increase the time in the Transmission Retry text box to 90.

The Spool Settings button opens a dialog box that allows you to turn on print spooling (for faster printing) or print directly to the printer. Normally you should use print spooling unless you have trouble with a particular print job.

The Port Settings button lets you turn print spooling for DOS programs on or off.

8. Click on the Paper tab, and do any of the following:

In the Paper Size list, click on the desired paper or envelope size you want to print on.

Under Orientation, select Portrait to print text across the page, as in a personal or business letter, or click on Landscape to print text sideways on a page (so the page is wider than it is tall).

Open the Paper Source drop-down list, and click on the type of paper feed you intend to use. If (for example) you have a printer with two or more paper trays, you can select a specific tray.

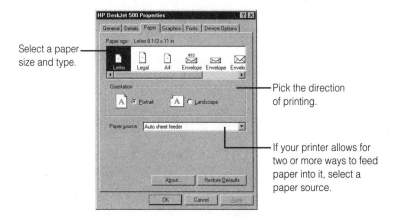

Select a paper size and type.

Pick the direction of printing.

If your printer allows for two or more ways to feed paper into it, select a paper source.

9. Click on the Graphics tab to change the following options for printing pictures (your Graphics options may differ greatly depending on the type of printer you have):

From the Resolution drop-down list, select the desired print quality for pictures. (Print quality is measured in dots per inch.

The more dots, the higher the quality, but it takes longer to print.) This does not affect text quality unless you choose to print text as graphics.

Under Dithering, select None for black-and-white graphics (no gray shading), Coarse if you selected a resolution of 300 dots per inch or more, Fine if you selected a resolution of 200 dots per inch or less, or Line Art if you want clearly defined lines to appear between shaded areas. Error Diffusion makes the picture look fuzzy.

Drag the Intensity slider to control the lightness or darkness of graphic images.

10. If you purchased a font cartridge for your printer, you can click on the Fonts tab to install the cartridge. To install soft fonts (which come on a disk), refer to Chapter 40. (The fonts tab may offer additional options for your printer.)

Don't change Memory unless you installed memory on your printer

11. Click on the Device options tab to change options such as the print quality, the amount of printer memory, and any other printer-specific settings. Enter your preferences.

12. Click on the OK button to save your changes.

Creating and Using a Printer Shortcut

Remember shortcuts from Chapter 12? Well, you can create a shortcut for your printer as well—and print documents without opening them. To create a printer shortcut, here's what you do:

1. Display the Printers window (double-click on the Printers icon either in My Computer or in the Control Panel).

2. Right-drag the icon for your printer onto a blank area on the Windows desktop. When you release the mouse button, a shortcut menu appears.

3. Click on Create Shortcut(s) Here. Windows creates a shortcut icon for the printer and places it on the desktop.

Right-click on printer shortcut to control printer

To print a document using the printer shortcut, the document's file type must be associated with a particular program. Refer to Chapter 37 to learn how to create file associations. You can then print document files simply by dragging the document file's icon from a My Computer or Windows Explorer window onto the printer icon. When you release the mouse button, Windows runs the associated program, opens the document, enters the Print command, and then closes the document.

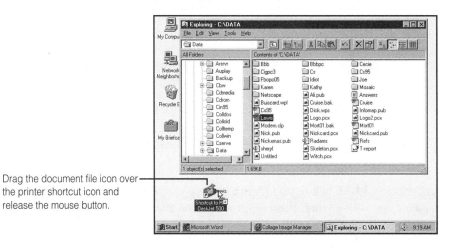

Drag the document file icon over the printer shortcut icon and release the mouse button.

Cheat Sheet

Viewing the Status of Print Jobs

- Windows is set up to print documents in the background, so you can continue with other tasks while your documents are being printed.
- Print jobs are stored in a *queue* (waiting line) as they are printing.
- You can view the print queue, rearrange documents, cancel print jobs, and resume printing.
- To view the print queue, double-click on My Computer, double-click on Printers, and then double-click on the icon for your printer.
- To quickly view the print queue, double-click on the printer icon next to the time on the right side of the Taskbar.

Pausing and Resuming a Print Job

1. To pause printing, double-click on the icon for your printer, open the Printer menu, and click on Pause Printing.
2. To resume printing, open the Printer menu and click on Pause Printing again.

Cancelling Printing

- To cancel the printing of a single document, click on it, open the Document menu, and then select Cancel Printing.
- To cancel the printing of several documents, Ctrl+click on each document you do not want to print, open the Document menu, and then select Cancel Printing.
- To stop printing entirely, open the Printer menu and select Purge Print Jobs.

47

Using the Windows Print Manager

Windows allows you to print documents (from Windows programs) in the background while you are working in other programs. Windows does this by printing the documents to a temporary file on your hard disk, and then *spooling* the documents to your printer. When you print a document from a Windows program, windows stores the document in a *queue* (a waiting line), and then feeds the document to the printer. In this chapter, you'll learn how to view the names of the documents waiting in the queue, and how to pause, resume, or cancel your print jobs.

Basic Survival

Turning Background Printing On or Off

Chances are good your printer is already set up to print documents in the background. Whenever you select the File/Print command in a Windows program, the file is sent to the queue and then spooled to your printer. If background printing is not turned on, the program sends the document directly to the printer; you have to wait until the program is done before you can do anything else or use other programs.

Normally you'll want to keep background printing on, so you can perform other tasks while waiting for the printer to finish up. If you have a slower computer, however, and you want to get the printing out of the way before you do anything else, you can turn off background printing. You might also try turning it off if your printer has trouble handling background printing.

Take the following steps to see whether background printing is on, and to turn it on or off:

1. Double-click on My Computer ▣.

2. Double-click on the Printers icon ▣.

3. Right-click on the icon for your printer, and select Properties.

4. Click on the Details tab, and then click on the Spool Settings button. The Spool Settings dialog box appears.

If this option is selected, you can print documents in the background.

With this option selected, you have to wait for the printing to finish before you can work.

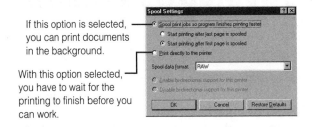

Low on memory? Choose Print Directly to Printer

5. Do one of the following to turn background printing on or off:

To turn on background printing, make sure Spool Print Jobs So Program Finishes Printing Faster is selected.

To turn background printing off (usually if your system has little memory), click on Print Directly to the Printer.

6. If you turned on background printing, you can select one of the following options to specify when you want the actual printing to start:

Start Printing After First Page Is Spooled waits till all pages are in the print queue before it starts sending pages to the printer.

Start Printing After Last Page Is Spooled starts sending the document to the printer as soon as the first page is in the print queue.

7. Click on the OK button to save your change and return to the printer Properties dialog box.

8. Click on the OK button to exit the printer Properties dialog box.

Pausing and Resuming Printing

Double-click on printer icon near the time in Taskbar

If your printer is set up to print documents in the background, they are added to a queue as you print them. If you look at the right side of the Taskbar, near the time, you'll see a tiny printer icon; double-click on it to view the queue (or you can double-click on your printer icon). Once the queue window is displayed, you can use it to pause, resume, cancel, or rearrange documents in the print queue. The following steps explain how to display the print queue and pause a print job:

1. Double-click on the printer icon next to the time in the Taskbar, or double-click on My Computer, double-click on the Printers icon, and double-click on the icon for your printer. The print queue window appears, showing the status of the documents in the print queue.

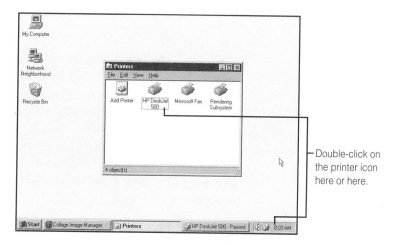

Double-click on the printer icon here or here.

2. Take one of the following steps to pause the printing of one or more documents in the queue:

    To pause all printing, open the Printer menu and click on Pause Printing.

    To pause the printing of a single document, click on it, open the Document menu, and select Pause Printing.

    To pause the printing of several documents, Ctrl+click on each document you want to pause, then open the Document menu and select Pause Printing.

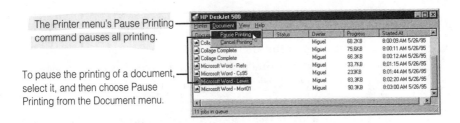

The Printer menu's Pause Printing command pauses all printing.

To pause the printing of a document, select it, and then choose Pause Printing from the Document menu.

3. To resume printing, take one of the following steps:

If you paused all printing, open the Printer menu and select Pause Printing.

If you paused the printing of one or more documents, select the paused documents, open the Document menu, and select Pause Printing.

You can use the Pause/Resume feature to print when you're at lunch or taking a break. Before you start printing, open the print queue window for your printer (open My Computer, double-click on Printers, and then double-click on your printer icon). Open the Printer menu and select Pause Printing. Now print your documents as you normally would. As you print, the documents are added to the print queue, but are not printed. Before you leave for lunch, return to the print queue window, open the Printer menu, and click on Pause Printing. (One more thing before you leave: make sure your printer has plenty of paper.)

Beyond Survival

Cancelling a Print Job

Sometimes you may start printing a document by mistake, or something gets fouled up at the printer and it starts printing strange text and symbols. If that happens, you'll want to cancel the print job and start over. Here's how you do it:

1. Double-click on the printer icon next to the time in the Taskbar, or double-click on My Computer, double-click on the Printers icon, and double-click on the icon for your printer. The print queue window appears, showing the status of the documents in the print queue.

2. Take one of the following steps to cancel the printing of one or more documents in the queue:

To cancel all printing, open the Printer menu and click on Purge Print Jobs. All documents are removed from the print queue, and printing is stopped.

To cancel the printing of a single document, click on it, open the Document menu, and select Cancel Printing.

To pause the printing of several documents, Ctrl+click on each document you want to cancel, then open the Document menu and select Cancel Printing.

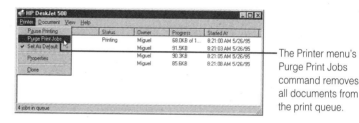

The Printer menu's Purge Print Jobs command removes all documents from the print queue.

Changing the Order of Print Jobs

If you print more than one document, the documents are added to the print queue in the order in which they were printed. You can rearrange the items in the list to print them in a different order. Here's what you do:

1. Double-click on the printer icon next to the time in the Taskbar, or double-click on My Computer, double-click on the Printers icon, and then double-click on the icon for your printer. The print queue window appears, showing the status of the documents in the print queue.

Pause before rearranging queue

2. Move the mouse pointer over the document whose position you want to change.

3. Hold down the mouse button while dragging the document to its new position in the queue.

4. Release the mouse button.

Drag a document up to print it sooner, or down to print it later.

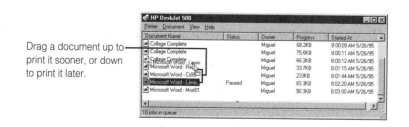

295

Cheat Sheet

Setting Up a New Piece of Hardware

1. Exit all running programs.
2. Click on the Start button.
3. Move the mouse pointer over Settings, and then click on Control Panel.
4. Double-click on the Add New Hardware icon.
5. Click on the Next button.
6. Make sure Yes (Recommended) is selected, and then click on the Next button.
7. Click on the Next button to have the Wizard search for new hardware.
8. Wait until the detection process is complete (several minutes), and then click on the Finish button.

Calibrating Your Joystick

1. Click on the Start button.
2. Move the mouse pointer over Settings, and then click on Control Panel.
3. Double-click on the Joystick icon.
4. Open the Joystick Selection drop-down list, and click on the type of joystick you have.
5. Click on the Calibrate button.
6. Move the joystick and press the buttons as instructed on the screen.
7. Click on the Finish button.
8. Click on OK to save your changes.

48

Installing New Hardware (Plug-and-Play)

When you installed Windows 95, the setup program searched for hardware devices (sound card, modem, printer, and so on) on your computer, and set up these devices to work in Windows. If you add a sound card, game card, or other device to your system, however, you must run through the hardware setup again.

Fortunately, Windows 95 offers a Wizard that can lead you through the process of installing a new device, and help you resolve any problems that might occur. In this chapter, you'll learn how to run the Add New Hardware Wizard, troubleshoot problems, and even calibrate your joystick.

Basic Survival

Understanding Plug-and-Play Hardware

Windows 95 is currently ushering in the era of *plug-and-play* hardware. With plug-and-play devices, you no longer have to worry about setting up the device to get along with all your other devices. You simply turn off the computer, connect the device, turn on your computer, and you're ready to roll.

With Windows 95, will installing devices be this easy for you? That depends. In order for plug-and-play to work, your system (and the device you want to install) must meet the following requirements:

- Your computer must have PCI or VLB expansion slots (or some other type of expansion slot that is capable of handling plug-and-play expansion boards).

- Your computer must have a BIOS (a set of instructions that tells the various computer components how to work together) that supports plug-and-play.

- Your operating system must support plug-and-play standards (Windows 95 is your operating system in this case; it does).

To plug and play, you need the right hardware

- The device you are connecting to your computer must be plug-and-play-compatible.

The good news is that Windows provides help for installing devices that are not plug-and-play-compatible. You can run the Add New Hardware Wizard, and have it lead you through the process of installing the devices. If you have two devices that won't work together, the Wizard will help you track down and correct the problem.

Letting the Hardware Wizard Set Up the Device

After you connect a new piece of equipment to your computer, you can have the Add New Hardware Wizard search for it and set it up to work in Windows 95. The Wizard takes care of all the complicated settings (like interrupts and I/O settings) to prevent the new device from interfering with the operation of any existing devices. To run the Add New Hardware Wizard, take the following steps:

1. Exit all running programs. This prevents you from losing any data in case Windows locks up during the process.

2. Click on the Start button.

3. Move the mouse pointer over Settings, and then click on Control Panel. The Control Panel window appears.

4. Double-click on the Add New Hardware icon 🖳 . The Add New Hardware Wizard appears, informing you about what the Wizard will do.

5. Click on the Next button. Wizard asks whether you want it to search for new hardware on your system.

Wizard sniffs out new hardware for you

6. Make sure Yes (Recommended) is selected, and then click on the Next button. If you know the type of hardware you want to install, you can select No; then you can skip ahead to the next section and select the item yourself (rather than having the Wizard search for it).

7. Click on the Next button to have the Wizard search for new hardware. Wizard searches your computer for any new hardware that's installed. This takes a long time. Don't panic.

8. Wait until the detection process is complete (several minutes), and then click on the Finish button. The Wizard installs the new device. If the device conflicts with another device in your system, Windows displays

a dialog box that informs you of the conflict; skip ahead to the section called "Troubleshooting Device Conflicts" to figure out what to do.

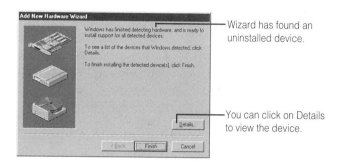

Wizard has found an uninstalled device.

You can click on Details to view the device.

9. Shut down the computer, turn off the power, and restart.

Calibrating Your Joystick

If you've ever played any computer games using a joystick, you know that you can't use the joystick effectively until you calibrate it. Calibrating ensures that the joystick moves objects on-screen according to the way you move the joystick. Windows 95 comes with its own joystick calibrator. To use it, take the following steps:

1. Click on the Start button.

2. Move the mouse pointer over Settings, and then click on Control Panel.

3. Double-click on the Joystick icon ⬚. The Joystick Properties dialog box appears.

4. Open the Joystick Selection drop-down list, and click on the type of joystick you have.

5. Click on the Calibrate button. The Joystick Calibration dialog box appears.

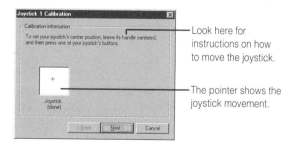

Look here for instructions on how to move the joystick.

The pointer shows the joystick movement.

6. Keep the joystick in the center position; click one of its buttons. (This sets the center position.)

7. Move the joystick around in several full circles, and then click one of its buttons. (This sets the joystick's full range of motion.)

8. Return the joystick to the center position, and click one of its buttons to confirm the center position.

9. Click on the Finish button.

10. Click on OK to save your changes.

Beyond Survival

Picking a Device to Install Yourself

If you don't like waiting for the Add New Hardware Wizard to search your system for new hardware, you can pick the device you want to install, and then let the Wizard complete the installation. Here's what you do:

1. Exit all running programs. This prevents you from losing any data in case Windows locks up during the process.

2. Click on the Start button.

3. Move the mouse pointer over Settings, and then click on Control Panel. The Control Panel window appears.

4. Double-click on the Add New Hardware icon . The Add New Hardware Wizard appears, informing you about what the Wizard will do.

5. Click on the Next button. Wizard asks if you want it to search for new hardware on your system.

6. Make sure No is selected, and then click on the Next button. The Wizard displays a list of devices you can install.

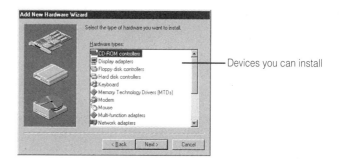

Devices you can install

7. Click on the type of device you want to install, and then click on the Next button. The Wizard displays a list of manufacturers and devices for which Windows 95 has drivers (programs that tell Windows 95 how to communicate with the device).

8. Take one of the following steps to select a driver:

In the Manufacturers list, click on the manufacturer of the device, and then click on the model of the device in the Models list.

If the device came with its own Windows 95 driver on a disk, insert the disk in the drive, and click on the Have Disk button; open the Copy Manufacturer's Files From drop-down list, click on the drive letter, and then click on OK.

9. Click on the Next button. Wizard informs you that it will install the driver using the factory default settings (the settings on the card, unless you flipped switches or changed jumpers).

10. Click on the Next button. If the driver for this device is not available, Wizard prompts you to insert one of the Windows installation disks (or the manufacturer's disk) into one of the drives.

11. Insert the required disk, and click on the OK button. Wizard copies the necessary files from the disk to the Windows directory, and indicates that it is about to finish.

Shut down Windows/Turn off computer/ Restart

12. Click on the Finish button. A dialog box appears, indicating that the changes won't be entered till you restart your computer.

13. Shut down the computer, turn off the power, and restart.

301

Understanding Device Conflicts

So, what are all these device conflicts I'm talking about? Each circuit board (called an *expansion board* or *card*) has a set of tiny switches or *jumpers* (posts over which you can slide connectors to turn the jumpers on or off). These switches control various settings that tell the computer where it can find the device, and which system resources the device is allowed to use. If two devices use the same settings, they are said to *conflict*. If your sound card and mouse use the same settings, for example, your mouse may lock up when the sound card attempts to emit a sound.

If two devices conflict, you have to make two changes. First, you must change the settings on one of the cards (using the switches or jumpers). Then you must change the settings for the card in Windows 95, so the settings match those of the card. Here are the settings you'll have to deal with:

IRQ stands for *interrupt request* and is a number that enables a device to demand attention from the central processing unit. If two devices have the same IRQ, they demand attention at the same time, confusing the CPU.

DMA Channel is a path to your computer's RAM. Most computers have eight DMA channels. If two devices have the same DMA channel, usually only one device gains access to RAM. The other device simply won't work.

I/O Port Address is a designation that allows a device to take in and put out information at a certain location. As with IRQs and DMAs, if two devices use the same I/O (input/output) setting, problems occur.

Conflicts occur when two devices use the same settings

The Add New Hardware Wizard can't help you set the switches on the card; you have to get inside the computer and flip the switches (or set the jumpers) yourself. The Wizard can enter the card's settings in Windows, however, so the device will not conflict with another device. The Wizard can also help you determine which settings to use on the card itself.

Troubleshooting Device Conflicts

If you install a device that conflicts with another device on your computer, Wizard displays a button called Start Conflict Troubleshooter. If you click on this button, a Help window appears that can help you track down and resolve the conflict.

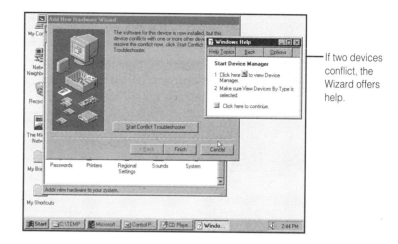

If two devices conflict, the Wizard offers help.

The Help window you see informs you of the conflict and provides a button for running the Conflict Troubleshooter (which is actually the Device Manager discussed briefly in Chapter 45). Click on the button next to Start the Hardware Conflict Troubleshooter, and then click on the button for the Device Manager. Carefully read the instructions in each Help window, and continue to click on buttons as you go through the process of tracking down the problem.

If you don't have the Help windows on your screen, take the following steps to use Device Manager to track down the conflict:

1. If the Add New Hardware Wizard is still displayed, click on the Finish button to complete the installation of the device (even though there's a conflict).

2. Click on the Start button, point to Settings, and click on Control Panel.

3. Double-click on the System icon. The System Properties dialog box appears.

4. Click on the Device Manager tab. A list of devices installed on your computer appears.

5. Click on the plus sign to the left of the type of device that's causing the conflict; you will see a display that names all devices of that type.

6. If the device you installed is listed twice (and you have only one in your computer), click on the second occurrence of the device, and then click on the Remove button.

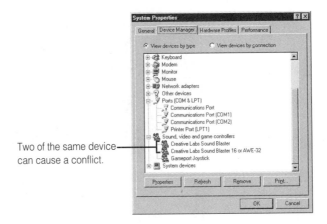

Two of the same device can cause a conflict.

7. If the device is listed only once, double-click on it. The Properties dialog box for the selected device appears.

8. Under Device Usage, make sure Original Configuration (Current) has a check mark next to it. This tells Windows to enable the device.

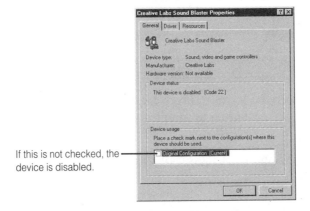

If this is not checked, the device is disabled.

9. Click on the Resources tab to find out whether this device is still conflicting with another device.

10. Look at the Conflicting Device List at the bottom of the dialog box to determine which settings are causing conflicts.

11. If any conflicts are listed, open the Setting Based On drop-down list, and click on a different configuration.

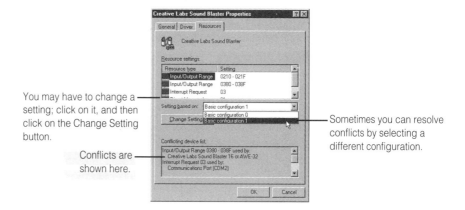

You may have to change a setting; click on it, and then click on the Change Setting button.

Conflicts are shown here.

Sometimes you can resolve conflicts by selecting a different configuration.

12. If there is still a conflict, click on the setting that is causing the conflict, and then click on the Change Setting button. Use the dialog box that appears to change the setting to one that is not in use. Click on the OK button.

(Be sure to write down the settings you entered; you'll probably have to change to those on the expansion card as well.)

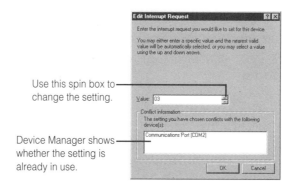

Use this spin box to change the setting.

Device Manager shows whether the setting is already in use.

13. Click on the OK button to save your changes.

If you resolved the conflict by removing a duplicate driver or by turning on Original Configuration (Current), chances are good that you're done. If you changed an IRQ, I/O, or DMA setting, however, you'll probably have to shut your computer off, remove the expansion card, and set the jumpers to match the settings you changed. Refer to the documentation that came with the device to determine which jumper positions to use for each setting.

Cheat Sheet

Changing the Accessibility Properties

1. Click on the Start button.
2. Move the mouse pointer over Settings, and then click on Control Panel.
3. Double-click on the Accessibility Options icon ![accessibility icon].
4. Enter your preferences.
5. Click on the OK button.

Using Special Keyboard Features

1. Click on the Keyboard tab in the Accessibility Properties dialog box.
2. To make it so that you don't have to hold down Ctrl, Alt, or Shift when pressing a key combination, click on Use StickyKeys.
3. To have Windows ignore errant keypresses, click on Use FilterKeys.
4. If you want to hear a tone when you press a key that toggles on or off (like CapsLock and NumLock), click on Use ToggleKeys.
5. To have programs display more keyboard help than usual, click on Show Extra Keyboard Help in Programs.
6. Click on the OK button.

Displaying Sounds On-Screen

1. Click on the Sound tab in the Accessibility Properties dialog box.
2. To make the screen (or a portion of it) flash to display a sound warning, click on Use SoundSentry.
3. To have programs display captions for the sounds they play, click on Use ShowSounds.
4. Click on the OK button.

Using Alternative Input Devices

1. Turn off the computer, and connect the alternative device.
2. In the Accessibility Properties dialog box, click on the General tab.
3. Click on Support SerialKey Devices to turn it on.
4. Click on the Settings button, choose the serial port and communications speed of the device, and click on OK.
5. Click on the OK button.

49

Configuring Windows for Users with *Special Needs*

If your vision or hearing is impaired, or if you have trouble using the keyboard or mouse, Windows 95 offers several features that can help. For example, if you have trouble seeing the display, you can turn on a special high-contrast option. If you have trouble hearing the warning sounds that Windows makes, you can have the sounds "displayed" on-screen. In addition, Windows allows you to set up your keyboard and mouse so they are more responsive to your movement, and install special input devices. In this chapter, you'll learn how to turn on the various accessibility options.

Basic Survival

Making Your Keyboard More Manageable

Whether you have trouble pressing keys, or you're still rusty on the keyboard, Windows provides features that can make your keyboard more forgiving and more responsive to your needs. To turn any of these special keyboard features on, take the following steps:

1. Click on the Start button.

2. Move the mouse pointer over Settings, and then click on Control Panel.

3. Double-click on the Accessibility Options icon 📇. The Accessibility Properties dialog box appears with the Keyboard tab selected.

4. If you have trouble holding down one key while pressing another, click on Use StickyKeys. With this feature on, you can press and release the Ctrl, Alt, or Shift key and then press the second key of the combination; you don't have to hold down the Ctrl, Alt, or Shift key.

5. If you commonly hit two keys when you intended to press only one, or if you hold keys down too long causing them to repeat, click on Use FilterKeys.

6. If you want to hear a tone when you press a key that toggles on or off (like CapsLock and NumLock), click on Use ToggleKeys.

Click on Apply to leave dialog box open and enter your changes

7. To have programs display more keyboard help than usual, click on Show Extra Keyboard Help in Programs. (Some Windows programs support this feature, some don't.)

8. Click on the OK button to save your changes, or leave the dialog box on-screen and proceed to the next section to make additional changes.

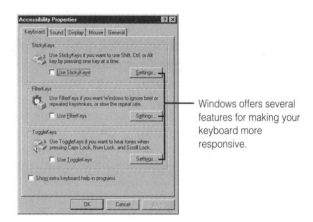

Windows offers several features for making your keyboard more responsive.

Seeing Sounds

Windows likes to make sounds to warn you or ask for your confirmation. If your hearing is impaired, or you like to crank up Pearl Jam tunes while you work, you can have Windows display messages whenever it emits a system sound. Here's what you do:

1. Click on the Start button.

2. Move the mouse pointer over Settings, and then click on Control Panel.

3. Double-click on the Accessibility Options icon 🖳.

4. Click on the Sound tab.

SoundSentry flashes screen in warning

5. To make the screen, border, or text flash whenever Windows emits a sound warning, click on Use SoundSentry. (You can click on the Settings button to select whether you want Windows to flash the whole screen, the border, or the text. Then click on the OK button.)

6. To have programs display captions for the sounds they play, click on Use ShowSounds.

7. Click on the OK button to save your settings, or leave the dialog box on-screen and go to the next section to enter additional preferences.

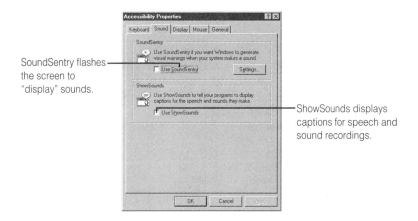

SoundSentry flashes the screen to "display" sounds.

ShowSounds displays captions for speech and sound recordings.

Increasing the Display Contrast

Do you have trouble reading the small print? Then try turning on the high-contrast display. With high-contrast, you can display large black text on a white background, so you can read your screen from a block away. Take the following steps:

1. Click on the Start button.

2. Move the mouse pointer over Settings, and then click on Control Panel.

3. Double-click on the Accessibility Options icon [icon].

4. Click on the Display tab.

5. Click on Use High Contrast to turn on the high-contrast display.

6. To customize the high-contrast display, click on the Settings button, and choose any of the following:

> **Use Shortcut** lets you turn high contrast on or off quickly by pressing the left Alt key, the left Shift key, and the Print Screen key at the same time.

> **White On Black** displays white text on a black background, and is somewhat difficult to read.

See Chapter 40 to increase/decrease screen text size

Black On White displays large black text on a white background, making it very easy to read.

Custom lets you set up your own background and foreground colors.

7. Click on the OK button.

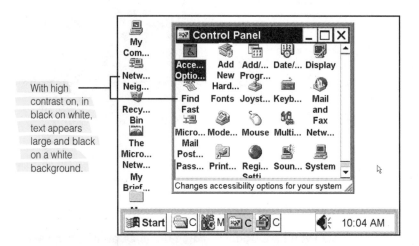

With high contrast on, in black on white, text appears large and black on a white background.

Beyond Survival

Using the Numeric Keypad to Move the Mouse Pointer

If you don't have a mouse or trackball, or if you have trouble using one, you can set up your numeric keypad to move the mouse pointer. Here's what you do:

1. Click on the Start button.

2. Move the mouse pointer over Settings, and then click on Control Panel.

3. Double-click on the Accessibility Options icon.

4. Click on the Mouse tab.

5. Click on Use MouseKeys to use the numeric keypad to move the mouse.

6. Click on the Settings button, and use the dialog box that appears to enter any of the following preferences:

Keyboard Shortcut lets you quickly turn MouseKeys on or off by pressing the key combination Left Alt+Left Shift+NumLock.

Pointer Speed drag the sliders to set the top speed of the mouse pointer and its acceleration (when you hold down one of the numeric keypad keys). By default, you can hold down the Ctrl key to speed up the mouse pointer or Shift to slow it down.

Use MouseKeys When NumLock Is lets you specify when you want the numeric keypad to move the mouse pointer: when NumLock is on or off.

Show MouseKeys Status On Screen tells Windows to display a mouse icon near the time in the Taskbar, whenever MouseKeys is on.

No trackball on your notebook PC? Turn on MouseKeys

7. Click on the OK button.

8. Click on the OK button to save your changes, or leave the Accessibility Properties dialog box on-screen and proceed to the next section.

Setting Up an Alternative Input Device

If you can't use a keyboard or mouse, and you have an alternative (or *augmentative*) input device connected to one of your computer's serial ports (a COM port), you can set up Windows to recognize this device. Take the following steps:

1. With the computer off, make sure that the alternative device is connected to one of the COM ports at the back of your computer.

2. Turn on your computer, wait for Windows to start, and then click on the Start button.

3. Move the mouse pointer over Settings, and then click on Control Panel.

4. Double-click on the Accessibility Options icon 🦽.

5. Click on the General tab. This displays preferences for automatically turning off Accessibility options and for installing an alternative device.

6. Click on Support SerialKey Devices to turn it on.

7. Click on the Settings button. A dialog box appears, prompting you to select a serial (COM) port and specify the speed of the device.

8. Open the Serial Port drop-down list, and click on the communications (COM) port into which you plugged the device.

9. Open the Baud Rate drop-down list, and click on the highest speed at which the device can send and receive signals. (Check the documentation that came with the device to find out.)

Pick a serial port. 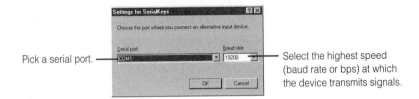 Select the highest speed (baud rate or bps) at which the device transmits signals.

10. Click on the OK button to save the COM port and baud rate settings. You return to the Accessibility Properties dialog box.

11. Click on the OK button to put your changes into effect.

PART
6

Maintaining Your Computer

Windows 95 comes with a complete suite of computer maintenance tools that can help you back up and restore your files, wring more storage space out of your hard disk, improve your hard drive's performance, and even fix damaged disks. In this section, you'll learn how to perform all the following tasks:

Cheat Sheet

Starting Microsoft Backup

1. Click on the Start button.

2. Move the mouse over Programs, and then over Accessories.

3. Move the mouse over System Tools, and then click on Backup.

4. Read the screen message, and then click on the OK button.

5. Read the next screen message, and then click on the OK button.

Backing Up All Files on a Drive

1. Start Backup, and then click inside the check box next to the icon for the drive you want to back up.

2. Click on the Next Step button.

3. Click on the icon for the floppy or tape drive you want to use to store the backup files.

4. Click on the Start Backup button.

5. Follow the on-screen instructions.

Click on this check box to back up all the folders and files on drive C.

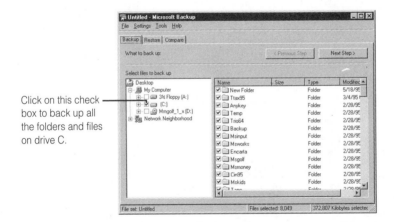

Backing Up Your Files

50

Most computer users know they should back up all the files on a hard disk, just in case the computer crashes and destroys the original files. Few users take the time to back up their files, however—until the computer does crash, and they realize how much more time they're going to spend re-creating their data files and reinstalling their programs.

To avoid deep feelings of regret for not having backed up, you should back up your computer files on a regular basis. In this chapter, you'll see just how easy Windows 95 has made it to back up the files on your computer to floppy disks, to a tape backup drive, or to another hard drive on your computer.

Basic Survival

Starting Microsoft Backup

The most difficult part of using the Windows Backup program is weaving through the menus to start it. Here's what you do:

1. Click on the Start button.

2. Move the mouse over Programs, and then over Accessories. The Accessories submenu opens.

3. Move the mouse over System Tools, and then click on Backup. The Welcome to Microsoft Backup dialog box appears, informing you that the backup operation takes three simple steps.

4. Read the screen message, click on Don't Show This Again (so it won't come up next time), and then click on the OK button. A dialog box appears, indicating that Backup created a file set for backing up all your system files (you'll learn about file sets later in this chapter).

5. Read the screen message, click on Don't Show This Again, and click on the OK button. The Backup screen appears, allowing you to start backing up files.

Create a shortcut on the desktop for Backup

Backing Up All Folders and Files

You should have at least one complete backup of every file on your computer, including the root directory of drive C, the DOS directory, your WINDOWS directory, all your programs, and all the data files you created. To back up everything on a hard disk drive, take the following steps:

1. Start Backup as explained in the previous section.

2. Click on the check box next to the drive you want to back up. A dialog box appears, showing you that Backup is selecting files; then, a check mark appears next to the drive icon.

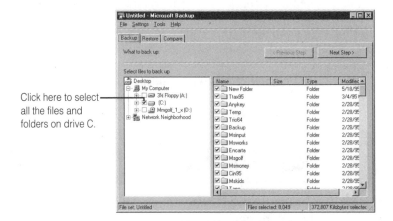

Click here to select all the files and folders on drive C.

3. Click on the Next Step button. Backup displays a dialog box that asks which drive you want to back up to. You can select a floppy disk drive, a tape backup drive (if you have one), another hard disk drive, or a network drive (if your computer is on a network).

4. Click on the icon for the drive you want to use to store the backup files.

5. If you're backing up to a floppy drive or a tape backup unit, make sure you have a disk or tape in the drive.

6. Click on the Start Backup button. A dialog box appears, prompting you to type a name for the backup set. A record of the backup will be stored under this name, allowing you to restore files quickly later.

7. Type a name for the backup set, and then click on the OK button. Backup starts backing up the files, and displays messages telling you what to do. If (for example) you are backing up to floppy disks, Backup informs you that you must insert a disk into the drive.

Microsoft Backup leads you through the backup operation.

8. Follow the on-screen instructions until the operation is complete.

Backing Up Selected Folders and Files

In the previous section, you learned how to back up all the folders and files on your hard drive. Backing up all your files can, however, take a tremendous amount of time (and an enormous number of floppy disks), so you won't want to do that every day. But you will want to back up your data files (the files you create and edit) on a daily basis. Fortunately, Backup lets you back up selected folders and files. Here's what you do:

1. Start Backup as explained earlier.

2. Click on the plus sign next to the icon for the drive that contains the folders and files you want to back up. The tree expands to show the first layer of folders on the selected drive.

3. To back up an entire folder, click on the check box next to its icon. If you click on the check box next to a folder that has subfolders, all its subfolders and files are selected.

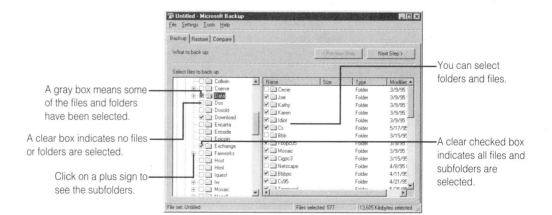

A gray box means some of the files and folders have been selected.

A clear box indicates no files or folders are selected.

Click on a plus sign to see the subfolders.

You can select folders and files.

A clear checked box indicates all files and subfolders are selected.

4. To back up only some files in a folder, click on its icon, and then click on the check box next to each file you want to back up.

5. Click on the Next Step button. Backup asks which drive you want to use to store the backup files.

6. Click on the icon for the drive you want to use to store the backup files. This can be a floppy drive, tape backup drive, network drive, or another hard disk drive.

7. If you're backing up to a floppy drive or a tape backup unit, make sure you have a disk or tape in the drive.

8. Click on the Start Backup button. A dialog box appears, prompting you to type a name for the backup set. A record of the backup will be stored under this name, allowing you to quickly restore files later.

9. Type a name for the backup set, and then click on the OK button. Backup starts the backup operation, and displays on-screen instructions to help you complete the process.

10. Follow the on-screen instructions until the backup operation is finished.

As you select files and folders to back up, keep the following guidelines in mind:

- If you click on a plus sign next to a drive or folder icon, the directory tree expands to show the next layer of folders under the selected drive or folder.

- If you click on a check box next to a drive or folder icon that is not expanded (you can't see its subfolders in the directory tree), all its subfolders and their files are selected.

- If you click on a check box next to a drive or folder that is expanded, none of the drive's or folder's subfolders are selected.

- An empty check box means *no* files or folders are selected. A white box with a check mark in it indicates *all* files and subfolders are selected. A gray box with a check mark shows that *some* files and subfolders are selected.

Another way to back up only selected groups of files is to exclude certain file groups from the backup. To exclude a group of files, open the Settings menu and click on File Filtering. To exclude files that were modified during a certain time period, click on Last Modified Date, and then use the From and To spin boxes to set the dates. To exclude certain file types (files whose names end in a specific extension), click on each file type you want to exclude in the File Types list, and then click on the Exclude button. Click on OK when you're done.

You can exclude groups of files by date.

Select each file group you want to exclude.

Press F5 to refresh list of files to back up

If you exclude one or two groups of files, but the backup tree doesn't change, don't panic. Simply open the File menu and click on Refresh to have Backup redetermine which files it should back up.

Beyond Survival

Setting the Backup Preferences

So far you have been performing backups with Backup's default settings. These settings work fine for most backup operations, but you might want to change the settings later for faster backups, or to avoid some warning messages. To change the Backup preferences, take the following steps:

1. Start Backup, as explained earlier.

2. Open the Settings menu and select Options. The Settings - Options dialog box appears, allowing you to enter settings for backing up, comparing, and restoring files.

3. Click on the Backup tab to change the backup options.

4. Select Quit Backup After Operation Is Finished if you want Backup to shut down automatically after performing the backup.

5. Under Type of Backup, choose the backup method you want to use:

Full backs up all the files in the folders you selected.

Incremental backs up only new files or files that have changed since the last backup operation. (You might want to perform a full backup at the beginning of the week, and incremental backups every day to save time while ensuring that you have timely backups.)

6. Under Advanced Options, turn on any or all of the following:

Verify Backup Data… compares the backup files to their original files to make sure your backup files are good.

Use Data Compression compresses files as it backs them up, so the files take up less storage space, and you require fewer disks or less tape for the backup. (If you turn this off, backups proceed faster, but you'll need more disks.)

Format When Needed on Tape Backups formats backup tapes if you try to back up to an unformatted tape.

Always Erase on Tape Backups erases any data on the backup tape if you attempt to back up to a tape that contains data. (If you turn this off, Backup tries to add the backup files to the tape without writing over existing backups.)

Always Erase on Floppy Disk Backups erases any data on the floppy disks you're using (if you try to back up to disks that contain data).

7. Click on the OK button to save your changes.

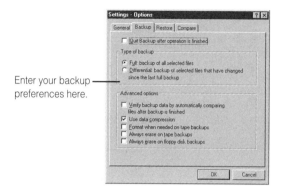

Enter your backup preferences here.

Backing Up Quickly with File Sets

Backing up an entire drive is easy. You simply select the drive you want to back up, and then click on the Next Step button. Say, however, that you want to back up all the data files you create—and they're stored in 14 different folders on your hard disk. In addition, you don't want to back up any existing backup files (files that end in .BAK or BK!). Performing a *selective backup* like this requires some time and patience; you'll have to select the folders individually. You don't want to have to select the folders each time you perform another backup. To help, Backup allows you to save your settings in a *file set*. When you want to back up the files again, you simply open the file set and start the backup. To create a file set, take the following steps:

1. Start Backup, as explained earlier.

2. Select the folders and files you want to back up.

3. Click on the Next Step button, and select a destination drive for the backup files.

4. Enter any other preferences, as desired.

5. Open the File menu and select Save As. The Save As dialog box appears, prompting you to name the file set.

6. Type a name for the file set; click on the Save button.

7. You can now complete the backup operation by clicking on Start Backup, or you can click on Previous Step if you want to use your new file set.

Now that you have a file set, you can use it to back up the same folders quickly, excluding the same file groups from the backup. To perform a backup with a file set, take the following steps:

1. Start Backup, as explained earlier in this chapter.

2. Open the File menu and select Open File Set. The Open dialog box appears, prompting you to pick the file set you want to use.

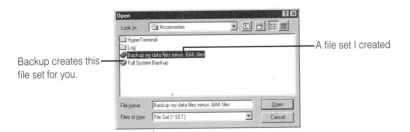

Backup creates this file set for you.

A file set I created

3. Click on the name of the file set you created, and then click on the Open button. Backup returns you to the main backup screen, and the file set selects all the files according to the settings you entered.

4. Click on the Next Step button. Backup prompts you to select the drive you want to use for the backup files.

5. Click on the drive you want to use as the backup destination, and then click on the Start Backup button. Backup starts backing up the files.

6. Follow the on-screen instructions to complete the backup operation.

To set preferences: open Settings, select Drag and Drop

Once you have file sets for all the backups you perform, you can back up files quickly by dragging the file set's icon from the Program Files/Accessories folder over the Backup icon (also in the Program Files/Accessories folder). If you back up your data files every day, consider dragging the Backup icon onto the Windows desktop to create a shortcut for it. Then Ctrl+drag the file set's icon you use for backing up your data files. You can then start the backup by dragging the file set shortcut over the Backup shortcut.

Cheat Sheet

Starting Backup to Restore Files

1. Click on the Start button.
2. Move the mouse over Programs, and then over Accessories.
3. Move the mouse over System Tools, and then click on Backup.
4. Click on the Restore tab.

Restoring All Files on the Backup Disks

1. Start Backup and click on the Restore tab.
2. Insert your backup tape (or the last floppy disk of the backup set) into the drive.
3. In the Restore From list, click on the drive that contains the backup disk or tape.
4. Click on the Next Step button.
5. Under Select Files From the Backup Set, click on the check box next to each folder in the list.
6. Click on the Start Restore button.
7. Follow the on-screen instructions.

Restoring Selected Folders and Files

1. Start Backup, and click on the Restore tab.
2. Insert your backup tape or the last floppy disk of the backup set into the drive.
3. In the Restore From list, click on the drive that contains the backup disk or tape.
4. Click on the Next Step button.
5. Under Select Files From the Backup Set, click on each plus sign to display all the folders and subfolders that were backed up.
6. To restore the contents of an entire folder, click on its check box.
7. To restore selected files in a folder, click on the folder under Select Files From the Backup Set, and then click on each file you want to restore in the Contents Of list.
8. Click on the Start Restore button.
9. Follow the on-screen instructions.

51

Restoring Files from Backups

It's inevitable. Sooner or later, your computer will crash, and you'll lose all your files... or you'll inadvertently wipe out a folder and all its contents (and then empty the Recycle Bin). When the inevitable occurs, it's time to dig out your backup disks (or tape), and restore the files you destroyed. This chapter will show you just what you need to do.

One word of warning: If you accidentally deleted a file or group of files, you probably don't need to restore them from backups. Instead, double-click on the Recycle Bin icon, and restore the files from the Bin. This gives you the most recent version of the file. Backup files might be older, and may not contain your latest changes.

See Chapter 7 to recover accidentally deleted files

Basic Survival

Restoring All Files From a Backup

If you wiped out all the files in a directory—or all the files on your hard disk—and you have a backup of all those files, you will want to restore *all* the files (not just a selected file or folder). In such a case, you can restore all the files you backed up and place them on your hard disk. If Backup finds any existing files whose names match the backup files, Backup replaces the files only if they are older than the files on the backup disks. (You can change this option, as explained later in this chapter.) To restore all files from a backup, take the following steps:

1. Click on the Start button.

2. Move the mouse over Programs, and then over Accessories.

3. Move the mouse over System Tools, and then click on Backup.

4. Click on the Restore tab.

5. Insert your backup tape or the last floppy disk of the backup set into the drive. (If you backed up to a network drive or another hard drive on your computer, you can skip this step.)

6. In the Restore From list, click on the drive that contains the backup disk or tape.

Click on the drive that contains the backup files.

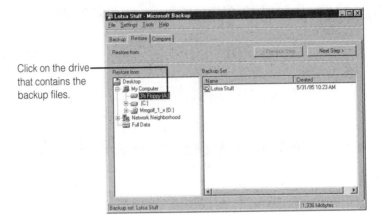

7. In the Backup Set list, if names exist for more than one backup set, click on the name of the backup set you want to restore. (You entered a backup set name when you performed the backup.)

8. Click on the Next Step button. A list appears, showing all the folders and files that are on the backup tape or disks.

9. Under Select Files From the Backup Set, if there is a minus sign next to the drive you want to restore, click on it to hide any folders under it. (Hiding the folders lets you select all files and folders on the drive simply by clicking on the check box next to the drive. If the folders are shown, you have to select each one.)

10. Click on the check box next to the drive whose files you want to restore. A check mark appears next to the drive letter, indicating that all files and folders on this drive are selected.

11. Click on the Start Restore button. A dialog box appears, telling you which disk (if any) to insert in the floppy drive. If you're restoring from another hard drive, network drive, or tape drive, Backup starts the restore operation.

12. Follow the on-screen instructions.

Restoring Selected Files

If you lose (or accidentally destroy) a folder or a couple of files, you won't want to restore all the files in a backup set. You'll want to restore only the files you lost. In such a case, you can perform a selective backup. Here's what you do:

1. Click on the Start button.

2. Move the mouse over Programs, and then over Accessories.

3. Move the mouse over System Tools, and then click on Backup.

4. Click on the Restore tab.

5. Insert your backup tape (or the last floppy disk of the backup set) into the drive. (If you backed up to a network drive or another hard drive on your computer, you can skip this step.)

6. In the Restore From list, click on the drive that contains the backup disk or tape.

7. If the Backup Set list shows names for more than one backup set, click on the name of the backup set you want to restore. (You entered a backup set name when you performed the backup.)

8. Click on the Next Step button. A list appears, showing all the folders and files that are on the backup tape or disks.

9. Under Select Files From the Backup Set, click on each plus sign to display all the folders and subfolders that were backed up. With all folder and subfolder names displayed, you can select individual folders to restore.

10. To restore the contents of an entire folder, click on its check box under Select Files From the Backup Set.

11. To restore selected files in a folder, click on the folder under Select Files From the Backup Set, and then click on the check box next to each file you want to restore in the Contents Of list.

Restore all files only if you wiped out entire folder or disk

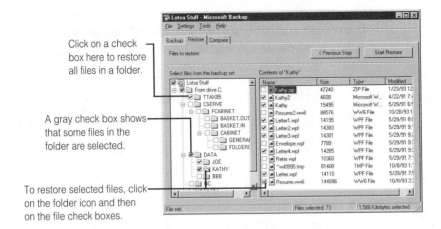

Click on a check box here to restore all files in a folder.

A gray check box shows that some files in the folder are selected.

To restore selected files, click on the folder icon and then on the file check boxes.

12. Click on the Start Restore button. If you are restoring from floppy disks, a dialog box appears, telling you which disk to insert.

13. Follow the on-screen instructions.

Beyond Survival

Entering Your Restore Preferences

Up to this point, you've restored files to their original drives and folders, replacing existing files only if they were older than the backed-up files. You can, however, enter Backup settings that restore files to different folders or drives, and replace all or none of the existing files. Here's how you set the restore options:

1. Click on the Start button.

2. Move the mouse over Programs, and then over Accessories.

3. Move the mouse over System Tools, and then click on Backup.

4. Open the Settings menu and select Options. The Settings - Options dialog box appears, allowing you to enter settings for backing up, comparing, and restoring files.

5. Click on the Restore tab.

6. Select Quit Backup After Operation Is Finished if you want Backup to shut down automatically after restoring files.

7. Under Restore Backed Up Files To, select any of the following options:

Original Locations restores the files to the disks and folders from which they were backed up.

Alternate Location restores files to a different disk or folder. If the backed-up files are in subfolders, they will be placed in subfolders on the alternate disk or folder.

Alternate Location, Single Directory restores files to a different disk or folder. All files are placed in the specified folder, even if they were originally in subfolders.

Restore to alternate location so you don't replace existing file of same name

8. Under Advanced Options, pick any of the following:

Verify Restored Data... tells Restore to compare the restored files to the backed-up files automatically, to make sure the files were restored properly.

Never Overwrite Files prevents any existing files on the hard disk from being replaced by backed-up files of the same name. Restore simply skips over any existing files.

Overwrite Older Files Only is the default selection. Backup will replace an existing file with a backed-up file having the same name only if the backed-up file is newer.

If Overwrite files is on, turn on Prompt before overwriting files

Overwrite Files tells Restore to restore all files on the backed-up disks or tape to the hard drive, and replace any files on the hard disk that have the same name as the backed-up files. If you choose this option, be sure to turn on Prompt Before Overwriting Files, so Backup will warn you when it is about to replace an existing file.

9. Click on the OK button to save your changes.

Once you've set your restore preferences, you can restore your files with the new settings in place.

Cheat Sheet

Starting DriveSpace

1. Click on the Start button.
2. Move the mouse pointer over Programs, and then over Accessories.
3. Move the mouse pointer over System Tools, and then click on DriveSpace.

Compressing an Existing Drive

1. Back up all files on the drive before you begin.
2. If you want to compress a floppy disk, insert the disk into the drive.
3. Start DriveSpace, and click on the letter of the drive you want to compress.
4. Open the Drive menu and select Compress.
5. Click on the Start button.
6. Click on Compress Now, and then wait until the compression is complete.
7. If Windows asks whether you want to restart your computer, click on Yes.

Creating a New Compressed Drive

1. Start DriveSpace, and click on the letter of the drive on which you want to create the new compressed drive.
2. Open the Advanced menu, and click on Create Empty.
3. Open the Create a New Drive Named drop-down list, and click on the letter you want to give the new drive.
4. Tab to the Using _____ MB text box, and type the amount of free space you want to use on the selected drive to create the new compressed drive.
5. Click on the Start button, and then wait until the compression is complete.

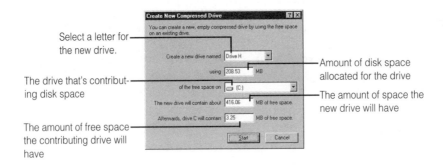

Select a letter for the new drive.

The drive that's contributing disk space

The amount of free space the contributing drive will have

Amount of disk space allocated for the drive

The amount of space the new drive will have

Creating More Storage
with DriveSpace

Back up all
files before
compressing a
disk

With the size of Windows 95 and today's programs, you can never have enough disk space for all your files and data. To help, Windows 95 offers DriveSpace, a program that can compress the files on your disk so they take up less space. DriveSpace works behind the scenes, compressing and decompressing files as you use them, so your computer won't seem much different to you—you'll just have more disk space. In this chapter, you'll learn how to use DriveSpace to compress existing disks, create a new compressed drive (using a section of your existing hard disk), and even compress floppy disks.

Basic Survival

**Planning a
Compression
Strategy**

Before you start compressing disks, you should come up with some sort of strategy for this task. Some users like to compress drive C so they have only one disk drive to deal with. Compressing drive C gives you the full benefits of DriveSpace, because you compress all the files on your hard disk.

I prefer to create a separate compressed drive, leaving the program and data files I commonly use on the uncompressed drive C, and placing programs I rarely use on the new compressed drive (E). This strategy serves two purposes. First, it prevents any glitches in DriveSpace from crippling my system (including Windows 95). Second, it allows my essential programs to run faster, because my computer doesn't have to wait for DriveSpace to decompress files before running them. The only drawback with this approach is that you don't reap the full benefits of data compression, because you don't compress *all* your files.

As you develop your own strategy, consider how much disk space you have. If you have little free space, you should probably compress drive C. If you have 100MB or more of free hard disk space, you may want to create a separate compressed drive.

331

Compressing an Existing Drive

You can use DriveSpace to compress any existing drive (hard drive or floppy). Before using DriveSpace, however, you should back up all the files on the disk, just in case your files get fouled up during compression. Although glitches rarely occur, a complete backup will give you the peace of mind to proceed.

If you have a large hard drive, keep in mind that a compressed drive can be no larger than 512 megabytes. If you compress a one-gigabyte drive, for example, Windows will create one 512-megabyte compressed drive and keep the additional storage space as an uncompressed *host*.

Once you've backed up the files on the disk, take the following steps to compress it:

Compression can take minutes or hours; can't stop once you start

1. Click on the Start button.

2. Move the mouse pointer over Programs, and then over Accessories.

3. Move the mouse pointer over System Tools, and then click on DriveSpace. The DriveSpace dialog box appears, showing you a list of the drives you can compress.

4. If you want to compress a floppy disk, insert the disk into the drive.

5. Click on the letter of the drive you want to compress.

6. Open the Drive menu and select Compress. A dialog box then shows you graphs of how much free space the drive currently has, and how much space it will have after compression. If you are compressing a large hard disk, the graphs are confusing (as shown here). From the graphs, you'd think you're going to lose disk space, but if you look in the lower-right corner of the dialog box, you'll see that after compression you will gain a new uncompressed drive that more than makes up for the free space you're about to lose.

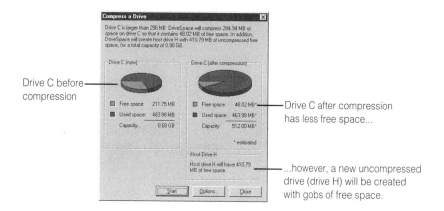

Drive C before compression

Drive C after compression has less free space...

...however, a new uncompressed drive (drive H) will be created with gobs of free space.

7. Click on the Start button. A dialog box appears, cautioning you to back up your files before compressing them. Assuming you already did this (or you're feeling very lucky), move on to step 8.

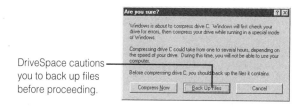

DriveSpace cautions you to back up files before proceeding.

8. Click on the Compress Now button; wait until the compression is complete. Depending on the size of the compressed drive and the amount of data needing compression, this can take from several minutes to several hours.

Creating a New Compressed Drive

If you're one of the many users who don't trust data compression—or you have a huge hard drive and you want to compress only a portion of it—you can create a separate compressed drive. Whenever you copy or move files to this drive, they will be compressed. In addition, any programs you install on the new drive will be compressed. To create a separate compressed drive, here's what you do:

1. Start DriveSpace, and click on the letter of the drive on which you want to create the new compressed drive.

2. Open the Advanced menu, and click on Create Empty. A dialog box appears, asking you to pick a letter for the drive, and asking how much space you want to use to create it.

3. Open the Create a New Drive Named drop-down list, and click on the letter you want to give the new drive.

4. Tab to the Using _____ MB text box, and type the amount of free space you want to use on the selected drive to create the new compressed drive.

5. Click on the Start button; wait until the compression is complete. When compression is done, a dialog box appears, showing the size of the new drive.

Start small; can change size of compressed drive later

6. Click on the Close button. Another dialog box appears, informing you that your system configuration has changed and asking whether you want to restart your computer.

7. Click on the Yes button.

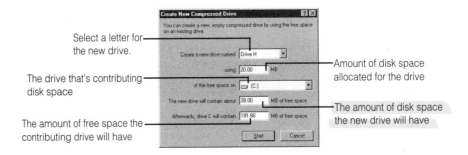

Select a letter for the new drive.

The drive that's contributing disk space

The amount of free space the contributing drive will have

Amount of disk space allocated for the drive

The amount of disk space the new drive will have

Uncompressing a Drive

If you compress a drive and decide later that you don't like the way the drive works with compressed files, you can uncompress the drive or delete it (which is more dangerous). To uncompress a drive, take the following steps:

1. Start DriveSpace as explained earlier.

2. Click on the letter of the drive you want to uncompress.

3. If you want to uncompress a floppy disk, make sure it is in the drive.

4. Open the Drive menu and select Uncompress. A dialog box appears, showing the effects of uncompressing the drive.

5. Click on the Start button. DriveSpace decompresses the drive. Other dialog boxes may appear after the decompression. Follow the on-screen instructions to proceed.

If you created a separate compressed drive on your hard disk, you can quickly remove it. If the compressed drive contains any files, however, the files will be deleted when you delete the compressed drive. Therefore back up the compressed drive (or move all its files to another drive) *before* you delete it. Once you've done that, take the following steps to delete the empty compressed drive:

1. Start DriveSpace, as explained earlier.

2. Click on the compressed drive you want to delete.

3. Open the Advanced menu and click on Delete. A dialog box appears, indicating that the compressed drive will now be deleted; it also informs you that if it contains any files, these files will be gone forever.

4. Click on Yes to remove the compressed drive, or click on No to stop. DriveSpace deletes the compressed drive, and informs you of the deletion.

5. Click on the OK button. Another dialog box appears, informing you that your system has changed, and that if you want it to work right, you had better restart your computer.

6. Click on the Yes button to restart Windows and your computer.

Beyond Survival

Changing the Compression Ratio

By default, DriveSpace scrunches data in a 2-to-1 ratio, so it can fit approximately twice as much data on a disk. DriveSpace can, however, compress data at ratios up to 16-to-1. Of course, this all takes more time than the 2-to-1 ratio default, but if you're really strapped for disk space, a higher ratio can help you hang on till you can afford a bigger hard disk. To change the compression ratio, here's what you do:

1. Start DriveSpace, and click on the letter of the compressed drive whose ratio you want to change. (If you're working with a floppy drive, make sure it has a compressed disk.)

2. Open the Advanced menu and click on Change Ratio. A dialog box appears, showing the current compression ratio.

3. Drag the Estimated slider to the left or right to change the compression ratio. The further to the right you drag, the higher the compression ratio.

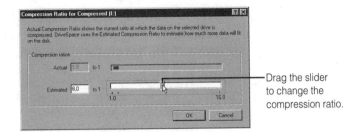

Drag the slider
to change the
compression ratio.

*Change
compression
ratio only if
you need disk
space bad*

4. Click on the OK button. A dialog box appears, indicating that you must restart your computer before the change will take effect.

5. Click on the Yes button to restart your computer.

Changing the Size of a Compressed Drive

You can change the relative sizes of the compressed and uncompressed portions of your hard drive. If (for example) you want to make the compressed drive larger—and the uncompressed drive smaller—you can increase the size of your compressed drive. Here's how:

1. Start DriveSpace, as explained earlier.

2. Click on the compressed drive whose size you want to change.

3. Open the Drive menu and click on Adjust Free Space. A dialog box appears showing the size of the host (uncompressed) drive and the compressed drive.

4. Drag the slider below the graphs to the left or right to change the relative sizes of the compressed and uncompressed drives.

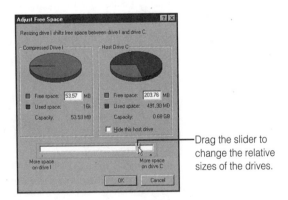

Drag the slider to
change the relative
sizes of the drives.

*Increasing
compressed drive
size decreases
uncompressed
drive size*

5. Click on the OK button. DriveSpace adjusts the sizes as specified.

Mounting and Unmounting a Compressed Floppy Disk

DriveSpace is not set up to recognize (*mount*) a compressed floppy disk automatically. If you insert a compressed disk into drive A, for example, and then click on it in My Computer or Explorer, you won't be able to work with the files on that disk. To have DriveSpace mount floppy disks automatically, take the following steps:

1. Run DriveSpace, as explained earlier.

2. Open the Advanced menu and click on Settings. The Disk Compression Settings dialog box appears.

3. Click on Automatically Mount New Compressed Devices; a check mark appears in the box.

4. Click on the OK button. Another dialog box appears, indicating that the change won't take effect till you quit DriveSpace.

5. Click on the OK button, and then exit DriveSpace.

If you change to drive A in My Computer or Explorer, and you get a window that contains the files **Dblspace.000** and **Readthis**, DriveSpace has not automatically mounted the drive. In such a case, you must tell DriveSpace to mount the drive. Open the Advanced menu and select Mount. To unmount the drive, open the Advanced menu and select Unmount.

If you see these files in My Computer or Explorer, DriveSpace has not mounted the drive.

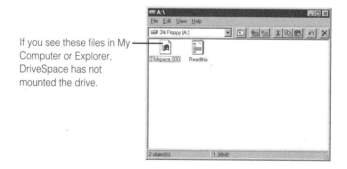

337

Cheat Sheet

Why Defragment a Disk?

- As you add and remove files from a disk, parts of files become scattered over the disk, making it more difficult for the drive to read each file.
- Disk Defragmenter rearranges the parts of each file, so the files are no longer fragmented. This speeds up your disk.
- By placing parts of each file in close proximity, your computer is better able to recover accidentally damaged files later.

Defragmenting a Disk

1. Click on the Start button.
2. Move the mouse pointer over Programs, and then over Accessories.
3. Move the mouse pointer over System Tools, and then click on Disk Defragmenter.
4. Open the Which Drive Do You Want to Defragment? drop-down list, and click on the desired drive.
5. Click on the OK button.
6. Click on the Start button.
7. Wait until the defragmentation is complete.

Setting Your Defragmentation Preferences

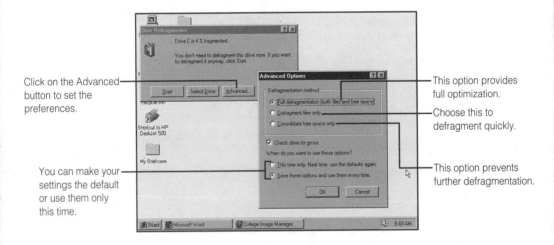

Click on the Advanced button to set the preferences.

You can make your settings the default or use them only this time.

This option provides full optimization.

Choose this to defragment quickly.

This option prevents further defragmentation.

Speeding Up Your Disk with Defragmenter

Whenever you save a file to your disk, Windows places the first part of the file in the first empty space on your disk. Additional parts of the file are saved in the next empty spaces. As you delete and save files, the files become more and more fragmented—their parts are scattered all over the disk. This slows down your computer, because the disk drive has to hunt around for pieces of a file each time you try to run or open the file. Fragmentation also makes it more likely that the computer will "misplace" a portion of the file and cause the file to become corrupted.

Defragment at least once per month

To reduce or eliminate fragmentation, you can use the Windows 95 Disk Defragmenter program. In this chapter, you'll learn how to defragment disks and set the defragmentation options.

Basic Survival

Defragmenting Files on a Disk

Unless you change the defragmentation settings (as explained later in this chapter), Disk Defragmenter performs a complete defragmentation operation. That is, Defragmenter shuffles pieces of files around to place all of each file's parts in one place, and then moves all the files to one section of the disk, so any files you save in the future will not be fragmented. To defragment your files in this way, take the following steps:

1. Click on the Start button to open the Start menu.

2. Move the mouse pointer over Programs, and then over Accessories.

3. Move the mouse pointer over System Tools, and then click on Disk Defragmenter. A dialog box appears, asking which disk drive you want to defragment.

Click on All
Hard Drives
to defragment
all drives

4. Open the Which Drive Do You Want to Defragment? drop-down list, and click on the desired drive. You can defragment all your disks by clicking on All Hard Drives. (There's no need to defragment floppy disks.)

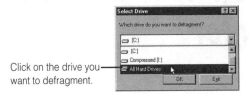

Click on the drive you want to defragment.

5. Click on the OK button. Another dialog box appears, indicating the percent of file fragmentation on the disk and telling you whether or not you need to defragment the disk.

Percentage of file fragmentation

6. Click on the Start button. Defragmenter starts to defragment the files on the disk. You can click on the Show Details button if you want to watch Defragmenter perform.

7. Wait until the defragmentation is complete.

Beyond Survival

Setting Defragmentation Preferences

Full
defragmentation
best, but takes
most time

The best way to optimize a disk is to perform a complete defragmentation, which defragments existing files and collects the free space on the drive, to prevent future fragmentation. Disk Defragmenter does, however, offer other options. If you click on the Advanced button in the Disk Defragmenter dialog box, you'll see the Advanced Options dialog box shown here. Select any of the following options to control the way Defragmenter operates:

- Full Defragmentation is the default setting. With this option on, Defragmenter defragments existing files and consolidates free space to prevent future fragmentation.

- Defragment Files Only places all the pieces of each file together, but leaves the files scattered over the disk. Because the disk's free space is also scattered around the disk, this option promotes future fragmentation.

- Consolidate Free Space Only does not defragment the files. It does consolidate the free space, so to reduce further file fragmentation.

- Check Drive for Errors tells Defragmenter to check the drive for any lost or missing file pieces or directories before continuing. If Defragmenter finds a problem on a disk, it will prompt you to run ScanDisk to correct the problem before proceeding.

Select your defragmentation preferences.

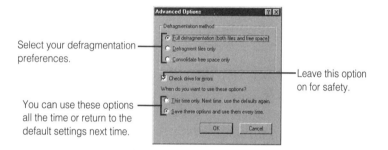

Leave this option on for safety.

You can use these options all the time or return to the default settings next time.

The last two options in this dialog box allow you to save these defragmentation settings for the future or return to the default settings next time. Choose the desired option, and then click on the OK button to return to the Disk Defragmenter dialog box. You can now defragment your disk (using the new settings) by clicking on the Start button.

Cheat Sheet

Quick Fixing a Disk

1. To fix a floppy disk, insert the disk into one of the floppy disk drives.
2. Click on the Start button, point to Programs, point to Accessories, point to System Tools, and then click on ScanDisk.
3. Click on the letter of the drive you want to check.
4. Make sure Standard is selected.
5. To have ScanDisk repair errors without asking for confirmation, click on Automatically Fix Errors.
6. Click on the Start button.
7. Follow the on-screen instructions.

Checking and Fixing the Surface of a Disk

1. To fix a floppy disk, insert the disk into one of the floppy disk drives.
2. Click on the Start button, point to Programs, point to Accessories, point to System Tools, and then click on ScanDisk.
3. Click on the letter of the drive you want to check.
4. Click on Thorough.
5. Click on the Options button, if desired, and specify how you want ScanDisk to check the disk. (If you don't understand an option, right-click on it, and then click on What's This?) Click on the OK button.
6. Click on the Start button.
7. Follow the on-screen instructions.

Fixing Disk Problems with ScanDisk

Occasionally a disk will go bad. Some of the magic storage dust they sprinkle on a disk during manufacturing may flake off. More frequently, your computer will just lose track of a file or directory or mistakenly "think" that two files are stored in the same place. Whether the problem is with the disk or with your computer's file management system, ScanDisk can help you find and repair problems—and even recover data from bad storage areas.

Basic Survival

When Should You Run ScanDisk?

The obvious answer to this question is: When your disk goes bad. Say (for example) you have a floppy disk that has a bunch of files on it. You insert the disk into the drive; you get an error message saying your computer can't read the disk, or that the disk has bad sectors. This is a good sign that the disk is bad, and that you'll need to run ScanDisk on it before you can use the files.

Other signs that a disk is having problems may not be so obvious. If a program consistently crashes or freezes up your system, the problem might be that your disk has lost track of some of its files. Often you can run ScanDisk at this point and solve the problem almost miraculously. Running ScanDisk on a regular basis (say, every month) can prevent such problems from ever occurring.

Fixing a Disk Quickly

If you receive an error message stating that a disk has a bad sector, you should skip ahead and thoroughly check your disk for errors and defects. A *thorough* disk check examines the actual surface of the disk to make sure each of its areas can store data securely.

If you're just having trouble with a file (or if your system is acting strange), a quick check is usually all you need to repair any problems. A *quick* disk check looks only for logical errors on the disk. If the computer lost track of a file or directory, for example, a quick disk check can help reorient the computer. To do a quick check of a disk, here's what you do:

1. To fix a floppy disk, insert the disk into one of the floppy disk drives; if necessary, close the drive door.

2. Click on the Start button.

3. Move the mouse pointer over Programs, and then over Accessories.

4. Rest the mouse pointer on System Tools, and then click on ScanDisk.

5. Click on the letter of the drive you want to check.

6. Make sure Standard is selected.

7. To have ScanDisk repair errors without asking for confirmation, click on Automatically Fix Errors. (If you leave this unchecked, ScanDisk will let you choose how to repair the error. For example, if ScanDisk finds a lost file cluster, it lets you delete the cluster or save it.)

Select Standard.

To have ScanDisk repair errors automatically, turn this option on.

8. Click on the Start button. ScanDisk starts checking the disk. If ScanDisk finds a problem, it either corrects the problem or displays a prompt asking you how you want to correct the problem.

9. Follow the on-screen instructions until the operation is complete. When ScanDisk is done, it displays a log of all the problems it found and the corrections it made.

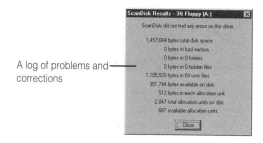

A log of problems and corrections

Beyond Survival

Checking a Disk for Surface Errors and Defects

If disk keeps giving you problems, check it thoroughly

If you have a floppy disk that contains files you can't seem to access, or if you keep getting disk errors for a disk you already checked with ScanDisk, you might need to perform a more thorough check of the disk. When ScanDisk performs a *thorough* check, it not only looks for pieces of lost folders and files, but it also tests the storage areas of the disk to make sure they're not defective. If you're checking a large hard disk (over 100MB), this thorough test can take a couple of hours. You might want to start it before leaving work for the night, or before going to bed. To start the test, here's what you do:

1. To fix a floppy disk, insert the disk into one of the floppy disk drives.

2. Click on the Start button.

3. Move the mouse pointer over Programs, and then over Accessories.

4. Rest the mouse pointer on System Tools, and then click on ScanDisk.

5. Click on the letter of the drive you want to check.

6. Click on Thorough. The Options button is now activated.

7. Click on the Options button. The Surface Scan Options dialog box appears, asking how thorough a job you want ScanDisk to do.

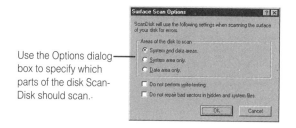

Use the Options dialog box to specify which parts of the disk Scan-Disk should scan.

8. Select one of the following options to specify which areas of the disk you want to check:

> **System and Data Areas** checks the entire disk.
>
> **System Area Only** checks only the area of the disk that is used to store the files for booting your computer. If ScanDisk finds problems in the surface area, you might have to replace the disk— ScanDisk won't be able to fix the problem.
>
> **Data Area Only** checks only the area of the disk used for storing program files and the files you create. If ScanDisk finds a problem in the data area, usually it can move the data from the bad spot to a good spot on the disk.

9. You can select one, both, or neither of the following options:

> **Do Not Perform Write Testing** tells ScanDisk to test storage areas on a disk by reading data off the storage areas. If you leave this option off, ScanDisk will perform a more thorough check by reading and writing data to each storage area.
>
> **Do Not Repair Bad Sectors in Hidden and System Files** tells ScanDisk to leave system and hidden files where they are, even if they are stored on bad sectors. (If you move some system or hidden files, the program that uses them might not work properly— but if the file is stored on a bad sector, the program probably won't work properly anyway.)

10. To have ScanDisk repair errors without asking for confirmation, click on Automatically Fix Errors. (If you're letting ScanDisk run overnight, you'll probably want to select this option.)

11. Click on the Start button. ScanDisk checks the specified disk for file and folder problems, and then scans the surface of the disk for defects. If Automatically Fix Errors is off, ScanDisk may display dialog boxes, asking for your input.

12. Follow the on-screen instructions. When ScanDisk is done, it displays a log of all the problems it found and the corrections it made.

Telecomputing with Windows 95

Windows 3.1 didn't offer much for modem users. With Windows Terminal, you could connect to another computer and transfer files awkwardly over the phone lines. Windows 95 has finally caught up with the current technology, offering a new and improved Terminal (called HyperTerminal), a phone dialer (which acts as a programmable telephone), a connection to Microsoft's online service (Microsoft Network), a fax program, and even a remote computing program (for connecting your PC at home to your PC at work). In this part, you'll learn how to use the Windows 95 telecomputing programs:

Cheat Sheet

Installing a Modem

1. Click on the Start button.
2. Move the mouse pointer over Settings, and then click on Control Panel.
3. Double-click on the Modems icon 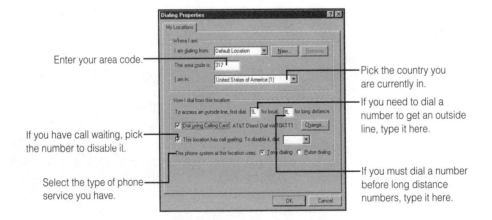.
4. Click on the Add button.
5. Click on the Next button, and wait until the Install New Modem Wizard finds your modem.
6. Click on the Next button.
7. Click on the Finish button.

Entering Dialing Preferences

1. Click on the Start button.
2. Move the mouse pointer over Settings, and then click on Control Panel.
3. Double-click on the Modems icon.
4. Click on the modem whose dialing preferences you want to set.
5. Click on the Dialing Properties button.
6. Use the dialog box (as displayed here) to enter your preferences, and then click on the OK button.

Enter your area code.

Pick the country you are currently in.

If you need to dial a number to get an outside line, type it here.

If you have call waiting, pick the number to disable it.

Select the type of phone service you have.

If you must dial a number before long distance numbers, type it here.

55

Setting Up Your Modem

If your modem was connected when you installed Windows 95, chances are that Windows already set up the modem. If you have a new modem, however—or you're not satisfied with the way Windows (or your modem program) is responding to your modem—you can proceed through modem setup again to install the modem or change its setup. This chapter leads you through the entire process.

Basic Survival

Installing a New Modem

If you just purchased a modem, follow the instructions that came with it to connect it to your computer. Once that's done, you'll have to run Modem Setup to tell Windows the type of modem you have. You might also run Modem Setup if you're having problems dialing out with your modem. Modem Setup can help you pick the correct modem and troubleshoot any other problems that might be causing trouble. To install a new modem or change a previous setup, take the following steps:

1. Click on the Start button.

2. Move the mouse pointer over Settings, and then click on Control Panel.

3. Double-click on the Modems icon 📇. The Modems Properties dialog box appears, showing a list of the modems that Windows thinks are installed on your computer.

4. If the modem type that's listed looks as though it matches the manufacturer and model of the modem you have, skip the rest of the steps. If the modem type is Standard or differs from the modem you have, click on the Add button. If you clicked on the Add button, the Install New Modem dialog box appears.

5. If you know the manufacturer and model name of your modem, click on Don't Detect My Modem; I Will Select It From a List. If Don't Detect My Modem… is off, you'll have to wait while Windows tries to determine the modem type.

6. Click on the Next button. If you clicked on Don't Detect My Modem…, the next dialog box presents a list of modems to choose from. Otherwise Windows pokes around to find your modem, and then picks the modem type it thinks you have.

7. Take one of the following steps:

> If Windows picked a modem type and you agree with it, click on the Next button, and then click on the Finish button. You're done.

> If Windows picked a modem type that does not match your modem (or if it picked Standard), click on the Change button and proceed to step 8.

> If you chose to pick a modem type from a list, proceed to step 8.

8. Click on the brand name of the modem in the Manufacturers list, and click on the model in the Models list. (If the precise model is not listed, pick a model that looks close. If the modem came with a disk, insert the disk, click on Have Disk, and follow the instructions.)

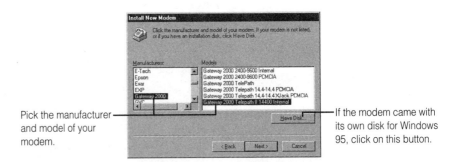

Pick the manufacturer and model of your modem.

If the modem came with its own disk for Windows 95, click on this button.

9. Click on the OK button. You're returned to the Verify Modem dialog box, where the name of the selected modem is displayed.

10. Click on the Next button. Windows indicates that it is about to complete the installation.

Remove any modem types that don't match yours

11. Click on the Finish button. You return to the Modem Properties dialog box.

If two modems are listed in the Modem Properties dialog box (and you have only one modem), click on the modem type that does not match your modem, and click on the Remove button.

Entering Information for Dialing Out

Depending on your phone system, there could be a number of preliminaries you must perform before you dial an actual phone number. You might (for example) have to dial a 9 to get an outside line, or dial an 8 before making long-distance calls. To have Windows perform these preliminary actions for you, you can enter dialing properties. Here's what you do:

1. Click on the Start button.

2. Move the mouse pointer over Settings, and then click on Control Panel.

3. Double-click on the Modems icon .

4. Click on the modem whose dialing preferences you want to set.

5. Click on the Dialing Properties button. The Dialing Properties dialog box appears.

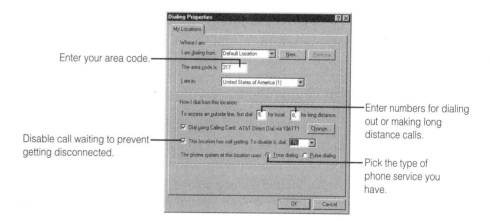

Enter your area code.

Disable call waiting to prevent getting disconnected.

Enter numbers for dialing out or making long distance calls.

Pick the type of phone service you have.

6. If you take your computer on the road to different states or countries, you can enter a set of dialing preferences for each area:

To create a new set of dialing preferences, click on New, type a name for the set, and click on OK.

Create set of dialing preferences for each area code you dial from

To pick a set of dialing preferences, open the I Am Dialing From drop-down list, and click on the named set.

7. In The Area Code Is text box, drag over the current area code, and type the area code for your current location.

8. Open the I Am In drop-down list; pick the country from which you are currently dialing.

9. In the ___ For Local text box, type any number you have to dial to reach an outside line, followed by a comma to pause for a second. (At some companies, for example, you must dial 9 before dialing any phone number.)

10. In the ___ For Long Distance text box, type whatever number you must dial to get an outside line for calling a long distance number; follow it with a comma, which creates a one-second pause. (**Note:** This number is not the 1 you normally have to dial to make a long distance call. This number is only needed if you work at a place that requires you to dial a special number to get an outside line for calling long distance.)

11. If you plan to charge the cost of your calls with a calling card, click on Dial Using Calling Card. Then click on the Change button, use the dialog box that appears to choose the type of calling card you're using, enter your calling card number, and then click on the OK button.

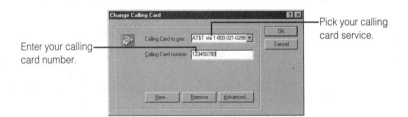

Enter your calling card number.

Pick your calling card service.

Call waiting can disconnect modem in the middle of a session

12. If you have call waiting, you should disable it. Click on This Location Has Call Waiting, and type the number you must dial to disable call waiting (usually ***70**). (After you hang up, call waiting is automatically enabled.)

13. Pick the type of phone service you have:

Tone Dialing, if you hear tones of various pitch when you dial your phone.

Pulse Dialing, if you hear clicks of various lengths when you dial your phone.

14. Click on the OK button. You're returned to the Modems Properties dialog box.

15. Click on the Close button to save your changes and exit.

Beyond Survival

Checking Your Modem's Properties

Your modem has several settings that control its operation, including where it is connected, how fast it sends and receives data, its speaker volume, and so on. To check and/or change these settings, take the following steps:

1. Double-click on the Modems icon 🖼 in the Control Panel window. The Modems Properties dialog box appears.

2. Click on your modem in the Modems list (if more than one modem is listed).

3. Click on the Properties button. The Properties dialog box for your modem appears.

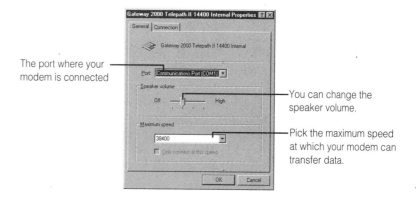

The port where your
modem is connected

You can change the
speaker volume.

Pick the maximum speed
at which your modem can
transfer data.

4. If your modem does not respond to commands, chances are that it's set for the wrong COM port. You can select a different port from the Port drop-down list.

5. If your modem is too loud or too quiet, drag the Speaker Volume slider left or right to change the volume.

6. Open the Maximum Speed drop-down list, and click on the fastest speed at which your modem can send and receive data. (Most modems can adjust to lower speeds automatically, if required, so pick the highest speed. Picking a speed that's too high usually won't cause any problems; if you're not sure, guess high.)

7. Click on the Connection tab. A list of modem connection settings appears. Windows uses the most common communications settings for your modem; you shouldn't have to change them unless you'll be connecting to a modem that uses some weird settings.

Leave modem settings alone unless you know what you're doing

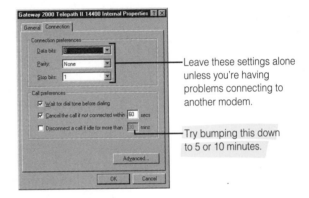

Leave these settings alone unless you're having problems connecting to another modem.

Try bumping this down to 5 or 10 minutes.

8. If you plan on connecting to another modem, find out the settings that the modem uses, and then enter the same settings for the following:

> **Data Bits** indicates the number of bits (pieces of information) in each transmitted character. The common setting is 8.

> **Parity** tests the integrity of the data sent and received. The common setting is None.

> **Stop Bits** indicates the number of bits used to signal the end of a character. The common setting is One.

> The **Port Settings** and **Advanced** buttons at the bottom of the dialog box let you change advanced settings such as buffers (for faster data transfer) and error-control preferences. Leave these options alone unless you run into trouble later.

9. Under Call Preferences, change any of the following settings to enter your calling, connecting, and disconnecting preferences:

Wait for Dial Tone Before Dialing tells the modem not to dial until it "hears" a dial tone. (It's a good idea to keep this on.)

Cancel the Call if Not Connected Within ___ Secs tells the modem to hang up if the remote modem does not answer or respond within the specified amount of time. (60 seconds is a good setting, unless the modem is hanging up before the remote modem has a chance to respond.)

Disconnect a Call if Idle for More Than ___ Mins tells the modem to hang up if no data is sent or received during the specified amount of time. (30 minutes is a little excessive, especially for long distance calls. Try bumping this down to 5 or 10.)

10. Click on the OK button to save your settings. You return to the Modems Properties dialog box.

11. Click on the Close button.

Troubleshooting Modem Problems

If you try to use your modem to connect to an online service (such as PRODIGY or America Online) or to dial the phone for you (as explained in the next chapter) and it doesn't respond, Windows can help you track down the problem and correct it. Take the following steps:

1. Double-click on the Modems icon ▣ in the Control Panel window. The Modems Properties dialog box appears.

2. Click on the Diagnostics tab. A list of the serial and communications ports appears, showing the names of the serial devices (including the modem) installed on your system.

3. Click on the Help button. The Modem Troubleshooter's Help screen appears, providing a list of questions about the problem you're having.

4. Click on the button next to a question to select it and track down your problem. (Keep clicking on buttons as needed until you find the cause of your modem problem and correct it.)

Use Modem Toubleshooter to track down any problems

Cheat Sheet

Starting Phone Dialer

1. Click on the Start button and move the mouse pointer over Programs.

2. Move the mouse pointer over Accessories, and then click on Phone Dialer.

Dialing a Phone Number

1. Start Phone Dialer.

2. Type the phone number (or click on numbers in the number pad).

3. Click on the Dial button.

4. Lift the phone receiver and click on the Talk button.

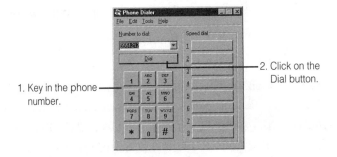

1. Key in the phone number.

2. Click on the Dial button.

Entering Speed Dial Numbers

1. Click on a blank button in the Speed Dial list.

2. Type the name of the person you want to call.

3. Tab to the Number to Dial text box, and type the phone number.

4. Click on the Save button.

56

Dialing Your Phone with Dialer

If you have a modem, you can plug your phone into it and use Phone Dialer to transform your computer into a programmable telephone. You simply enter the number you want to dial, click on a button, and Phone Dialer dials the phone for you. All you have to do is pick up the receiver and start talking. In this chapter, you'll learn how to dial out with Phone Dialer and program numbers for placing quick phone calls.

Basic Survival

Dialing Phone Numbers with Phone Dialer

Make desktop shortcut for Phone Dialer (it's in Windows directory)

Although you can program phone numbers into Phone Dialer so you can place calls quickly (as explained in the next section), you can also use Phone Dialer's keypad (or type numbers) to place calls. Here's what you do:

1. Click on the Start button and move the mouse pointer over Programs.

2. Move the mouse pointer over Accessories, and then click on Phone Dialer. Phone Dialer appears.

3. Type the phone number (or click on numbers in the number pad).

You can click on numbers here or type them in.

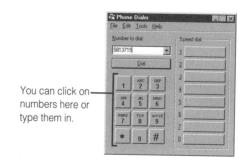

4. Click on the Dial button. Phone Dialer starts to dial the phone, displaying the Dialing dialog box. Don't pick up the receiver yet.

5. Wait until the Call Status dialog box appears.

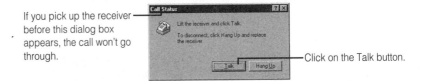

If you pick up the receiver before this dialog box appears, the call won't go through.

Click on the Talk button.

6. Lift the phone receiver and click on the Talk button. You can now talk to your party.

Programming Speed Dial Numbers

Using the Phone Dialer to key in numbers is cool, but you can do that yourself on the phone. If you don't have a programmable phone, however, Phone Dialer lets you program numbers so you can dial them quickly with a click of a single button. To program a phone number, take the following steps:

1. Click on a blank button in the Speed Dial list. The Program Speed Dial dialog box appears, prompting you to type a name and phone number.

2. Type the name of the person you want to call in the Name text box.

3. Tab to the Number to Dial text box, and type the person's phone number.

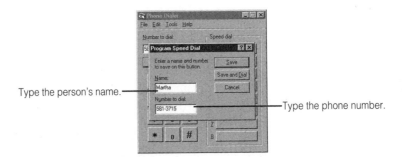

Type the person's name.

Type the phone number.

4. Click on the Save button. The Speed Dial list now has a button that contains the name of the person whose number you just programmed in. To place a call, simply click on the name.

If you no longer call a particular person in the Speed Dial list (or if the person's phone number changed), you can edit the entries in the list. Here's what you do:

1. Open the Phone Dialer's Edit menu and click on Speed Dial. The Edit Speed Dial dialog box appears.

2. Click on the button for the person whose number you want to change. The person's name and current number appear in the text boxes at the bottom of the dialog box.

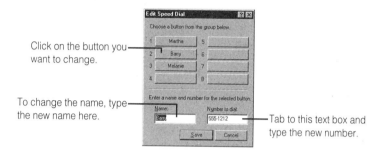

Click on the button you want to change.

To change the name, type the new name here.

Tab to this text box and type the new number.

3. If you're replacing this button with a button for a different person, type the person's name in the Name text box.

4. Tab to the Number to Dial text box, and type the new number.

5. Repeat steps 2 to 4 for each number you want to change.

6. Click on the Save button. All the numbers you changed are saved, and the Speed Dial list is updated as specified.

Beyond Survival

Entering Dialing Preferences

To further automate Phone Dialer, you can enter special dialing preferences. For example, if you have to dial a 9 before dialing any phone number, you can enter the 9 as a dialing preference, so that Phone Dialer dials that number automatically whenever you place a call. To enter dialing preferences, take the following steps:

1. Start Phone Dialer.

2. Open the Tools menu and select Dialing Properties. The Dialing Properties dialog box appears.

3. Follow the instructions in Chapter 55, in the section called "Entering Information for Dialing Out," to set your dialing preferences.

Cheat Sheet

Creating a Connection with HyperTerminal

1. Click on the Start button and move the mouse pointer over Programs.
2. Move the mouse pointer over Accessories, and then click on HyperTerminal.
3. Double-click on the Hypertrm icon .
4. Type a name for the connection you want to establish.
5. Click on an icon for the connection, and click on the OK button.
6. Type the phone number you must dial to connect to the remote computer, and then click on the OK button.
7. Click on the Dial button.

Disconnecting from the Remote Computer

1. Open the Call menu.
2. Click on Disconnect.
3. Open the File menu and click on Exit.

Sending a File

1. Tell the person in charge of the remote computer to prepare to receive a file. (Agree on a protocol to use: Text, Kermit, Zmodem, or Ymodem.)
2. Open the Transfer menu and select Send File.
3. Click on the Browse button; when a dialog box appears, use it to select the file you want to send. Click on the Open button.
4. Open the Protocol drop-down list and click on the agreed-upon protocol.
5. Click on the Send button.

57

Making Modem Connections with HyperTerminal

If you have a modem connected to your computer and to the phone line, you can use HyperTerminal to transfer files to and from another computer—as well as to connect to an electronic bulletin board, your city library's computerized card catalogue, or any other system that allows computers to call in and connect. In this chapter, you'll learn how to dial out with your modem and transfer files.

Although you can use HyperTerminal to establish an Internet connection and to connect to some online services, HyperTerminal is not the best tool to use. You can connect to such services more efficiently by using the specialized programs such services offer. You can also purchase and acquire specialized Internet software that provides better tools for connecting to and navigating the Internet. Use HyperTerminal to connect to a friend's computer, to bulletin board systems (BBSs), and to local computers (such as your library).

Basic Survival

Starting HyperTerminal

When you first start HyperTerminal, it asks a series of questions to enable you to connect to a remote computer immediately. Then, in the future, you can simply click on an icon to dial that same number again. To start HyperTerminal and create a new connection, take the following steps:

1. Click on the Start button and move the mouse pointer over Programs.

2. Move the mouse pointer over Accessories, and then click on HyperTerminal. A Windows Explorer window opens, displaying a collection of HyperTerminal icons.

3. Double-click on the Hypertrm icon. HyperTerminal starts and displays a dialog box that asks for a description of the new connection.

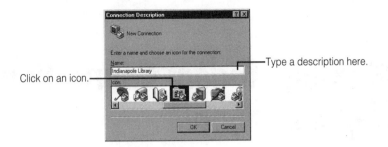

Click on an icon.

Type a description here.

4. Type a name for the connection you want to establish. The name should describe the remote computer you want to hook up to.

5. Click on an icon for the connection, and then click on the OK button. Another dialog box appears, asking for the phone number of the remote computer.

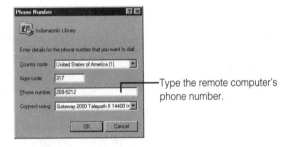

Type the remote computer's phone number.

6. Type the phone number you must dial to connect to the remote computer, and click on the OK button. Another dialog box appears, showing the number that HyperTerminal will dial.

7. Click on the Dial button. HyperTerminal dials the number and establishes a connection.

How Hyper-Terminal screen looks will depend on computer you connect to

What you do next depends on the type of connection you established. If you connected to a remote computer that has its own menu system (such as a library computer), you'll see a menu that you can use to get around in the system. If you connected to a friend's or colleague's computer, you can type messages to have them appear on the other user's screen. Whatever the other user types in response will appear on your screen. To hang up the phone (and disconnect), open the Call menu and select Disconnect.

Saving Your Settings

When you choose to exit HyperTerminal, a dialog box appears and asks whether you want to save your session. If you choose Yes, then Hyper-Terminal creates an icon in the HyperTerminal folder that contains the name of the connection, the phone number you entered, and any other settings you may have changed. The next time you want to dial the same number, you simply select HyperTerminal from the Programs/Accessories menu, and then double-click on the icon for the connection.

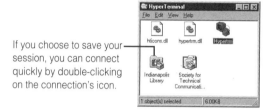

If you choose to save your session, you can connect quickly by double-clicking on the connection's icon.

Entering Communications Settings

When you installed your modem, you may have entered communications settings that control the way your modem communicates with other modems. If you didn't enter communications settings, Windows enters the most common settings for you. If you are not having any problems connecting to a remote computer, you should leave the settings as they are. If problems arise with a particular connection, however, you can check and change your settings as follows:

1. Open HyperTerminal's File menu and select Properties. The New Connection Properties dialog box appears.

2. Click on the Configure button. The Properties dialog box for your modem appears.

3. If your modem does not dial or seem to respond to other modem commands, open the Port drop-down list and try a different COM port setting.

4. Open the Maximum Speed drop-down list and click on the fastest speed at which your modem can send and receive data. (Pick the highest speed; most modems can adjust automatically to lower speeds if necessary.)

5. Click on the Connection tab. If your modem dials, but has trouble communicating with the remote modem, find out the settings that the remote modem uses. Then enter the same settings for the following:

> **Data Bits** indicates the number of bits (pieces of information) in each transmitted character. The common setting is 8.
>
> **Parity** tests the integrity of the data sent and received. The common setting is None.
>
> **Stop Bits** indicates the number of bits used to signal the end of a character. The common setting is One.

6. If your modem disconnects before the other modem has a chance to answer, double-click inside the Cancel the Call If Not Connected Within ___ Secs text box, and type a larger number.

7. Click on the OK button to save the modem configuration.

8. Click on the OK button to save the new connection properties.

Any time you enter changes, open File menu and select Save

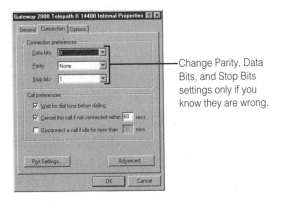

Change Parity, Data Bits, and Stop Bits settings only if you know they are wrong.

Selecting a Terminal Emulation

Large mainframe computers (used for online services, libraries, and other institutions) sometimes require the computer that's calling to act like (*emulate*) a certain type of computer. HyperTerminal is set up to determine automatically which emulation is required, and to make your system emulate the specified terminal type. If your computer is having trouble connecting, however, you may have to select an emulation yourself. Here's how:

1. Open HyperTerminal's File menu and select Properties. The New Connection Properties dialog box appears.

Terminal emulation makes your computer act like a different type of computer

2. Click on the Settings tab. Auto Detect should be highlighted in the Emulation drop-down list.

3. If Auto Detect is not selected, open the Emulation drop-down list and select it. (If you know the required emulation type, select it from the drop-down list.)

4. Click on the OK button to save your change.

Beyond Survival

Sending Text Files

Many word processing programs, including Windows Notepad and WordPad, allow you to create *plain-text files* (these contain characters, but no fancy formatting commands). You can send and receive these files quickly by using your modem and HyperTerminal. To send a file, take the following steps:

1. Make sure the remote computer is ready to receive the text file. (You can phone your friend, or type and send a message in HyperTerminal.)

2. Run HyperTerminal and connect to the remote computer.

3. Open the Transfer menu and select Send Text File. A dialog box appears, asking you to pick the file you want to send.

4. Change to the folder that contains the file, and then click on the file's name.

5. Click on the Open button. HyperTerminal opens the file and sends it.

Before sending file, make sure remote computer is prepared to receive it

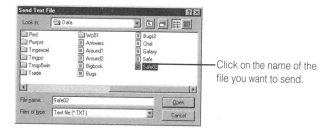

Click on the name of the file you want to send.

Sending Binary Files

A *binary file* is any file that's not a text file. If you want to transfer a program, sound, graphic file, or a document that contains special formatting codes, you must use the binary file-transfer method. Here's what you do:

1. Make sure the remote computer is ready to receive the text file. (You can phone your friend, or type and send a message in HyperTerminal.)

2. Run HyperTerminal and connect to the remote computer.

3. Open the Transfer menu and click on Send File. The Send File dialog box appears.

4. Open the Protocol drop-down list and select the protocol setting that matches that of the remote computer. (Zmodem is one of the faster, more reliable protocols.)

Binary file transfers work for most file types

5. Click on the Browse button; when a dialog box appears, use it to select the file you want to send. Click on the Open button.

6. Click on the Send button. HyperTerminal begins transmitting the file to the remote computer.

Preparing to Receive a File

To receive a file, first make sure you are using the proper settings for the desired file transfer. (You'll have to contact the person who's sending the file and determine whether she's sending a text or binary file, as well as what type of protocol she's using.) You must also type a name and select a location for the new file. The following steps lead you through the process:

1. Run HyperTerminal and connect to the remote computer (as explained earlier).

2. Open the Transfer menu and select one of the following options:

   Receive File to receive a binary file.

   Capture Text to receive a text file.

3. If you picked Receive File, open the Protocol drop-down list; then click on the protocol that matches that of the remote computer.

For binary files, the protocol must be the same for both the sending and receiving computers.

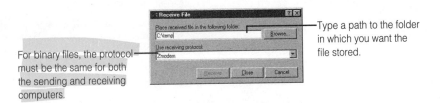

Type a path to the folder in which you want the file stored.

4. Click inside the File or Place Received File in the Following Folder text box, and then take one of the following steps:

> For a text file, type a path to the folder in which you want the file saved, followed by a name for the file. For example, you might type **C:\DATA\TEXTFILE\AARON.TXT**.

> For a binary file, type a path to the drive and folder in which you want the file placed. The file will have the same name as the file that is sent. For example, type **C:\DATA\BINARY**.

5. Click on the Receive button. HyperTerminal waits until the file data starts to come in; then HyperTerminal receives the file and stores it in the specified folder.

Cheat Sheet

Starting an Account with The Microsoft Network

1. Double-click on The Microsoft Network icon 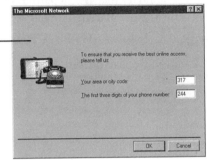 on the Windows desktop.

2. Follow the on-screen instructions to open your account.

The first time you run The Microsoft Network, it displays a series of dialog boxes that lead you through the process of starting an account.

Signing In

1. Once you've set up an account, double-click on The Microsoft Network icon.

2. Tab to the Password text box and type your password.

3. Click on the Connect button.

4. You can sign off by opening the File menu and selecting Sign Out.

Moving Around in Microsoft Network

- When you connect to The Microsoft Network, you're greeted by a collection of on-screen buttons. Click on a button to see what's offered.

- Most buttons open a window that contains a collection of folders. Double-click on a folder to open it, or double-click on an area to go to it.

- You can return to a previous screen by clicking on the Up One Level button in the toolbar (the button that has the folder with the up arrow on it).

58

Connecting to Microsoft Network

The Microsoft Network is the newest entry in the ever-growing list of online services you can connect your modem to. This new online service looks and acts very much like the veteran online services, offering the standard fare of e-mail, bulletin boards, special interest groups, information databases, and chat rooms.

The Microsoft Network—pay service you can connect to with modem

What gives The Microsoft Network its real marketing edge, however, is that the software comes as an integrated part of Windows 95. When you start Windows 95, The Microsoft Network icon appears on your desktop, allowing you to connect quickly and start using the service in a matter of minutes. This chapter shows you how to set up a new account on The Microsoft Network.

Basic Survival

Connecting for the First Time

Before you can take advantage of The Microsoft Network's offerings, you must set up an account. This consists of providing your credit card number so Microsoft can bill you for the service. Take the following steps to set up your account.

1. Double-click on The Microsoft Network icon ▨. A dialog box appears, offering to lead you through the sign-up procedure.

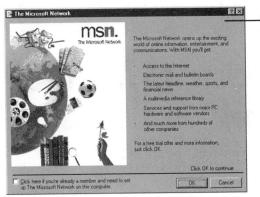

Windows will lead you through the setup procedure.

2. Click on the OK button to continue. The next dialog box asks for your area code and first three digits of your phone number.

3. Type the requested information in the text boxes, and click on OK. (This information is used to determine a local number you can dial to connect.) Your modem will now dial a local number to obtain a list of local connect numbers.

4. Click on the Connect button to connect temporarily to the service and fetch the local numbers. After obtaining the local phone numbers, the setup program displays a dialog box asking for some personal information.

5. Click on the Tell Us Your Name and Address button. A dialog box appears, allowing you to enter your name, address, and phone number.

6. Type the requested information in each text box. You can move to the next text box by clicking inside it or by pressing the Tab key. Click on OK when you're done. You return to the previous text box; a check mark appears next to the first button.

7. Click on the Next, Select a Way to Pay button to enter your credit card information.

You'll need credit card number to start account

8. Choose the type of credit card you're using from the Choose a Payment Method list, and then enter the required credit card information. Click on the OK button to return to the previous dialog box.

9. Click on the Then, Please Read the Rules button; read the long legal statement explaining your responsibilities as a user and Microsoft's responsibilities as a provider.

10. Click on the I Agree button (assuming you agree to the service agreement). (If you don't agree, you won't be able to use the service.)

11. To view details about the service and pricing information, click on the Details or Price button.

12. When you're ready to sign on, click on the Join Now button. A dialog box appears, showing the primary and secondary local connect phone numbers. Click on the OK button.

13. Another dialog box appears, showing the number that will be dialed. Click on the Connect button. Your modem connects to The Microsoft Network, and you're asked to enter the name you want to use for the account (Member ID) and a password.

14. Type the name that you want to use as your pseudonym, and then tab to the Password text box, and type your password. (Use a password that is easy for you to remember, but difficult for others to guess.)

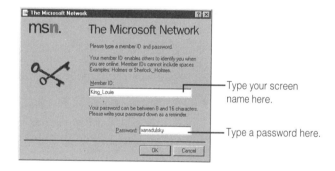

Type your screen name here.

Type a password here.

15. Click on the OK button. A dialog box appears, announcing that you are now a member of The Microsoft Network.

16. Click on the Finish button.

Live near major city? Connect using a local phone number to avoid long-distance charges

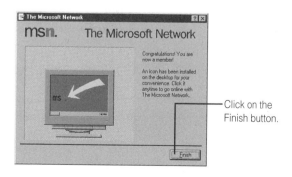

Click on the Finish button.

You can create another account for a member of your family or a colleague by running the Sign Up program again. In My Computer, go to the Program Files/Microsoft Network folder, and then double-click on the Signup icon. Follow the same steps given here to create another account.

Connecting Once You've Set Up an Account

Once you've set up an account with The Microsoft Network, signing on is easy. Take the following steps:

1. Double-click on The Microsoft Network icon . The Sign In dialog box appears, asking you to type your member ID and password.

Type your member ID here.

Type your password here.

2. If the supplied member ID is correct, skip to step 3. If the name is incorrect, drag over it and type the correct member ID.

3. Tab to the Password text box and type your password. As you type, the password appears as a series of asterisks so nobody can read it as you type.

Prevent unau-thorized use of your account: remove check mark from Remember My Password check box

4. To have the Sign In dialog box remember your password (so you won't have to type it next time), click on the Remember My Password option to place a check in the box.

5. Click on the Connect button. Your modem dials the local connect number, and connects to The Microsoft Network. The opening Microsoft Network screen provides a list of buttons that you can click on to view the various offerings or retrieve your electronic mail.

Beyond Survival

Solving Sign-In Problems

If you have trouble signing in to The Microsoft Network, Windows can help you track down the problem and correct it. Take the following steps:

1. Double-click on The Microsoft Network icon 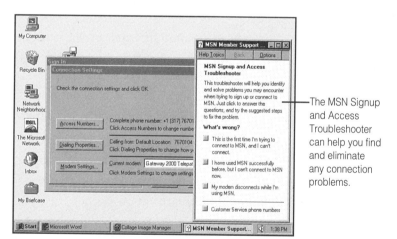. The Sign In dialog box appears, asking you to type your member ID and password.

2. Click on the Settings button. The Connection Settings dialog box appears.

3. Click on the Help button. The MSN Signup and Access Troubleshooter appears. The Troubleshooter asks a series of questions to help narrow down the problem.

4. Click on the buttons to answer the questions until the Troubleshooter determines the cause of the problem and helps you correct it.

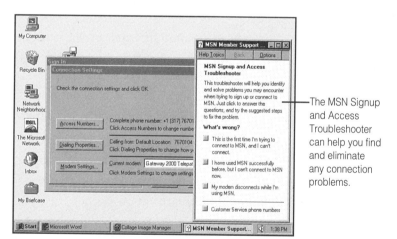

The MSN Signup and Access Troubleshooter can help you find and eliminate any connection problems.

Once you sign on, you'll see The Microsoft Network opening screen. Move on to the next chapter to figure out how to navigate The Microsoft Network's vast resources.

Cheat Sheet

Moving Around in The Microsoft Network

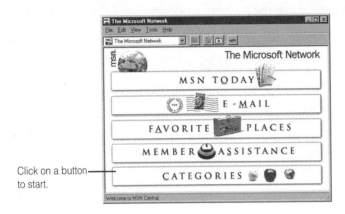

Click on a button to start.

Create a List of Favorite Places

1. Go to the area you want to record as a favorite place.

2. Click on the Add to Favorite Places button 🖳. (If the toolbar is not visible, open the View menu and click on Toolbar.)

3. To go to a favorite place on the list, click on the Go to Favorite Places button 🖳.

4. Double-click on the desired icon to shoot to your favorite place.

Send E-Mail

1. Sign in to The Microsoft Network, and then click on the E-Mail button.

2. Click on the New Message button 🖳.

3. In the To text box, type the recipient's member ID.

4. Click inside the Subject text box; then type a brief description of the message.

5. Click inside the message area near the bottom of the dialog box; type your message.

6. Click on the Send button 🖳.

59

Navigating Microsoft Network

As you saw in Chapter 58, when you connect to The Microsoft Network, you're greeted with several buttons that enable you to sample the offerings of the Network. You can click on the Categories button to try out some of the information services and bulletin boards (where you can read and post messages), click on the E-Mail button to send and receive electronic mail, or click on Member Assistance to get answers to your questions.

You can send e-mail to its destination in seconds

In this chapter, you'll learn how to browse around on The Microsoft Network, create a list of your favorite places, send and receive e-mail, post and read messages on a bulletin board, and download (copy) files from the service.

Basic Survival

Wandering The Microsoft Network

Wandering The Microsoft Network is fairly simple. You click on a button, and you see a list of folder icons. Double-click on a folder icon, and you get more icons. Just keep clicking on what you want till you get to the desired area. The following steps show you how:

1. Connect to The Microsoft Network (as explained in Chapter 58), and then click on the Categories button. The Microsoft Network window changes to show a collection of folders.

When you click on the Categories button, your screen shows a collection of folders.

2. To open a folder, double-click on it. The screen changes to show the contents of the folder. This may include icons for additional subfolders and for specific areas you can visit.

3. Double-click on an icon to open the subfolder or go to that area. If you double-click on an icon for a specific area, you are transported to that area, where you can obtain the information you want (or exchange information with other users who share your interests).

4. To return to the previous screen, click on the Up One Level button. You can also return to a place you've visited by selecting it from the drop-down list to the left of the Up One Level button.

The Up One Level button displays the previous screen.

The Go to MSN Central button takes you back to the beginning.

Select a place you visited from this drop-down list.

These buttons let you pick an icon arrangement.

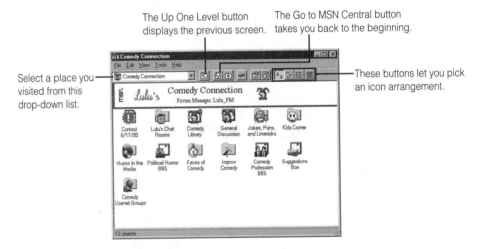

5. To return to the opening screen, click on the Go to MSN Central button. You can then start wandering from the beginning.

6. To change the way folder and area icons are arranged on the screen, click on one of the icon buttons at the right end of the toolbar.

7. You can disconnect from the service at any time by clicking on the Sign Out button, or you can select Sign Out from the File menu. When you choose to sign out, a dialog box appears, asking for your confirmation.

Click and double-click to wander The Microsoft Network

8. Click on Yes.

Sending Electronic Mail

Like all the major online services, The Microsoft Network allows you to send mail to and receive mail from other users of the service and anyone who has an Internet e-mail address. Here's what you do to send a message:

1. Sign in to The Microsoft Network, and then click on the E-Mail button. Windows runs Microsoft Exchange, its built-in e-mail manager.

2. Click on the New Message button ![icon], or open the Compose menu and click on New Message. The New Message dialog box appears, prompting you to type your message and the recipient's e-mail address.

Type the person's e-mail address or member ID here.

Type the message itself.

Click here to attach a file (if desired).

Type a description of the message.

3. In the To text box, type the recipient's member ID or e-mail address.

4. Click inside the Subject text box, and type a brief description of the message. This description will appear in the recipient's e-mail box.

5. Click inside the message area near the bottom of the dialog box, and then type your message.

6. (Optional) If you want to send a file along with your message, click on the Insert File button ![icon] (or open the Insert menu and select File).

7. (Optional) Use the Insert File dialog box to select the folder and name of the file you want to send. Click on the OK button. (If you're sending to an Internet address, you can only send a text file.)

You can attach a file to send along with message

8. Click on the Send button ![icon], or open the File menu and select Send. Microsoft Exchange sends the message and any files you attached.

377

Reading Incoming Mail

Whenever someone sends an e-mail message to your address, the message is stored on the computers that make up The Microsoft Network. To view a list of waiting messages, take the following steps:

1. Connect to The Microsoft Network, and click on the E-Mail button. Windows runs Microsoft Exchange automatically, and it checks for any new e-mail messages.

2. Double-click on a message description to read the message. A dialog box appears, showing the contents of the message.

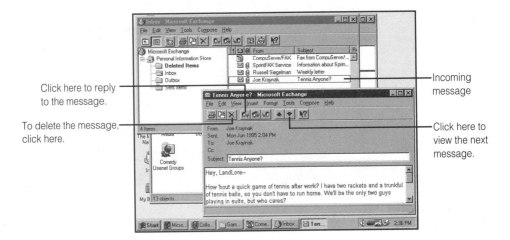

Click here to reply to the message.

To delete the message, click here.

Incoming message

Click here to view the next message.

3. When the message is displayed, you can click on the Next or Previous button to read additional e-mail messages.

4. To reply to an e-mail message, click on the Reply to Sender button, type your response, and then click on the Send button.

5. You can delete the message by clicking on the Delete button. Note, however, that you won't be able to read a message again after you delete it.

6. After reading your mail, click on the Close button to exit Microsoft Exchange. You remain connected to The Microsoft Network.

Reading and Posting Bulletin Board Messages

Several areas in The Microsoft Network contain electronic bulletin boards where you can read messages from other members, respond to those messages, and post your own notes and questions. The icon for a bulletin board area typically looks like a piece of paper with a thumbtack stuck in it. If you encounter a bulletin board, take the following steps to read and post messages:

1. Connect to the Microsoft Network, and go to a bulletin board area. A list of the recent postings appears.

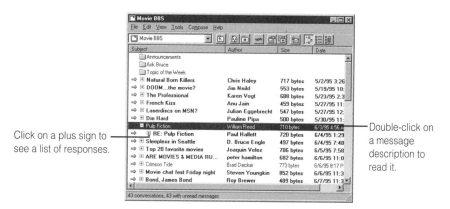

Click on a plus sign to see a list of responses.

Double-click on a message description to read it.

2. If a message has a plus sign next to it, you can click on the plus sign to view a list of responses.

3. To read a message, double-click on its description. The message is displayed in its own dialog box.

4. To respond to a message, click on the Reply to BBS button, type your response, and then click on the Post button. The message is placed on the bulletin board, where it can be read by all.

5. To start your own conversation on a message board, open the Compose menu and select New Message.

6. Type a description of the message in the Subject text box.

7. Click inside the message area, and then type the full text for the message. Click on the Post button, or open the File menu and select Post Message. The message is placed on the bulletin board where other members can read it.

Reply privately to BBS message by opening Compose menu and selecting Reply by E-mail

Beyond Survival

Creating a List of Your Favorite Places

The Microsoft Network makes it easy to return quickly to your favorite haunts. Take the following steps to mark an area as one of your favorite places:

1. Go to the area you want to add to your list of favorite places.

2. Click on the Add to Favorite Places button, or open the File menu and select Add to Favorite Places. The Microsoft Network creates an icon for the place, and then inserts it into the Favorite Places screen.

3. To go to a favorite place on the list, click on the Go to Favorite Places button 🔘. A window opens, showing icons for all the areas you added as favorite places.

4. Double-click on the desired icon to shoot to your favorite place.

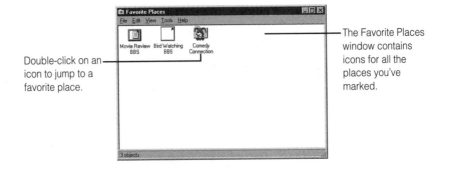

Double-click on an icon to jump to a favorite place.

The Favorite Places window contains icons for all the places you've marked.

Chatting with Other Members

The Microsoft Network contains a variety of electronic meeting places where members can gather to carry on live conversations. These places (called *chat rooms*) allow you to carry on telephone conversations by using your keyboard (instead of your voice) and by using a local connection free of long-distance charges. To chat on The Microsoft Network, take the following steps:

1. Connect to The Microsoft Network, and click on the Categories button.

2. Double-click on The MSN Member Lobby icon to view a collection of icons for the various chat areas. Another collection of icons appears.

3. Double-click on The Chat Garden folder. A list of tables appears. You can sit at a table and start chatting with other people who are sitting at the same table.

To change relative dimensions of panes that make up window, drag their borders

4. Double-click on one of the table icons. You've now pulled up a chair at the table. The member IDs of the people sitting at the table are listed on the right. The main conversation takes place in the big window in the middle.

Look here for the conversation.

The names of fellow members who are sitting at the table.

Type your message here and click on Send.

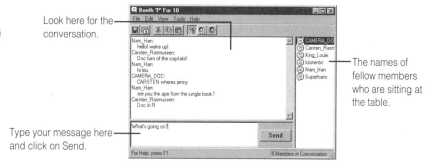

5. To contribute your own witty comments to the conversation, type in the message area, and then click on the Send button.

6. You can view personal and professional information about a person by double-clicking on his or her member ID. Read the information, and then click on the OK button.

7. To leave a chat table, say your good-byes, and then click on the Close button.

Retrieving Files

Many areas in The Microsoft Network contain files you can copy to your computer. These files might include pictures of your favorite movie and TV stars, update files for programs and computer devices, catalogs, movie clips, sound effects, and anything else that can be transmitted electronically. To retrieve a file, take the following steps:

1. Go to the area that contains the file you want to retrieve.

2. Double-click on the name of the file you want to copy. (Files are marked with a paper-clip icon.) A dialog box appears, showing a brief description of the file.

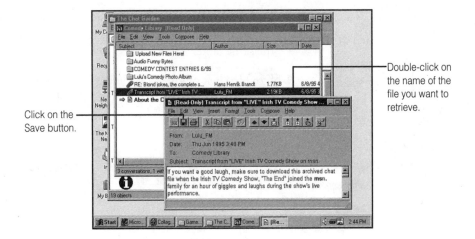

Click on the
Save button.

Double-click on
the name of the
file you want to
retrieve.

3. Click on the Save button (the button with the diskette on it). The Save As dialog box appears, prompting you to name the file and select a location for it.

4. Under Save, click on Attachments. The filename under Attachments is inserted into the Filename text box.

5. Use the Folders list to select the folder in which you want the file stored.

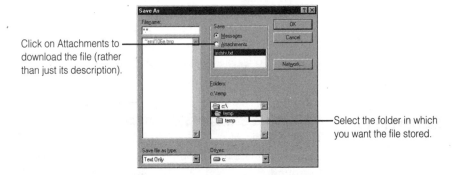

Click on Attachments to
download the file (rather
than just its description).

Select the folder in which
you want the file stored.

6. Click on the OK button. A dialog box appears, showing the status of the downloading operation. Wait until the file transfer is complete.

Downloading the file places a copy of it in the selected folder on the specified drive. You can now open the file in a program that can handle the downloaded file's format. For example, if you downloaded a text file (whose name ends in .TXT), you can open it in Notepad or WordPad. If the file is a bitmapped graphic (whose name ends in .BMP), you should be able to open it in Paint.

Cheat Sheet

Sending a Fax

1. Click on the Start button and move the mouse pointer over Programs.
2. Rest the mouse pointer first on Accessories, and then on Fax.
3. Click on Compose New Fax, and then click on the Next button.
4. Type the name of the person to whom you are sending the fax.
5. Click inside the Fax # text box, and then type the fax phone number.
6. Click on the Add to List button, and then click on the Next button.
7. Click on Yes, and then select the type of cover page you want. Click on the Next button.
8. Type a description of the fax in the Subject text box.
9. Click inside the message area, and type the message that you want to appear on the cover page. Click on the Next button.
10. To attach a file to the fax, click on the Add File button, select the file you want to attach, and then click on Open. Click on the Next button.
11. Click on the Finish button.

Receiving Faxes with Microsoft Exchange

1. Click on the Start button, point to Programs, and click on Microsoft Exchange.
2. Click on the fax-machine icon in the Taskbar (next to the time display).
3. Wait for the phone to start ringing, and then click on the Answer Now button.

60

Sending and Receiving Faxes

To send and receive faxes in previous versions of Windows, you had to purchase a special fax program such as WinFax PRO. Windows 95 comes with two programs (Microsoft Fax and Microsoft Exchange) that together provide the basic tools you need to send and receive faxes. Although not as full-featured as a specialized fax program, Microsoft's fax features can get the job done with no added expenses. As long as you have a modem that's capable of sending and receiving faxes, you'll be able to fax right now.

You must have a modem that can send and receive faxes

If, as you work through this chapter, you cannot find Microsoft Exchange or Microsoft Fax, you may not have installed the programs when you installed Windows. Both of these programs must be installed in order for you to send and receive faxes. To install these programs, refer to the installation appendix at the back of this book.

Basic Survival

Sending Faxes with Microsoft Fax

The Windows Compose New Fax Wizard provides a quick-and-easy way to send a fax. You start the Wizard, and it displays a series of dialog boxes that you respond to. The Wizard then dials the recipient's phone number and sends the fax. To send a fax with the Compose New Fax Wizard, here's what you do:

1. Click on the Start button, and then point to Programs, Accessories, and Fax.

2. Click on Compose New Fax. The Compose New Fax Wizard appears, displaying the current dialing properties.

3. If you take your computer on the road to different area codes, you can click on the Dialing Properties button and change your current area code and other information (see Chapter 55 for details). If you don't take your computer on the road, click on I'm Not Using a Portable Computer…, so the Wizard won't display this dialog box again.

4. Click on the Next button. The Wizard displays a dialog box asking you to enter the fax recipient's name and fax number.

5. Type the name of the person to whom you are sending the fax.

6. Click inside the Fax # text box, and type the fax phone number. (If you are faxing to a different area code, type it in the Area Code text box. When you click outside the text box, a check mark appears in the Dial Area Code box.)

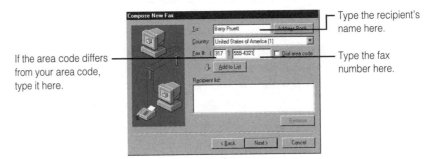

If the area code differs from your area code, type it here.

Type the recipient's name here.

Type the fax number here.

7. Click on the Add to List button to insert the name in the Recipient List, and then click on the Next button. The Wizard displays a dialog box that asks whether you want to attach a cover page.

8. To attach a cover page to your outgoing fax, click on Yes..., and select the type of cover page you want.

9. Click on the Next button. The next dialog box allows you to type a description of the fax and a message for the cover page.

10. Type a description of the fax in the Subject text box.

11. Click inside the Note area; type the message you want to appear on the cover page.

12. Click on the Next button. The Wizard asks whether you want to attach a file to the fax. Wizard can transform some document files (such as those created in Microsoft Word or WordPad) into faxable documents. You can't send sound files or movie clips, however, or any other files that can't be sent to a fax machine.

13. To attach a file to the fax, click on the Add File button, use the dialog box to select the file you want to attach, and click on Open. You return to the Wizard, and the name of the selected file appears in the Files to Send list. (You can repeat this step to attach more files.)

Select the file you want to attach.

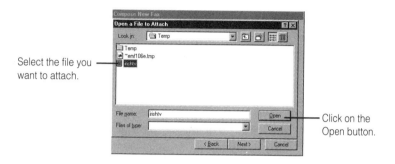

Click on the Open button.

Resend failed fax: double-click on its name in Microsoft Exchange; click on Send Again

14. Click on the Next button. The Wizard displays a dialog box saying that it is nearly ready to send the fax.

15. Click on the Finish button. The Wizard creates the cover page, transforms any attached files into faxable data, dials the recipient's fax number, and sends the fax.

If you chose to attach a file, it may take the Wizard a while to transform the attachments into faxable data. The Wizard runs the program used to create the file, then works with that program to turn the text into a graphic image that a fax machine can print. If you have trouble with attached files, you may not have associated the file type to a program. Turn back to Chapter 37 to learn how to associate file types to programs, and then try faxing the attachment again.

There are many other ways to run the Compose New Fax Wizard and use it to transmit a fax. The following list explains these alternative methods:

Fax a file: right-click on it in My Computer or Windows Explorer; select Send To

- Run Microsoft Exchange (Start, Programs, Microsoft Exchange). Then open the Compose menu and select New Fax; this starts the Wizard. Perform the same steps as those just given to complete the operation.

- To fax files, select one or more files you want to fax in Windows Explorer or My Computer. Right-click on the name of one of the selected files, move the mouse pointer over Send To, and then click on Fax Recipient. Perform the same steps above to send the fax. (If you use this method, the Wizard does not display a dialog box to ask you to attach files.)

- Some programs (such as Microsoft Word for Windows 95) have a Send command on the File menu. Open the document you want to fax, and then select the Send command. You'll get a dialog box that prompts you to enter the recipient's name and fax number. Enter the requested information, and then click on the option for sending the fax.

- If you want to fax from a program that does not have a Send command, select Microsoft Fax as your printer, and then use the program's Print command to print as you normally would.

Receiving Faxes with Microsoft Exchange

Microsoft Exchange is a powerful communications program that can manage all your e-mail and fax messages. To use Microsoft Exchange to receive an incoming fax, you can set it up to answer the phone automatically (after a specified number of rings), or you can enter a command to have it answer the phone now.

If your phone is ringing and you know it's because of an incoming fax, take the following steps to have Microsoft Exchange answer the call:

1. Click on the Start button, point to Programs, and click on Microsoft Exchange. A tiny fax-machine icon appears next to the time in the Taskbar.

2. Click on the fax-machine icon. The Microsoft Fax Status dialog box appears.

3. Click on the Answer Now button. Microsoft Exchange answers the phone and starts receiving the incoming fax.

If you use your phone line primarily for voice calls, you should answer incoming fax calls using the steps just given. If you use the phone line mostly to receive faxes, however, you may want to set up Microsoft Exchange to answer incoming calls automatically. Here's how you do it:

1. Run Microsoft Exchange (click on Start, point to Programs, and click on Microsoft Exchange).

2. Right-click on the fax-machine icon in the Taskbar (next to the time display), and then click on Modem Properties. The Modem Properties dialog box appears, allowing you to turn on the auto-answer feature.

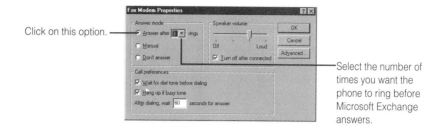

Click on this option. ——

Select the number of times you want the phone to ring before Microsoft Exchange answers.

To receive incoming faxes, your computer must be on and running Microsoft Exchange

3. Click on Answer After ___ Rings, and then open the drop-down list, and select the number of times you want the phone to ring before your modem answers.

4. Click on the OK button to accept your change.

5. Leave Microsoft Exchange running, so it can answer incoming calls. (You can minimize the window or use other Windows programs while Microsoft Exchange is running.)

The Modem Properties dialog box offers additional Answer Mode settings. If you pick Manual, Microsoft Exchange displays a dialog box whenever the phone rings, asking whether you want to receive the incoming fax. If you know that the call is not an incoming fax, you can click on No, pick up the receiver, and start talking. The Don't Answer option tells Microsoft Exchange not to answer any calls; you can answer the calls manually, as explained earlier.

Viewing Your Faxes

Now that you've received a fax, how do you view it? Take the following steps:

1. Run Microsoft Exchange (click on Start, point to Programs, and click on Microsoft Exchange). When Microsoft Exchange starts, it displays a list of all faxes and e-mail that were received.

2. Double-click on the name of the fax you want to view. Microsoft Exchange displays the fax.

3. Use the button bar (as shown in the figure) to flip pages, print the fax, and zoom in and out.

Click here to print the fax.

Use these buttons to zoom in and out.

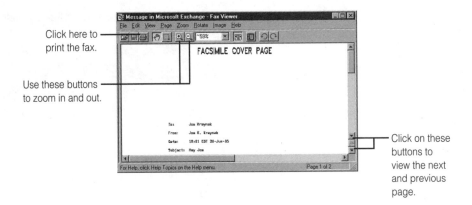

Click on these buttons to view the next and previous page.

PART
8

Tricks and Traps

Are you starting to feel like a Windows expert yet? If so, this section
contains some more advanced information that can help you solve
problems and optimize Windows. You'll learn how to solve printer,
mouse, and modem problems, clear useless files off your hard drive,
and make Windows run faster (as well as more reliably). In addition,
you'll learn some cool Windows tricks to wow your friends. Here's
what you'll get:

Cheat Sheet

Recovering from a Program Crash

1. Wait a couple of minutes.
2. If the program still does not respond, press Ctrl+Alt+Del.
3. Click on the problem program's name.
4. Click on the End Task button.

Solving Memory Problems

- Exit any programs that you're not using.
- If you added programs to the Startup group (so they run automatically when you run Windows), remove them from the Startup group and restart Windows.
- Click on the Start button, point to Settings, and click on Control Panel. Double-click on the System icon, click on the Performance tab, and click on Virtual Memory. Make sure Let Windows Manage My Virtual Memory Settings is selected. Click on OK.
- Free up some disk space on your hard drive. See Chapter 63, "Uncluttering Your Disk," for details.

Using Windows Troubleshooters

1. Click on the Start button and click on Help.
2. Click on the Contents tab.
3. Double-click on Troubleshooting.
4. Double-click on the description of the problem you're having.
5. Follow the on-screen instructions.

Troubleshooting Common Windows Problems

Windows 95 can do some fairly amazing things to prevent you from being caught in the usual software-and-hardware snares of personal computing. It can detect and install new hardware devices, lead you through the process of installing new programs, and correct most startup problems automatically.

Sometimes, however, Windows 95 needs help. Maybe Windows chose the wrong driver for your mouse, or maybe you changed a setting when you shouldn't have. Whatever the case, you're encountering some problems, and you need to figure out what's going on. In this chapter, you'll learn how to correct the most common problems, and how to seek help from Windows itself.

Basic Survival

Recovering from Program Crashes

Program crashes aren't as exciting as they sound. You expect to hear some grinding and smashing, but you get just the opposite—no sound, no movement, nothing. You can't use your mouse or keyboard, and the program doesn't respond to a single command. To regain control of your computer, take the following steps:

1. Wait a couple of minutes. The program might be printing or performing some calculation in the background. It hasn't crashed; it's just busy. If you wait awhile, the program might start to respond.

2. If the program still does not respond, press Ctrl+Alt+Del. The Close Program dialog box appears, showing the names of all the programs you are currently running.

3. Click on the name of the program that's giving you problems. If you're not sure which program is causing the problem, look for the one that says **Not responding** next to it.

4. Click on the End Task button. Windows closes the program and returns you to the Windows desktop. You can now continue working or restart the program.

5. If the program crashes again, repeat the steps, shut down Windows, and then restart. Try running the program by itself (with no other programs running).

When a program crashes: press Ctrl+Alt+Del; click on program's name; select End Task

If you keep having problems with a particular program, you may be running low on memory. Skip ahead to the next section to determine what to do. If you still have problems, you may have some sort of hardware conflict. See "Troubleshooting Device Conflicts" in Chapter 48 for hints on how to deal with the problem.

If you notice that the program crashes when you use your mouse, there may be a problem with the mouse driver you're using. To correct the problem, skip ahead to "Solving Mouse Problems" in this chapter.

Obtaining Additional Memory

Windows 95 requires a bare minimum of 4 megabytes of RAM (8 or more megabytes would be better). If Windows 95 needs more memory than your system has, it uses the free space on your hard disk as temporary (virtual) memory. Although this memory is slower than the memory in RAM chips, it does allow your computer to run more programs.

Computer with 8 MB or more RAM = low-memory problems less likely

Most Windows 95 memory problems are related to virtual memory. Either your computer does not have enough disk space for Windows to create sufficient virtual memory, or someone changed the settings in your computer so Windows does not have full control of the virtual memory. Take the following steps to find the cause of the problem:

1. Click on the Start button, point to Settings, and click on Control Panel. The Control Panel appears.

2. Double-click on the System icon, and then click on the Performance tab.

3. Click on Virtual Memory. Make sure Let Windows Manage My Virtual Memory Settings is selected.

Click here to have Windows manage virtual memory.

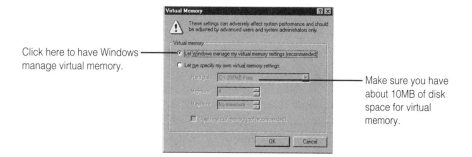

Make sure you have about 10MB of disk space for virtual memory.

4. Look inside the Hard Disk text box. You should have 10 megabytes or more of free disk space for virtual memory. If you have less, see Chapter 63, "Uncluttering Your Disk," to figure out how to free up some disk space.

5. Click on the OK button to save the virtual memory setting. You are returned to the System Properties dialog box.

Windows uses disk space as if it were RAM

6. Click on the OK button to close the System Properties dialog box and save your settings.

As long as Windows is in charge of managing your system's virtual memory—and you have sufficient space on your hard drive—your memory problems should be over. If you still have problems, try running fewer programs. Also, take the following steps to make sure you're not running any programs you don't use at startup:

1. Click on the Start button, point to Programs, and point to StartUp. The StartUp menu lists all the programs that start automatically when you fire up your computer.

2. To remove a program from the StartUp menu, click on the Start button, point to Settings, and click on Taskbar.

3. Click on the Start Menu Programs tab.

4. Click on the Remove button. A list of the Start menu items appears.

5. Click on the plus sign next to the StartUp folder to display the names of the programs on the StartUp menu.

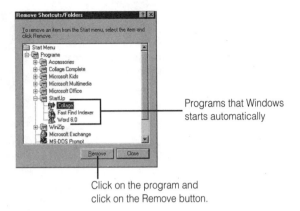

Programs that Windows
starts automatically

Click on the program and
click on the Remove button.

6. Click on the program you want to remove, and then click on the
   Remove button. Repeat this step to remove additional programs.

7. When you're done, click on the Close button. You return to the
   Taskbar Properties dialog box.

8. Click on the OK button.

After removing items from the StartUp menu, restart your computer by
clicking on the Start button, selecting Shut Down, and then selecting Restart
the Computer. Windows restarts, but does not run the programs you removed. You should now have some additional memory available for running
other programs.

*Each running
program
consumes
memory-run
fewer
programs*

Solving Display Problems

You may encounter two common problems with your display. First, you may
have selected the wrong display adapter in Windows, preventing the screen
from displaying Windows properly (if at all). Another common problem is
that video clips and graphics may look fuzzy. Take the following steps to
correct either of these display problems:

1. Right-click on a blank area of the Windows desktop, and then click on
   Properties. The Display Properties dialog box appears.

2. Click on the Settings tab to check the display driver, colors, and
   resolution.

3. Click on the Change Display Type button. The dialog box that appears
   allows you to change the adapter and monitor type. The *adapter* is the
   circuit board that the monitor plugs in to.

4. If the adapter type that's listed is incorrect (check your manual), click on the Change button. A dialog box appears, prompting you to pick your adapter from the list.

5. Take one of the following steps:

> If your adapter type is listed, click on it.

> If your adapter type is not listed, click on the Show All Devices option, and click on the manufacturer and model of your display adapter. (If your adapter is not listed, click on Standard Display types at the top of the Manufacturer's list.)

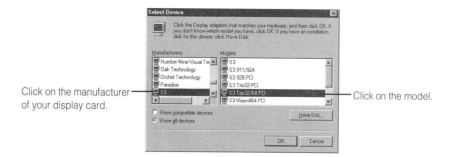

Click on the manufacturer of your display card.

Click on the model.

6. Click on the OK button to save your change and return to the Change Display Type dialog box.

7. If the monitor type that's listed is incorrect (check your manual again), click on the Change button under Monitor Type. A dialog box appears, asking you to pick your monitor from the list.

8. Take one of the following steps:

> If your monitor type is listed, click on it.

> If your monitor type is not listed, click on the Show All Devices option, and click on the manufacturer and model of your monitor. (If your monitor is not listed, click on Standard Monitor Types at the top of the Manufacturer's list.)

9. Click on the OK button to return to the Change Display Type dialog box, and then click on the Close button to return to the Display Properties dialog box.

If you pick wrong adapter or monitor, Windows will restart in Safe mode and use a standard display type

10. If graphics and video clips appear fuzzy, make sure 256 Color (or higher) is selected under Color Palette.

11. You can display higher resolution graphics by dragging the Desktop Area slider to the right to increase the resolution, but the pictures will appear smaller.

12. Click on the OK button to save your changes. If a dialog box appears, indicating you must restart your computer for the changes to take effect, click on the Yes button.

Solving Mouse Problems

If your mouse pointer skips around on the screen, chances are that your mouse is dirty. Open it, clean the mouse ball with rubbing alcohol and a clean towel, and pick the dirt off the rollers inside the mouse (dirt and lint appear as rings around the center of each roller; pick off the rings with a toothpick).

If your mouse pointer simply does not appear on the screen—or if it does some crazy gymnastics—Windows may have selected the wrong mouse driver for your mouse. To check the driver and select a different one, take the following steps:

1. If this mouse is new, use the Add New Hardware Wizard to install it. See Chapter 48 for details. If you installed the mouse and are still having problems, go to step 2.

2. Press Alt+F4 to close any windows and return to the Windows desktop.

3. Press the Tab key until My Computer is selected, and then press the spacebar. Press Enter to open My Computer.

4. Use the arrow keys to select the Control Panel icon, and then press Enter.

5. Use the arrow keys to highlight the Mouse icon, and then press Enter.

6. Press Ctrl+PgDn until the General tab is selected. This shows the current mouse driver.

7. Press Alt+C to select the Change button. A dialog box appears, showing a list of mouse manufacturers and models.

8. Use the down arrow key to highlight the name of the mouse manufacturer. If the manufacturer of your mouse is not listed, select Standard Mouse Types at the top of the list.

9. Press the Tab key, and then use the arrow keys to select the model name of your mouse. If in doubt, pick one of the serial or PS/2 models. (PS/2 mice typically have a round plug, whereas serial mice have a rectangular plug that connects to one of the COM ports.)

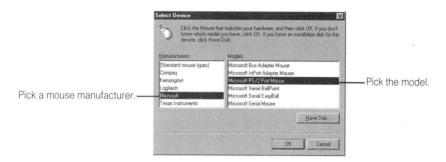

Pick a mouse manufacturer.

Pick the model.

10. Press Enter to save your change.

11. Press Enter again to close the Mouse Properties dialog box. If Windows tells you to restart your computer, press Enter.

If your mouse still doesn't work, repeat the steps to select a different mouse driver. If none of the mouse drivers seems to work, contact the manufacturer of your mouse to see if they have a mouse driver for Windows 95. Then, take steps 2 through 7 above, and press Alt+H to select Have Disk. When a dialog box appears, use it to install the mouse driver you received on disk from the manufacturer.

Beyond Survival

Other Problems and Solutions

If you didn't find the solution to your computer's problem in this chapter, check the following chapters for solutions to specific problems:

- If you installed a new device and you're having trouble getting it to work, see Chapter 48, "Installing New Hardware (Plug-and-Play)."

- If you have problems running games or DOS programs, see Chapter 62, "Running Stubborn DOS Games and Programs."

- For help with printing problems, see Chapter 65, "Solving Printer Problems."

- If Windows seems to be running more slowly than usual, see Chapter 64, "Speeding Up Windows."

- If you're having problems accessing files on a disk, see Chapter 54, "Fixing Disk Problems with ScanDisk."

- For any other problems, try using the Windows Troubleshooters, as explained in the following section.

Using the Windows 95 Troubleshooters

If you didn't find the answer to your problem in this chapter or other chapters in this book, try using one of the Windows Troubleshooters. These interactive tools ask a series of questions that can help you find and correct common problems. To run a Troubleshooter, take the following steps:

1. Click on the Start button and click on Help. This gets you into the Windows help system.

2. Click on the Contents tab.

3. Double-click on Troubleshooting. A list of common Windows problems appears. (You can view a longer list of problems by clicking on the Index tab and typing troubleshoot.)

4. Double-click on the item that best describes the problem you've encountered. The corresponding Troubleshooter appears, displaying a set of questions you can answer to start zeroing in on the problem.

5. Read all the choices, and click on the button next to the desired problem description or question.

Windows Troubleshooters can solve common problems.

Click on a button to proceed.

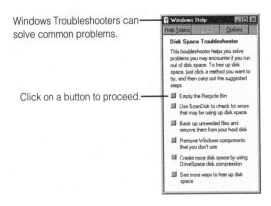

Look in the Help index for more trouble-shooting topics

6. Follow the on-screen instructions; keep clicking on buttons until you correct the problem or reach a dead end.

Cheat Sheet

Changing a Program's Properties

1. Use My Computer or Windows Explorer to display the icon for the program that's giving you trouble.
2. Right-click on the icon, and click on Properties.
3. Click on the tab for the properties you want to change.
4. To view helpful information about a property, right-click on it and click on What's This?

Running a DOS Program in Full-Screen Mode

1. Right-click on the program's icon, and then click on Properties.
2. Click on the Screen tab.
3. Click on Full Screen.
4. Click on the OK button.

Making a DOS Program Ignore Windows

1. Right-click on the program's icon, and then click on Properties.
2. Click on the Program tab.
3. Click on the Advanced button.
4. Click on Prevent MS-DOS-Based Programs from Detecting Windows.
5. Click on the OK button.
6. Click on the OK button.

Solving Mouse Problems in DOS Programs

1. Right-click on the DOS program's icon, and then click on Properties.
2. Click on the Misc tab.
3. Under Mouse, click on Exclusive Mode.
4. Click on the OK button.

62

Running Stubborn DOS Games and Programs

In Chapter 9, "Installing and Setting Up Programs," you learned how to install a DOS application to run in Windows and how to add a program to the Programs menu. If you installed your DOS program, and it is running according to your expectations, you can safely skip this chapter. However, if you can't install the program, or if the program doesn't run well (or run at all), this chapter can help.

Basic Survival

When You Can't Even Install the Program

As you saw in Chapter 9, Windows comes with an Add/Remove Programs utility that makes it easy to install new programs. In order for it to work, however, you must have a disk that has a file on it called Setup or Install. If the Add/Remove Programs utility does not work for a particular program, check the following:

- **Are you installing to a hard disk that has enough free space?** Double-click on the My Computer icon. Right-click on the icon for the drive to which you are installing the program, and click on Properties. The dialog box shows the amount of free space. Check your new program's documentation to find out how much disk space it requires.

- **Are you using the correct installation disk?** The setup or install file is usually on the first disk of the set. Try the other disks to determine whether you're using the right one.

- **Does the program have special installation instructions?** Check the documentation that came with the program to find out if you have to perform special steps to install it. If one of the disks has a ReadMe file, double-click on it to read it.

If everything checks out okay, but you still can't install the program using Windows Add/Remove Programs utility, take the following steps to install the program:

1. Insert the CD or the first floppy disk of the set into one of the disk drives.

2. Double-click on My Computer 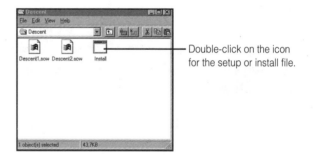.

3. Double-click on the icon for the drive into which you inserted the CD or floppy disk. My Computer shows the names of all the files on the disk.

4. Look for an icon that has the word **setup** or **install** in it (or an abbreviation of one of those words). If you see a folder icon named Setup or Install, double-click on it and look for the setup or install file.

Double-click on the icon for the setup or install file.

5. When you find a file that looks promising, double-click on it. This should start the installation program.

If the installation program still won't run, try running it from the DOS prompt. Open the Start menu, point to Programs, and click on MS-DOS Prompt. Type the letter of the drive that contains the CD or floppy disk, then type a colon and press Enter (for example, type **a:** and press Enter). Type the name of the setup or install file, and then press Enter.

Try running install or setup program from My Computer

Running a Program in Full-Screen Mode

If a DOS program or game won't run from Windows, there may be a simple solution—free up some memory. First, exit any other DOS or Windows programs that are running. (You can exit most programs quickly by right-clicking on their names in the Taskbar and choosing Close.)

Now, set up the DOS program to run in full-screen mode, rather than in a window. Full-screen mode requires less memory, and often can run a DOS program that cannot run in a window. Here's what you do to select full-screen mode:

1. Use My Computer or Windows Explorer to display the icon for the program that's giving you trouble. (Remember, DOS program icons typically look like small program windows.)

2. Right-click on the icon, and click on Properties. The program's Properties dialog box appears.

3. Click on the Screen tab.

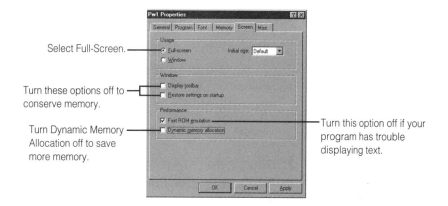

Select Full-Screen.

Turn these options off to conserve memory.

Turn Dynamic Memory Allocation off to save more memory.

Turn this option off if your program has trouble displaying text.

4. Under Window, click on Display Toolbar, and then on Restore Settings on Startup; this turns both options off to conserve memory.

5. Under Performance, turn Dynamic Memory Allocation off to make additional memory available for this program. If the program has trouble displaying text, turn off Fast ROM Emulation as well.

6. Click on the OK button.

Full-screen mode solves many DOS display problems

Selecting Full Screen Mode here ensures that your DOS program will start in full-screen mode whenever you run it. You can, however, switch quickly out of full-screen mode and back again by pressing Alt+Enter.

Program Won't Run Under Windows?

You installed the program okay, but whenever you try to run it, a message pops up saying this program won't run under Windows. Is there anything you can do? Yes—you can try to fool the program into thinking that Windows isn't running. Try the following:

1. Use My Computer or Windows Explorer to display the icon for the program that's giving you trouble. (Remember, DOS program icons typically look like small program windows.)

2. Right-click on the icon, and then click on Properties. The program's Properties dialog box appears.

DOS program icons usually look like tiny windows.

Right-click on the icon and choose Properties.

3. Click on the Program tab, and then click on the Advanced button. The Advanced Program Settings dialog box provides options for providing more system resources to your DOS program.

For info about options in Properties dialog box, right-click on an option and select What's This?

4. Click on Prevent MS-DOS Based Programs from Detecting Windows (this puts a check mark in the box).

5. Click on the OK button to close the Advanced Programs Settings dialog box, and then click on the OK button in the Properties dialog box.

6. Try running the program again.

Running a Program in MS-DOS Mode

Simply telling a program to ignore Windows doesn't always work. If the program still won't run, you can try running it in MS-DOS mode. In MS-DOS mode, the program is given full control of your computer's resources. When you run the program, Windows shuts down all other programs and fades into the background. When you exit the program, Windows restarts automatically. To set up a program to run in MS-DOS mode, here's what you do:

1. Perform the previous steps to turn off Prevent MS-DOS Based Programs from Detecting Windows.

2. Click on MS-DOS mode, to place a check mark in the box.

3. Click on the OK button to save your change.

4. Try running the program now.

If the program still won't budge, skip ahead in this chapter to the section called "Using Alternative Startup Files." Another option is to restart the computer in DOS mode. You can bypass Windows 95 by booting your computer and then pressing F8 when you see the **Starting Windows 95** message.

Dealing with Mouse Problems

If you have a DOS program that supports a mouse (that is, you've always been able to use your mouse with it) and you lose the mouse pointer when you run the program from Windows 95, try giving the program exclusive use of the mouse. (Of course, if you could not use the mouse in the DOS program before, you won't be able to use it when you run the program under Windows 95, either.) Take the following steps to give your DOS program exclusive use of the mouse:

1. Use My Computer or Windows Explorer to display the icon for the program that's giving you trouble.

2. Right-click on the icon, and click on Properties. The program's Properties dialog box appears.

3. Click on the Misc tab.

4. Under Mouse, click on Exclusive Mode to place a check mark in the box. This gives the DOS program exclusive use of the mouse. You won't be able to use the mouse in Windows.

5. Click on the OK button to save your changes.

More info about mouse problems: "Solving Mouse Problems," Ch.61

Beyond Survival

Insufficient File Handles?

If you try to run a DOS program and you receive a message indicating an insufficient number of file handles, you must change the FILES= command in the CONFIG.SYS file. Take the following steps:

1. Double-click on the My Computer icon, and then double-click on the icon for drive C. A window appears, showing the names of all the files and folders on drive C.

2. Right-click on the Config.sys icon, and then click on Open With.

3. Scroll down to NOTEPAD and click on it.

4. Click on the OK button. Windows runs Notepad and opens the Config.sys file.

5. Drag over the number after **FILES=** and type a number between 30 and 50.

6. Open the File menu and select Save. Then click on the Close button.

7. Restart Windows, and then try running the program. If you still receive the error message, try increasing the number after **FILES=** by 10.

Using Alternative Startup Files

Computer games are notorious for making you completely reconfigure your system just to run the game. Most games come with instructions telling you how to add specific commands to your AUTOEXEC.BAT and CONFIG.SYS files. Some games even require you to create a special start-up disk for your computer. Whenever you want to run the game, you have to reboot your computer with the special disk.

All this is pretty nerve-wracking. To help, Windows 95 allows you to enter specific startup commands for your DOS programs. These startup commands affect only the specific DOS program, not your entire system, so you don't have to worry about messing up your entire system to play a single game or run a single program.

First, look through the documentation that came with the game or program; try to find the specific startup commands you need to enter. Then take the following steps to enter those commands:

1. Use My Computer or Windows Explorer to display the icon for the program that's giving you trouble. (Remember, DOS program icons typically look like small program windows.)

2. Right-click on the icon, and then click on Properties. The program's Properties dialog box appears.

3. Click on the Program tab, and then click on the Advanced button.

4. Click on MS-DOS Mode to give this program control of all system resources.

5. Click on Specify a New MS-DOS Configuration to enter unique startup commands for this program.

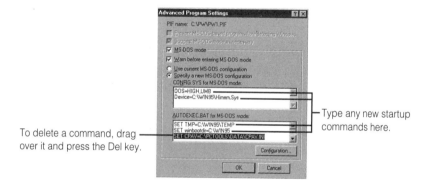

To delete a command, drag over it and press the Del key.

Type any new startup commands here.

6. Take one of the following steps to enter startup commands:

> In the CONFIG.SYS and AUTOEXEC.BAT text boxes, type the startup commands for this program. (Check the program's documentation.)

> Click on the Configuration button, and select the commands you want to enter from the command list. (With this technique, you don't have to enter the commands yourself.) Click on the OK button when you're done selecting commands.

7. Click on the OK button to save your changes.

Properties dialog box replaces PIF files used in older Windows versions to run DOS programs

Cheat Sheet

Types of Files You Can Delete

- Text, backup, and temporary files
- Fonts
- Windows 95 accessories
- Screen savers
- Wallpapers
- Games
- Programs you no longer use

Removing Windows Components You Don't Use

1. Double-click on the My Computer icon .
2. Double-click on the Control Panel icon .
3. Double-click on the Add/Remove Programs icon .
4. Click on the Windows Setup tab.
5. To remove all the parts of a component, click on the component's check box to clear it.
6. To remove parts of a component, click on the component's name, click on Details, and clear the check box for each part you want to remove (click on OK.)
7. Click on the OK button.

Finding and Removing TMP Files

1. Click on the Start button, point to Find, and click on Files or Folders.
2. Type *.tmp and press Enter.
3. Open the Edit menu and click on Select All.
4. Open the File menu and select Delete.
5. Click on the Yes button.

63

Uncluttering Your Disk

Windows and Windows programs come with lots of files that consume gobs of disk space. If you have a large hard disk with plenty of free space, you may not run into any problems. If you start running short on disk space, however, you may find that your computer is low on memory, that it can't save a document you create, or that it starts to lose files and data. Before this happens, you should clean up your disk.

Do complete backup before deleting files

If you know what you're doing, you can use the Windows Explorer or My Computer to perform disk surgery–removing any unnecessary files. If you don't know what you're doing, that could be dangerous. In this chapter, you'll learn how you do some disk cleaning, even if you're not really comfortable about deleting Windows files.

Basic Survival

Types of Files You Can Delete

Windows consists of two types of files: files that are essential for Windows to run, and those that are not. If you're running out of disk space, you may have no choice but to delete some of the inessential files:

- Files you've dumped in the Recycle Bin. Remember, these files are still on your disk!

- .TXT and .WRI (text) files that contain specific information about using Windows with some types of computers and printers.

- .BMP graphics files that are used as wallpaper. You may want to save one .BMP file to use as wallpaper.

- .HLP help files, if you never use the Windows Help system.

- .EXE files for Windows applications you don't use. These include CLOCK.EXE, NOTEPAD.EXE, SOL.EXE, WINMINE.EXE, and PBRUSH.EXE. Be careful about deleting EXE files. Use the Windows Setup application (as explained in this chapter), to avoid deleting any of your executable system or application files. Also, keep in mind that if you delete an EXE file, you won't be able to run the application.

- .FOT and .TTF TrueType font files for any fonts you do not use. For details about deleting font files, see Chapter 40.

Don't use Windows Calendar? Delete it!

Emptying the Recycle Bin

In Chapter 7, you learned how to use the Recycle Bin to dump and recover files. Unless you changed the Recycle Bin's properties, it uses about 10% of your hard disk space for any files you delete. You can often reclaim a good chunk of hard disk space by emptying the Recycle Bin:

1. Double-click on the Recycle Bin icon.

2. Select any files you think you might need, and drag them to a temporary folder.

3. Open the File menu and select Empty Recycle Bin.

4. If a confirmation message appears, click on the Yes button.

Removing Windows Files with Windows Setup

The easiest and safest way to delete inessential Windows files is to use Windows Setup. Windows Setup lets you delete groups of files or individual files.

Before deleting files, you may want to back up your WINDOWS directory. See Chapter 50, "Backing Up Your Files," for complete instructions. If you have the Windows installation disks, you can reinstall any of the Windows files you delete in this section.

Once you've backed up, here's what you do to delete files:

1. Double-click on the My Computer icon ⊟.

2. Double-click on the Control Panel icon 🗂. The Control Panel window appears.

3. Double-click on the Add/Remove Programs icon 🗔. The Add/Remove Programs Properties dialog box appears.

4. Click on the Windows Setup tab. A list of all the Windows components appears. You will probably see three types of check boxes:

A clear check box indicates that the component is not installed.

A gray check box with a check mark in it means that some parts of the component are installed.

A clear check box with a check mark in it means that all parts of the component are installed.

This component is not installed.

Some parts of this component are installed.

All parts of this component are installed.

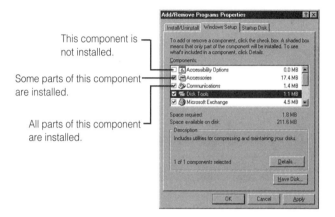

5. To remove all the parts of a component, click on the component's check box to clear it.

6. To remove parts of a component, click on the component's name, and click on the Details button. For each part of a component you want to remove, click on its box to remove the check mark. Click on OK.

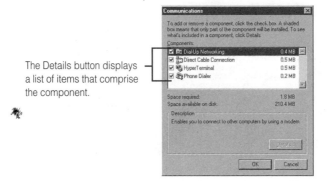

The Details button displays
a list of items that comprise
the component.

7. Click on the OK button to save your changes. A dialog box appears, asking for your confirmation.

8. Click on the Yes button to confirm.

Beyond Survival

Deleting Other Files

If you're really strapped for disk space, use My Computer or Windows Explorer to poke around in your other drives and directories. Look for any of the following files:

- Files that have the **.BAK** or **BK!** extension. These are *backup files* of documents you created in your applications. You can copy these files to a floppy disk (if you want them), and then delete them from your hard disk.

- Files that have the **.TMP** extension. These are *temporary files* that Windows and applications create as you work on a document. If you quit the application the wrong way, or Windows crashes, these .TMP files get stuck in a directory somewhere, and can take up a lot of disk space.

Delete TMP files in C:\WINDOWS\TEMP or C:\TEMP

Note: Windows creates and uses .TMP files as it works. If you try to delete a .TMP file that's in use, you'll get an error message saying that you can't delete the file. Just click on the OK button.

• Documents you no longer edit or refer to. Copy these documents to a floppy disk, write-protect the disk, and store it in a safe location. Then delete the document files from your hard disk.

• Programs you no longer use. Check around for folders that contain programs you no longer use. Some programs come with a Setup feature that lets you uninstall the application. See "Uninstalling Windows Programs," in Chapter 9.

The easiest way to locate and destroy .TMP or .BAK files is to have Windows find them for you. Take the following steps:

1. Click on the Start button, point to Find, and click on Files or Folders. The Find: All Files dialog box appears.

2. Type *.tmp or *.bak to search for files that end in .TMP or .BAK.

3. Open the Look In drop-down list, and click on the letter of the drive you want to search.

4. Make sure the Include Subfolders check box has a check mark in it. (If the check mark is missing, click on the option.)

5. Click on the Find Now button. Windows searches all folders on the specified drive, and displays a list of all the files that match your search entry.

6. Open the Edit menu and click on Select All. All the files in the list are highlighted. (You can deselect the files you want to keep by Ctrl+clicking on their names.)

7. Open the File menu and select Delete. Windows displays a dialog box asking if you're sure you want to move these files to the Recycle Bin.

8. Click on the Yes button.

Remember, any files you move to the Recycle Bin remain on your disk. To remove the files completely, empty the Recycle Bin.

Cheat Sheet

Ten Ways to Speed Windows Overall

- Add RAM to 16 megabytes.
- Make sure Windows recognizes the speed of your CD-ROM drive.
- Decrease the number of display colors.
- Try running without AUTOEXEC.BAT and CONFIG.SYS.
- Minimize windows you're not using.
- Run fewer programs at one time.
- Defragment your hard drive.
- Let Windows manage virtual memory.
- Use no wallpaper.
- Prevent DOS programs from hogging system resources.

Five Ways to Work Smarter

- Place shortcuts for often-used programs on the Windows desktop.
- Use the Documents menu to open recently edited documents.
- If you commonly store files in a particular folder, create a shortcut for the folder on the desktop.
- Place a shortcut for your printer on the desktop.
- Use the right mouse button.

64

Speeding Up Windows

Windows can make even the quickest PC seem a little sluggish. A graphical interface is designed to make your computer easier to use; accordingly, it places much heavier demands on a computer than does a simple text-based interface. If you have a 486 33MHz computer or slower, with only about 4 megabytes of RAM, you may find yourself waiting while Windows catches up with you. In this chapter, you'll learn about a few things you can do to speed up Windows.

Basic Survival

Upgrade to 16 Megabytes of RAM

Computer should have at least 8MB of RAM; 16MB = big performance boost

Although Microsoft claims that Windows 95 can run on a computer with as little as 4 megabytes of RAM, it requires 8 megabytes to do any real work. Any less, and Windows must rely on virtual memory (disk space) to do its job. This slows down your computer considerably and places added strain on your disk drive.

Studies show that increasing RAM from 8 megabytes to 16 megabytes results in a 25-30 percent overall performance increase. Performance reaches a plateau, however, at about 16 megabytes. Refer to your computer manual (or check with a qualified computer technician) before installing additional RAM chips.

Set Your CD-ROM Drive Speed and Cache Size

Although Windows 95 does a fair job of detecting most CD-ROM drives and adding the required drivers to operate them, Windows may not have detected the correct speed of your CD-ROM drive. If you have a 2X, 3X, 4X, or faster CD-ROM drive, enter the correct setting in Windows. Refer to "Optimizing CD-ROM Performance" in Chapter 45 for complete instructions.

While you're at it, check to make sure that Windows is using the maximum read-ahead buffer for your hard drive. Double-click on the System icon in the Control Panel. Then click on the Performance tab, and click on the File System button. Make sure that the Read-Ahead Optimization slider is pushed all the way to the right.

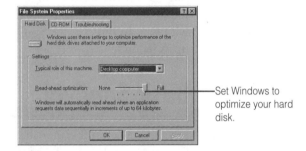

Set Windows to optimize your hard disk.

Use Fewer Display Colors

If you have a fancy display adapter and monitor—capable of displaying thousands of colors—these may also be slowing your system to a crawl. All those colors require a great deal of computer power to generate. You can often increase your system performance by sacrificing some colors. Try it:

1. Right-click on a blank area of the Windows desktop, and click on Properties.

2. Click on the Settings tab.

3. Open the Color Palette drop-down list, and click on 256 Color. (256 colors display a fairly good picture without hogging your system resources).

4. Click on the OK button.

5. When asked if you want to restart your computer, click on the Yes button.

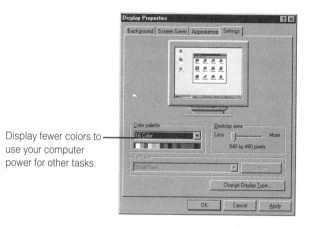

Display fewer colors to use your computer power for other tasks.

If you do not notice a significant performance increase, repeat the steps and enter the original color palette setting. You might also be able to increase the video speed by selecting a lower display resolution. Perform the same steps above, but instead of changing the color, drag the slider under Desktop Area to the left to decrease the resolution to 640-by-480 pixels (you don't want to go any lower than that).

Display info stored in video RAM, freeing computer's RAM for other tasks

One additional way to increase the performance of Windows is to buy a Windows accelerator or video accelerator card. Because Windows is so graphic, an accelerator card can take over much of the work that your system normally must perform just to create the graphic screens. Buy a card that offers at least 2 megabytes of video RAM.

Remove AUTOEXEC.BAT and CONFIG.SYS

Unlike the previous Windows version, Windows 95 enters many startup commands itself; it does not need the commands in the DOS startup files (CONFIG.SYS and AUTOEXEC.BAT) in order to operate. If your system can get by without these files, you can reclaim some memory by preventing the startup commands from loading. Try the following:

1. Make sure you have a Windows Startup disk on hand in case you have problems after changing your system. (See "Making a Floppy Startup Disk" in Chapter 1 for details.)

2. Run My Computer, and rename AUTOEXEC.BAT and CONFIG.SYS as AUTOEXEC.CS and CONFIG.CS. This prevents Windows from running these files at startup.

3. Shut down Windows and restart your computer.

Don't disable
AUTOEXEC.BAT
or CONFIG.SYS
unless you have
emergency startup
disk handy

Windows does not run the startup commands. This gives your computer an additional 8 kilobytes or so of RAM, which can help increase performance. If you find that a hardware device (such as a sound card or CD-ROM drive) does not operate after you make this change, give CONFIG.CS and AUTOEXEC.CS their old names back, and restart your computer.

Minimize Open Windows

Windows uses memory to keep all those pretty windows open on the desktop. It also uses resources to check all the windows on a regular basis to determine which one is active. By minimizing all windows except the one in which you are currently working, you can save memory and processing power.

To minimize all open windows, right-click on a blank area of the Taskbar, and click on Minimize All Windows. Then, in the Taskbar, click on the name of the window you want to work with.

Run Fewer Programs at Once

Minimizing windows helps, but it's even better to quit programs you're not currently using. This frees up all the system resources assigned to the program.

Defragment Your Hard Drive

A slow hard disk drive can slow down your entire system. One factor that is sure to slow down your disk drive is *file fragmentation*. If parts of each file become scattered over the surface of the disk, the drive must search for all the pieces each time it needs the file. Use Disk Defragmenter, as explained in Chapter 53, to optimize your disk.

Let Windows Manage Memory

If you or someone else fiddled with Windows' virtual-memory settings, fiddle them back. Windows can optimize memory on its own, and if you don't know what you're doing, you'll just get in the way. To make sure Windows is in charge of your memory, double-click on the System icon in the Control Panel. Click on the Performance tab, and then click on the Virtual Memory button. Make sure Let Windows Manage My Virtual Memory Settings is selected. Click on the OK button.

Turn Off Wallpaper and Patterns

If you pick a fancy graphic image to display as your Windows wallpaper, or if you pick a fancy background, you may be wasting system resources on looks. Open the Display Properties dialog box (right-click on a blank area of the desktop, and click on Properties). Select (none) in both the Patterns and Wallpaper drop-down lists. Click on the OK button.

Limit DOS Program Access to Resources

If you run DOS programs on a regular basis, they might be hogging your system resources (your computer's memory and processing power). Take the following steps to prevent your DOS programs from taking over:

1. Use My Computer or Windows Explorer to display the icon for the file that executes the DOS program. (Remember, DOS program icons typically look like small program windows.)

2. Right-click on the icon, and click on Properties. The program's Properties dialog box appears.

3. Click on the Memory tab. The Conventional, Expanded, and Extended memory settings are all set to Auto. Some DOS programs use this Auto setting as an excuse to take over all memory (RAM as well as virtual memory).

4. If the DOS program does not use expanded or extended memory, change the Expanded and Extended settings to None.

   If the DOS program does use expanded or extended memory, change the setting to 1024 or 2048. The idea is to provide some limit, preventing the program from taking up all the free disk space (some of which is used as virtual memory).

5. Click on the Misc tab.

6. Drag the Idle Sensitivity slider all the way to the right to change the setting to High. This tells Windows that when the DOS program is inactive, Windows can assign its system resources to other (active) programs.

7. Under Background, make sure there is a check mark in the Always Suspend box. This tells Windows to pull CPU time from the DOS program when it is inactive.

8. Click on the OK button.

To change properties of a running DOS program, right-click inside its title bar and click on Properties

Beyond Survival

Five Ways to Work Smarter

As you work with Windows 95 and Windows 95 programs, you'll develop your own time-saving techniques. Here are a few tips to get you started:

- Place shortcuts for often-used programs on the Windows desktop. Right-click on the program's icon, select Create Shortcut, and then drag the shortcut icon to the Windows desktop. If the desktop becomes too cluttered, right-click on it, point to New, and select Folder. Drag your shortcut icons into the new folder to get them off the desktop. You can double-click on the folder icon to display your shortcuts.

- Use the Documents menu to open documents you've edited recently. The Documents menu displays a list of the document files you opened most recently. To reopen the document, click on the Start button, point to Documents, and then click on the document's name.

- If you commonly store files in a particular folder, create a shortcut for the folder on the desktop. When you want to open the file, simply double-click on the shortcut icon, and then double-click on the file's icon.

- Place a shortcut for your printer on the desktop. You can then print a document by dragging it from a folder in My Computer or Windows Explorer over the printer icon. When you're printing, you can double-click on the printer icon to view a list of documents that are currently waiting to be printed.

- Use the right mouse button. The right mouse button is a real time-saver. It can save you several steps by allowing you to bypass complicated menu systems. For additional control over files and other objects, you can also drag with the right mouse button.

Use right mouse button to display shortcut menus

Cheat Sheet

Checking the Obvious

- Is the printer plugged in?
- Is the printer turned on?
- Does the printer have paper?
- Is the printer's On-Line indicator lit?
- Is the printer connected to the system unit?

Checking Print Manager's Print Queue

1. Double-click on the printer icon next to the time display in the toolbar.
2. Look for Paused or Stalled in the Print Manager title bar.

Possible Print Queue Problems

Printer stalled: Make sure the printer is on, and has paper; then click on Retry.

Printer paused: Display the Print Manager window, open the Printer menu, and click on Pause Printing.

Printer not selected or online: Turn the printer on, make sure the printer is selected in the program you're printing from, and then click on Retry.

Checking Your Printer Setup

1. Double-click on My Computer .
2. Double-click on the Printers icon .
3. Right-click on the icon for the printer you want to use, and then click on Set As Default.
4. Right-click on the icon for the printer you want to use, and then click on Properties.
5. Enter any changes, and then click on the OK button.

65

Solving Printer Problems

See Chapters 46 and 48 for details

If you followed the instructions in Chapter 46 ("Setting Up and Selecting a Printer") to select the correct printer driver and port for your printer, printing should proceed without a glitch. Even with the proper setup, however, you may run into problems when you attempt to print a document. In this chapter, you'll learn how to trace the problem back to its cause, and get on with your printing.

Basic Survival

Why Doesn't Your Printer Print?

If you have printed successfully in Windows before and are just now encountering problems, the cause of the problem may be very simple. Ask yourself the following questions:

- **Is the Printers Folder dialog box displayed?** If it is, make sure your printer has paper, turn the printer on, and press its On-Line button so the indicator lights. Click on the Retry button.

Check for problems, and then click on Retry.

- **Is the printer turned on?** If the printer is turned off, turn it on.

- **Is the printer plugged in?** If you can't get the printer to turn on, check to make sure it is plugged into a power source.

- **Does the printer have paper?** A printer won't even go through the motions unless it has paper. If your printer has more than one paper tray, the empty tray might be selected. Try changing the Paper Tray setting to AutoSelect rather than Upper or Lower. See Chapter 46, "Setting Up and Selecting a Printer," to learn how to change the printer setup.

Check printer's On-Line indicator

- **Is the printer On-Line indicator lit?** Most printers have an On-Line indicator that lights when the printer is ready to print. If the indicator is not lit, press the On-Line button.

- **Is the printer connected to the system unit?** Sometimes the cable that connects the printer to the system unit will wiggle loose from the system unit or printer. Exit Windows, turn off your computer, and check the connections at both ends.

Checking Your Printer Setup

If none of the obvious solutions work, go back to Chapter 46, "Setting Up and Selecting a Printer," and check your printer setup. You need to check for two things:

- **Correct printer driver.** Double-click on My Computer, and double-click on the Printers icon. Right-click on the printer you're trying to use; make sure there is a check mark next to Set As Default. If there is no check mark, click on Set As Default.

- **Correct printer port.** If your printer is set up to use port LPT2, and LPT1 is selected, the printed document will never reach the correct destination. To check the printer port, double-click on My Computer, double-click on the Printers icon, right-click on the printer icon, and click on Properties. Click on the Details tab. The Print to the Following Port drop-down list shows the currently selected port.

Check printer setup from the program

In addition to checking for a correct printer driver and port, keep in mind that most programs allow you to select a specific printer driver (other than the default). This is important because even if you select the correct printer driver as the Windows default, the program may be set up to use a different printer driver. Check the print setup from inside the program. (There is usually a Print Setup command on the File menu, or a Print Setup or Setup button in the Print dialog box when you select the File/Print command.)

Default printer ───
Specific printer is ─── chosen for this program

Resuming Your Print Jobs

Resume printing after correcting problem

Once you've solved the mystery, you can continue printing. If the Printers Folder dialog box is displayed, click on the Retry button to continue printing. If the Print Manager dialog box is not visible, take the following steps:

1. Double-click on the tiny printer icon next to the time display in the Taskbar. The Print Manager dialog box appears, showing all the documents waiting to be printed.

2. Click on Printer in the menu bar. The Printer menu opens. There's probably a check mark next to Pause Printing, meaning that the printing has been interrupted.

3. Click on Pause Printing to resume.

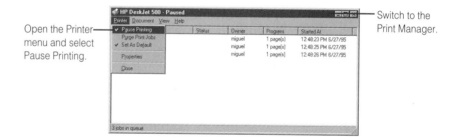

Open the Printer menu and select Pause Printing.

Switch to the Print Manager.

Beyond Survival

Printer Is Printing Partial Pages

Although laser printers are the best type of printers to own, some have trouble printing an entire page. Two factors usually cause this problem. If the printer seems to chop text off the left or right side of the page, your margin settings are probably too narrow. Try using wider margins. Also, check the page setup and printer setup to make sure they are both set to the correct orientation: portrait or landscape.

If you notice that the printer is printing only the first third or half of a page, the page contains too much data for your printer's memory. With laser printers, Windows must send entire pages to the printer. If a page has a lot of complex fonts and graphics, the printer's memory may be insufficient to store all the data. To correct this problem, try the following:

- For a quick fix, try using fewer fonts and less complicated graphics on the page that's giving you problems. (Or try printing one simple page. If you can print a simple page, but not one with complex fonts and graphics, your printer probably needs more memory.)

- Make sure your printer is set up to use the correct driver. See Chapter 46, "Setting Up and Selecting a Printer," for details.

- Open the printer's Properties dialog box, and click on the Graphics tab. If you see a Graphics Mode option, try changing its setting from Vector to Raster.

- Try increasing the Time Out settings for the printer. To prevent this miscommunication, display the Properties dialog box for your printer, and click on the Details tab. In the Transmission Retry text box, type **90**.

Printer Is S-L-O-W

All printers are fairly slow when compared to other computerized operations. Unlike other parts of the computer, the printer has components that move, and these mechanical components take some time to get in gear. However, if printing seems tediously slow, open the printer's Properties dialog box, and try the following:

- Click on the Details tab, and then click on the Spool Settings button. Make sure Spool Print Jobs... is selected, and click on the OK button. Click on OK again to save your changes.

- Click on the Graphics tab, and select a lower graphics resolution. (Your pictures may lose a little quality, but you'll gain some printing speed.)

- Click on the Details tab, and then click on the Spool Settings button. Under Spool Data Format, try changing from EMF to RAW. This controls the way data is sent to the printer. One or the other may be faster depending on your printer.

Hints and Tips for Stubborn Printing Problems

If you tried all the solutions up to this point and are still unable to print, here are some hints for tracking down the cause:

- **Problems in only one program?** If you can print from other programs, the problem is with the printer setup in the problem program (not with the Windows printer setup).

- **Problems in all Windows programs?** Try printing from DOS. Go to the DOS prompt (Start, Programs, MS-DOS Prompt), type the command **dir > LPT1** and press Enter. This prints the current directory list. If it prints okay, the problem is in the Windows printer setup. Use the Printers icon in My Computer to check your Windows printer setup.

- **Don't print from DOS and Windows programs at the same time.** DOS programs come with their own printer drivers that may try to print to the same printer that the Windows printer driver is using. This usually results in a garbled printout. Cancel the printing in the DOS program, exit Print Manager, turn your printer off, wait 30 seconds, and turn it back on.

- **Disable Print Spooling.** This may slow your printing operations and prevent you from working in other programs during printing. However, it does bypass the middleman. To disable print spooling, display the Properties dialog box for your printer, and click on the Details tab. Click on the Spool Settings button, and click on Print Directly to Printer. Click on the OK button twice.

To disable print spooling, turn this option on.

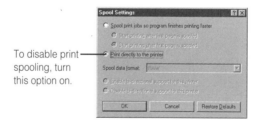

- **Do you get Time Out messages on long print jobs?** Some printers (especially PostScript laser printers) take awhile before they start printing. This can cause Windows to think that there's a problem with the printer. To prevent this miscommunication, display the Properties dialog box for your printer and click on the Details tab. In the Transmission Retry text box, type **90**.

Cheat Sheet

Make Your Own Wallpaper

1. Click on the Start button, and then point to Programs.
2. Point to Accessories and click on Paint.
3. Make your picture using Paint's drawing and painting tools.
4. Open the File menu and select Save.
5. Type a name for the picture file, and then click on the Save button.
6. Open the File menu and select Set As Wallpaper (Tiled) or Set As Wallpaper (Centered).

Drag-and-Drop Printing

1. Double-click on the My Computer icon .
2. Double-click on the Printers icon .
3. Drag the icon for the printer you want to use onto a blank area of the desktop.
4. Click on the Yes button.
5. Run Windows Explorer or My Computer.
6. Change to the drive and folder that contains the file you want to print.
7. Drag the icon of the file you want to print; put it over the printer icon.
8. Release the mouse button.

66

10 Cool Tricks

Time to play. In this chapter, you'll learn about ten cool, fun, mean things you can do with Windows.

Basic Survival

#1: Make Your Own Wallpaper

Use Paintbrush to make wallpaper picture

In Chapter 39, "Changing the Display Settings," you learned how to select the wallpaper design that you want to appear as a backdrop for Windows. You can use Paintbrush to create your own graphic image to use as wallpaper. Here's what you do:

1. Click on the Start button, and then point to Programs.

2. Point to Accessories and click on Paint. The Windows Paint program appears.

3. Use Paint's drawing and painting tools to make your picture (as explained in Chapter 16, "Making Pictures with Paint"), or open a picture file that you want to use as wallpaper.

4. Open the File menu and select Save. The Save As dialog box appears, prompting you to enter a name and location for the file.

5. Select the folder in which you want the picture file stored, and then type a name for the file in the File Name text box. Click on the Save button. Paint saves the file to the specified folder on the disk.

6. Open the File menu and select Set As Wallpaper (Tiled) or Set As Wallpaper (Centered). Windows uses the picture as the backdrop for the Windows desktop.

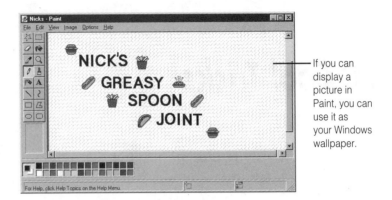

If you can display a picture in Paint, you can use it as your Windows wallpaper.

If you tire of your new wallpaper, you can quickly select a standard wallpaper (or no wallpaper) by resetting the display properties. Right-click on a blank area of the Windows desktop, and select Properties. Select the desired look from the Wallpaper list, and click on the OK button.

#2: Drag-and-Drop Printing

You can use My Computer or the Windows Explorer together with Print Manager to print files without opening them in a program. The only stipulation is that you must first have created file associations for the files you want to print. See Chapter 37, "Running Programs from Windows Explorer," for details. Once you have your file associations set up, here's how you use drag-and-drop to print:

1. Double-click on the My Computer icon 🖥️ .

2. Double-click on the Printers icon 📁 . Windows displays icons for all printers connected to your computer.

3. Drag the icon for the printer you want to use onto a blank area of the desktop. When you release the mouse button, a dialog box appears, asking whether you want to create a shortcut on the desktop.

4. Click on the Yes button. Windows creates the shortcut icon and places it on the desktop.

5. Run Windows Explorer or My Computer (see Chapters 25 and 26).

6. Change to the drive and folder that contain the file you want to print.

7. Drag the icon of the file you want to print; put it over the printer icon.

If Windows runs wrong program, your file association is wrong

8. Release the mouse button. Windows runs the program you used to create the document, and then prints the document from that program.

Trying to get the minimized printer icon on-screen with Windows Explorer or My Computer can take some time and patience. An easier way to print files is to select the file(s) in My Computer or Windows Explorer, and then right-click on a selected file and click on Print.

#3: Bypass the Screen Saver Password

In Chapter 39, "Changing the Display Settings," you learned how to add a password to the Windows screen saver to prevent meddlesome fellow workers from messing with your system. A neat trick, but I hope you didn't rely on that method to protect your supersecret secrets. Here's how easy it is to get around the screen-saver password:

Don't rely on screen saver password to protect you

- **Turn off the screen saver.** Reboot and start Windows. Before the screen saver has a chance to kick in, right-click on the Windows desktop and click on Properties. Click on the Screen Saver tab, open the Screen Saver drop-down list, and click on (none). Click on OK. The Screen Saver won't even come on, let alone demand a password.

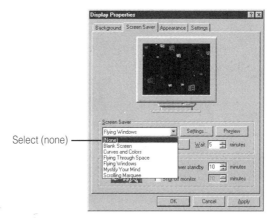

Select (none)

- **Remove password protection.** Reboot, and restart Windows. Before the screen saver has a chance to start, right-click on the Windows desktop, and click on Properties. Click on the Screen Saver tab and click on Password Protected. Click on OK. The Screen Saver might come on, but it won't be password-protected.

- **Reboot with the emergency startup disk.** If you created a startup disk before or after installing Windows 95, use it to restart your computer. Exit Windows and shut down. Insert the startup disk into drive A and turn on your computer.

#4: Additional Cheap Security Tricks

Swap left/ right mouse button for security

As you learned in the last section, anyone with any experience in Windows can get past the screen-saver password trick, and that's probably the first thing they'll look for. I have some other cheap security tricks that they may not think of:

- **Swap the left/right mouse buttons.** Chapter 41, "Controlling Your Mouse and Keyboard," explains how to set your mouse for left-handed use. If you swap the mouse buttons, a user can left-click on a menu until he gets Carpal Tunnel Syndrome, and nothing will happen.

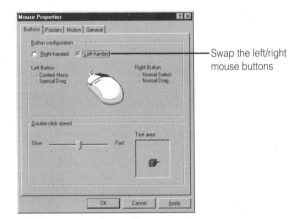

Swap the left/right mouse buttons

- **Make everything white.** Edit your screen colors (Chapter 39, "Changing the Display Settings") to make the menu bar and menu text white. This hides the names of all menus.

- **Rename group windows and program-item icons.** If you created an icon that runs your word processing program and loads your diary, don't name the icon Diary. Name it something really boring like Sales Rpt or Budget.

- **Clear your Documents menu.** Snoopy colleagues will look on your Documents menu for recently opened documents (that's where the juicy stuff will usually reside). To clear the Documents menu, right-click on a blank area of the Taskbar, and click on Properties. Then click on the Start Menu Programs tab and click on the Clear button.

Beyond Survival

#5: Prevent Changes to Your Desktop

Different Windows desktops for each user

If you share your computer with meddlesome coworkers, or with inexperienced users who like to foul up your carefully constructed Windows desktop, you can lock your desktop. Here's how you do it:

1. Double-click on the My Computer icon 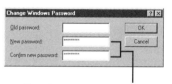.

2. Double-click on the Control Panel icon.

3. Double-click on the Passwords icon. The Passwords Properties dialog box appears.

4. Click on the User Profiles tab.

5. Click on Users Can Customize Their Preferences and Desktop Settings. With this option on, Windows asks you to enter your name and password when you sign on. Windows then uses your desktop settings for its display.

6. Under User Profile Settings, specify which settings you want to save with each password:

   Include Desktop Icons and Netware Neighborhood Contents in User Settings. Turn this option on to save the look and layout of the desktop.

   Include Start Menu and Program Groups Contents in User Settings. Turn this option on to save the structure and contents of the Start menu.

7. Click on the Change Passwords tab, and click on the Change Windows Password button. A dialog box appears, indicating that you can change your password.

8. Click on the OK button.

Type the same password in these two text boxes.

9. Type your password in the New Password text box and in the Confirm New Password text box. Click on the OK button. You are returned to the Passwords Properties dialog box.

10. Click on the OK button to save your new user profile settings.

#6: Cheat at Solitaire

This is a quick one. Okay, you have the game set to deal three cards at a time. If you get into a jam, and you know you're about to lose, hold down Ctrl+Alt+Shift, and click on the deck. This flips one card at a time, and it just might help you pull one out of the bag.

#7: Read Any .HLP File

Sometimes you'll get an application that comes with one or more .HLP files. These files are designed to display Help screens if you open the application's Help menu and select a topic. Even so, you may not be able to get to the application to view its Help system. In such a case, you can use Windows to view the .HLP file. Here's what you do:

1. Run My Computer or Windows Explorer.

2. Change to the drive and folder that contains the Help file.

3. Double-click on the Help file. Windows runs its Help program and displays the contents of the Help file.

#8: Drag a Program to the Start Menu

In Chapter 9, "Installing and Setting Up Programs," you learned how to add programs to the Start menu by using the Taskbar Properties dialog box. Although this method does allow you to add programs to the Start menu's submenus, there is a quicker way to add programs to the top of the Start menu:

1. In My Computer or Windows Explorer, display the icon for the program you want to add to the Start menu.

2. Drag the program's icon over the Start button, and release the mouse button. The program is now on the Start menu.

Another quick way to run a program is to click on the Start button and select Run. The drop-down list in the dialog box that appears contains the names of several programs you ran most recently using the Start/Run command. Simply select the program's name from the list, and then click on OK.

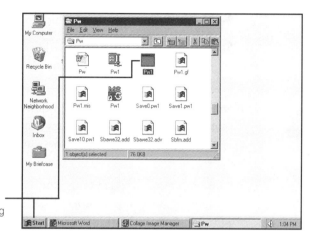

You can add a program quickly to the top of the Start menu by dragging its icon over the Start button.

#9: Copy and Paste "Scraps"

The Windows desktop can store more than program and printer icons. It can store portions of a document (such as selected text and graphics). You can drag selections from one document onto the desktop, and then drag them into other documents. Here's how:

1. Open the document that contains the text, graphic, or other object you want to copy.

2. Select the desired text, graphic, or object.

3. Drag the selection onto a blank area of the Windows desktop. Windows creates an icon for the selection on the desktop. This is called a *scrap*.

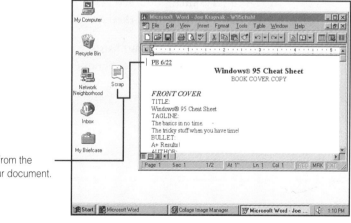

Drag the scrap from the desktop into your document.

4. Open the document into which you want to place the scrap.

5. Drag the scrap from the Windows desktop into the document, and release the mouse button. The scrap is inserted at the insertion point.

#10: Manage Programs with Taskman

If you miss the Task List from Windows 3.1, you can use Windows 95 secret Taskman as a substitute. When you run Taskman, a list of the running programs appears. You can quickly switch to a program by selecting it from the list.

Because Microsoft decided to use the Taskbar rather than Taskman as its main tool for switching to programs, it tucked Taskman out of the way. You won't find it on the Start menu (or any of its submenus). Instead, you have to place it on your desktop or on the Start menu yourself. Take the following steps to place Taskman in a convenient location:

1. Double-click on the My Computer icon, and then double-click on the icon for the drive that contains your Windows 95 files.

2. Double-click on the Windows folder to see its files.

3. Right-click on a blank area inside the Windows folder window, point to Arrange Icons, and click on By Type. This places all the program files together.

4. Drag the Taskman icon over a blank area of the desktop or onto the Start button (to place Taskman at the top of the Start menu). Windows creates a shortcut for Taskman on the desktop or Start menu.

5. To run Taskman, double-click on its shortcut on the desktop, or click on the Start menu and then on Taskman.

6. As you can see, Taskman lists the names of the programs you have running. To switch to a program, click on it.

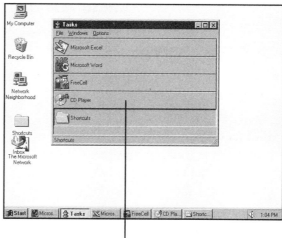

You can switch to a program by clicking on its name in the Taskman window.

Cheat Sheet

Installing Windows 95 from Windows 3.X

1. Insert the installation disk into your floppy drive or CD-ROM drive.
2. Select File, Run.
3. Click on the Browse button.
4. Open the Drives drop-down list; click on the letter of the drive that contains the installation disk.
5. Click on setup.exe in the File Name list, and then click on OK.
6. Click on the OK button.
7. Follow the on-screen instructions to complete the installation.

Installing Windows 95 from DOS

1. Insert the installation disk into your floppy drive or CD-ROM drive.
2. At the DOS prompt, type the letter of the drive that contains the installation disk; then type a colon and press Enter.
3. Type **setup** and press Enter.
4. Follow the on-screen instructions to complete the installation.

Adding and Removing Windows Components

1. Double-click on [icon] the My Computer icon.
2. Double-click on [icon] the Control Panel icon.
3. Double-click on the [icon] Add/Remove Programs icon.
4. Click on the Windows Setup tab.
5. To install or remove a component, click on its check box (a check indicates the component will be installed).
6. To install or remove parts of a component, click on the component's name, and then click on the Details button.
7. Click on the check box next to a component part to add or remove it (a check indicates the part will be installed).
8. Click on the OK button.
9. Follow the on-screen instructions.

Installing Windows 95

Windows 95 is fairly simple to install. You insert the installation disk, change to the drive that contains the disk, and then enter the **SETUP** command. Then you just follow the on-screen instructions to complete the process. What could be easier?

However (and there is always a "however"), the setup program seems to leave out a little information that could make your life easier. For example, Setup fails to tell you that the Typical installation option it offers does not install all the Windows components.

This chapter fills in some of the details so you can go through the setup process with the information you need. You won't get step-by-step instructions leading you through the entire process (the Setup program does that), but you will learn how to run the Setup program from Windows and DOS. You'll also learn how to add and remove Windows 95 components after you've initially installed the program.

Basic Survival

What You Need to Run Windows 95

If you just bought a new PC, it is probably Windows 95-ready. Most new PCs come with a 486 or Pentium processor, a large hard disk, an SVGA monitor, and Windows 3.1 or 3.11. If you have an older PC, however, check the documentation to make sure it meets the minimum requirements for running Windows 95.

- IBM PC or compatible with an 80386 25MHz or better processor. To run Windows 95, you should really have a 486 or better that runs at least at 33MHz. Otherwise Windows will run at a crawl.

- 4 megabytes of RAM (8 megabytes or more is recommended). To check for memory, type **mem** at the DOS prompt and press Enter.

Bare minimum: IBM PC, 386 or better, 4 megs of RAM

- VGA or SVGA graphics adapter and monitor. If your system has a graphics accelerator or Windows accelerator card, it will run Windows much faster.

- A hard disk with 30 to 40 megabytes free space. To check free disk space, type **dir** at the DOS prompt and press Enter. The number at the bottom of the directory list shows the amount of free space.

- At least one 1.2MB or 1.44MB diskette drive. A floppy drive is required to copy the Windows files from the disks you purchased to your hard disk. Installing from a CD-ROM version of Windows is best.

- MS-DOS 3.1 or higher. MS-DOS 5.0 or higher is recommended.

- A Microsoft (or compatible) mouse. You may be able to work without a mouse, but the process could drive you insane.

If you're not sure whether your computer has the necessary disk space, you can start the Setup program anyway. If your system is low on space, the Setup program will attempt to perform the Compact installation, installing as few Windows components as are necessary. After you get Windows 95 up and running, you can use it to remove unnecessary files and free up disk space (see Chapter 63, "Uncluttering Your Disk").

Pre-Installation Considerations

When you start the Windows 95 setup program, it's tempting to look at the screen and click on options without thinking. So, before you start, etch the following considerations onto your brain cells:

Before starting Setup: Back up entire hard disk, run ScanDisk or CHKDSK in DOS

- **Do you still want to use your old version of Windows?** The Setup program lets you install Windows 95 over your old version of Windows (3.1 or 3.11) to replace it. This sets up all your old programs to run in Windows 95. This is probably the best way to install Windows, and the Installation program recommends that you follow this method.

  An alternative: You can choose to install Windows 95 to a separate directory. This allows you to *dual-boot* your computer: start it with either Windows 95 or your old Windows. The drawback is that this option consumes more disk space, and does not set up your old programs to work in Windows 95. Pick your poison.

- **Do you want all the toys installed?** The Setup program recommends that you perform a Typical installation. This installs the Windows components used most commonly. If you want all the components installed (including components such as The Microsoft Network), select the Custom installation. (If you choose Typical, you can add components, as explained later in this appendix.)

- **Let Windows look for hardware devices.** The Setup program can poke around on your computer and look for devices such as sound cards, CD-ROM drives, printers, and other items. Let it. Don't try to set up this stuff yourself.

Starting Setup from Windows 3.1 or 3.11

If you already have an older version of Windows installed on your computer, you should run Windows 95 Setup from Windows. Take the following steps to start the Setup program:

1. Insert the installation disk into your floppy drive or CD-ROM drive; if necessary, close the drive door or disc caddy.

2. Open the Program Manager's File menu and select Run. The Run dialog box appears.

3. Click on the Browse button. A dialog box appears, allowing you to select the setup file from a file list.

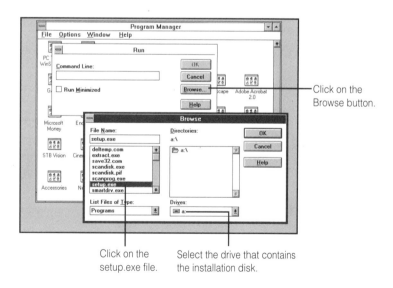

Click on the Browse button.

Click on the setup.exe file.

Select the drive that contains the installation disk.

4. Open the Drives drop-down list, and then click on the letter of the drive that contains the installation disk.

5. Click on setup.exe in the File Name list, and then click on the OK button. This returns you to the Run dialog box; Windows inserts setup.exe into the Command Line text box.

6. Click on the OK button. Windows starts the Setup program and displays the opening Setup dialog box.

7. Follow the on-screen instructions to complete the installation.

Starting Setup from the DOS Prompt

If you don't have a previous version of Windows on your computer, you can start the Setup program from the DOS prompt. Here's what you do:

1. Insert the installation disk into your floppy drive or CD-ROM drive; if necessary, close the drive door or disc caddy.

2. At the DOS prompt, type the letter of the drive that contains the installation disk; then type a colon and press Enter. For example, type **a:** and press Enter.

3. Type **setup** and press Enter. DOS starts the Setup program and displays the first Windows 95 installation dialog box.

4. Follow the on-screen instructions to complete the installation.

Beyond Survival

Adding and Removing Windows Components

If you find that you are not using some of the installed Windows components, or that you want to use a component that is not installed, you can update the installation by adding or removing components. If you installed the CD version of Windows 95, simply insert the disc into the CD-ROM drive and click on the Add/Remove Software button. Then, pick up at step 4 below.

When you insert the Windows 95 CD,
Windows displays this screen.

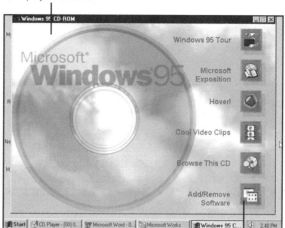

Click on the Add/Remove
Software button.

If you have Windows 95 on floppy disks, you'll have to take a few steps to start the configuration program. Here's what you do:

1. Double-click on ▨ the My Computer icon.

2. Double-click on ▨ the Control Panel icon.

3. Double-click ▨ on the Add/Remove Programs icon. The Add/Remove Programs Properties dialog box appears.

4. Click on the Windows Setup tab. A list of all Windows 95 components appears. The check boxes indicate which components are installed:

A clear check box indicates that the component is not installed.

A white check box with a check mark indicates that all parts of the component are installed.

A gray check box with a check mark indicates that some parts of the component are installed.

5. Take one of the following steps:

To remove all parts of a component, click on its check box until it appears clear.

To install all parts of a component, click on its check box until a check mark appears.

To install some parts of a component, click on the component's name (not on its check box), and click on the Details button. Add a check mark to each part you want to install; remove the check mark from each component you want to remove.

The component will not be installed.

All parts of the component will be installed.

Parts of the component will be installed.

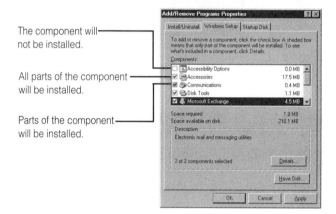

6. Click on the OK button.

7. Follow the on-screen instructions to complete the operation. (You may have to insert one or more of the installation disks.)

Index

M

W-X-Y-Z

Windows Anatomy

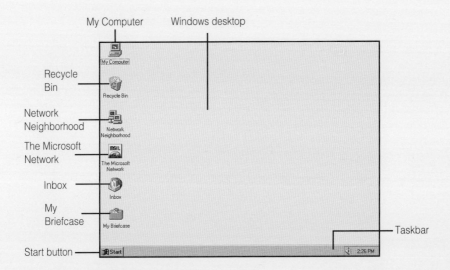

The **Windows desktop** is your work area. You open windows and place icons on the desktop to do your work.

Click on the **Start button** to display a menu that lets you run your programs. Click on the program's name to run it.

Double-click on **My Computer** to view icons for all the disk drives on your computer. To see what's on a disk, double-click on the disk's icon.

The **Taskbar** shows the names of all the programs you're currently using. Click on a program's name to go to it quickly.

You can drag files and icons into the **Recycle Bin** to delete them. Double-click on the Recycle Bin to see what's in it. You can even restore items you've accidentally deleted.

The **Network Neighborhood** icon appears only if you installed a networking tool. This icon allows you to tap the network resources (its drives and printers).

The Microsoft Network lets you subscribe to Microsoft's own online service. If you have a modem, you can connect to the service to transfer electronic mail, talk with other people, and do research on various topics.

The **Inbox** is an electronic mailbox that can retrieve mail from your network and from any online services you may subscribe to.

My Briefcase allows you to transfer files quickly between your laptop and desktop computer.

Using a Mouse

- **Point**   Roll the mouse on your desk until the tip of the mouse pointer touches the desired object on your screen.

- **Click**   Press and release the left mouse button once, without moving the mouse.

- **Right-click**   Point to an object; then press and release the right mouse button. In Windows 95, this usually displays a shortcut menu you can use to enter commands quickly.

- **Double-click**   Press and release the left mouse button twice quickly, without moving the mouse.

- **Drag**   Hold down the left mouse button while moving the mouse.

Running Programs

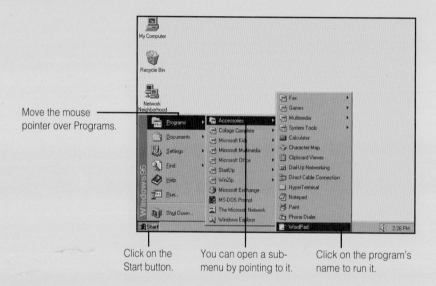

Move the mouse pointer over Programs.

Click on the Start button.

You can open a sub-menu by pointing to it.

Click on the program's name to run it.

Getting Help

- Click on the Start button and click on Help.

- Click on the Contents tab, and double-click on the type of help you want.

- The Index and Find tabs allow you to search for help about a specific task or topic.

Switching Between Running Programs

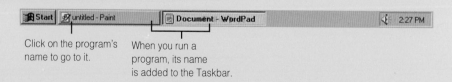

Click on the program's name to go to it.

When you run a program, its name is added to the Taskbar.